TEACHING ASIAN AMERICA IN ELEMENTARY CLASSROOMS

Asian American voices and experiences are largely absent from elementary curricula.

Asian Americans are an extraordinarily diverse group of people, yet are often viewed through stereotypical lenses: as Chinese or Japanese only, as recent immigrants who do not speak English, as exotic foreigners, or as a "model minority" who do well in school. This fundamental misperception of who Asian Americans are begins with young learners—often from what they learn, or do *not* learn, in school.

This book sets out to amend the superficial treatment of Asian American histories in U.S. textbooks and curriculum by providing elementary teachers with a more nuanced, thematically driven account. In chapters focusing on the complexity of Asian American identity, major moments in Asian immigration, war and displacement, issues of citizenship, and Asian American activism, the authors include suggestions across content areas for guided class discussions, ideas for broader units, and recommendations for children's literature as well as primary sources.

Noreen Naseem Rodríguez is an Assistant Professor of Elementary Education and Educational Justice in the College of Education and

Core Faculty in the Asian Pacific American Studies Program at Michigan State University. She studies the pedagogical practices of Asian American educators and how elementary educators teach so-called "difficult histories" through children's literature and primary sources. Before becoming a teacher educator, she was a bilingual elementary teacher in Austin, Texas for nine years.

Sohyun An is a Professor of Social Studies Education in the Department of Elementary and Early Childhood Education at Kennesaw State University. Her teaching and research centers on issues of race, war, migration, and imperialism within the context of social studies education. She is a founding member of Asian American Voices for Education, a grassroots collective in Georgia with a mission to advance K-12 Asian American studies and ethnic studies in public schools. Prior to migration to the US, she taught secondary social studies in South Korea.

Esther June Kim is an Assistant Professor and Program Coordinator for Secondary Social Studies in the School of Education and an affiliate faculty in Asian Pacific Islander American Studies at William & Mary. Her research explores how different communities are represented in Social Studies curriculum, particularly racial and religious communities. Prior to her work in teacher education, she was a high school history and humanities teacher in South Korea and California.

EQUITY AND SOCIAL JUSTICE IN EDUCATION SERIES

Paul C. Gorski, Series Editor

Routledge's Equity and Social Justice in Education series is a publishing home for books that apply critical and transformative equity and social justice theories to the work of on-the-ground educators. Books in the series describe meaningful solutions to the racism, white supremacy, economic injustice, sexism, heterosexism, transphobia, ableism, neoliberalism, and other oppressive conditions that pervade schools and school districts.

Teaching Asian America in Elementary Classrooms
Noreen Naseem Rodríguez, Sohyun An, and Esther June Kim

Literacy for All: A Framework for Anti-Oppressive Teaching
Shawna Coppola

Social Studies for a Better World: An Anti-Oppressive Approach for Elementary Educators
Noreen Naseem Rodríguez and Katy Swalwell

Equity-Centered Trauma-Informed Education:
Alex Shevrin Venet

Learning and Teaching While White: Antiracist Strategies for School Communities
Jenna Chandler-Ward and Elizabeth Denevi

Public School Equity: Educational Leadership for Justice
Manya C. Whitaker

TEACHING ASIAN AMERICA IN ELEMENTARY CLASSROOMS

Noreen Naseem Rodríguez
Sohyun An
Esther June Kim

Routledge
Taylor & Francis Group
NEW YORK AND LONDON

Designed cover image: © Getty Images

First published 2024
by Routledge
605 Third Avenue, New York, NY 10158

and by Routledge
4 Park Square, Milton Park, Abingdon, Oxon OX14 4RN

Routledge is an imprint of the Taylor & Francis Group, an informa business

Library of Congress Cataloging-in-Publication Data
Names: Rodríguez, Noreen Naseem, author. | An, Sohyun, author. |
Kim, Esther June, author.
Title: Teaching Asian America in elementary classrooms / Noreen Naseem
Rodríguez, Sohyun An, and Esther June Kim.
Description: New York, NY : Routledge, 2024. | Series: Equity and social
justice in education series | Includes bibliographical references.
Identifiers: LCCN 2023037528 (print) | LCCN 2023037529 (ebook) |
ISBN 9781032662688 (hardback) | ISBN 9781032597157 (paperback) |
ISBN 9781032662695 (ebook)
Subjects: LCSH: Asian Americans—History—Study and teaching (Elementary) |
United States—History—Study and teaching (Elementary) | Education,
Elementary—Social aspects—United States.
Classification: LCC E184.A75 R64 2024 (print) | LCC E184.A75 (ebook) |
DDC 973/.0495071—dc23/eng/20230926
LC record available at https://lccn.loc.gov/2023037528
LC ebook record available at https://lccn.loc.gov/2023037529

ISBN: 978-1-032-59715-7 (pbk)
ISBN: 978-1-032-66269-5 (ebk)

DOI: 10.4324/9781032662695

Typeset in Adobe Garamond Pro
by codeMantra

For Lola Lucia, Erum, and Jen - N.N.R.
For 부모님, Jean, Jacqueline, and Terrie - S.A.
For 엄마와 아빠 - E.J.K.

• Contents •

• Acknowledgments •

This book is the product of communities and efforts that extend far beyond the three of us as individuals. We conduct research in social studies education, a field that has not historically been supportive of this kind of scholarly work. Therefore, we have had to find resources, expertise, and encouragement beyond our field, and through each other. One nurturing academic community has been the Research on the Education of Asian and Pacific Americans (REAPA) Special Interest Group of the American Educational Research Association. We are grateful to our REAPA family for honoring and uplifting our work, particularly in recent years. We also want to thank the contributors who explored Asian American narratives and histories in our 2022 special issue of *Social Studies and the Young Learner*, as well as journal editor Scott Waring for entrusting us with the privilege of spotlighting such important scholarship. Thank you for giving us the opportunity to pass the mic to others so that we can all learn from them! The scholarship featured in these venues and shared within these communities has been foundational to the creation of this book.

Esther and Noreen would not know about Asian American histories if it were not for Madeline Hsu and the University of Texas at Austin Center for Asian American Studies. Madeline, thank you for being such a generous teacher, powerful connector, and incredible mentor. In everything we do related to Asian American history, we hope to make you proud. Erika Lee, while we do not know you personally, your work has inspired all three of us in countless ways, but especially for its accessibility and comprehensiveness. Thank you for writing books that have taught us so much that we can share with others interested in teaching Asian American histories. Thank you to Stop AAPI Hate and Russell Jeung for their tremendous advocacy for our communities and for entrusting Sohyun and Noreen with the Asian American Studies K–12 Framework. We hope that the framework, alongside this book, can offer elementary educators clear starting points for expanding their curriculum.

There are many individuals whose academic work has taught and inspired us and whose mentorship, support, and activism have deeply informed this book. Thank you to the following Asian American scholars and activists who we are so grateful to be in community with: Arshad Ali, Wayne Au, Poushali Bhadury, Patrick Camangian, Gerald Campano, Jason Chang, Edward Curammeng, Sarah Park Dahlen, E. J. R. David, Yến Lê Espiritu, Ameena Ghaffar-Kucher, Jennifer Ho, Betina Hsieh, Jung Kim, Erika Lee, Maxwell Leung, Lisa Lowe, Daryl Maeda, Cheryl Matias, Mohit Mehta, Rahul Mehta, Andrea Kim Neighbors, Mae Ngai, Leigh Patel, OiYan Poon, Ritu Radhakrishnan, Erika Saito, Sona Shah, Roland Sintos-Coloma, Binaya Subedi, Liza Talusan, Allyson Tintiangco-Cubales, Phitsamay S. Uy, Ellen Wu, Judy Wu, Connie Wun, and Cathery Yeh. To LaGarrett King: your Black Historical Consciousness Framework has greatly shaped our book, particularly Chapter 7 on teaching contention in Asian American histories. Thank you for your intellectual generosity and leadership. We appreciate Paul Gorski, Carol Collins, and Mariah Eppes for supporting this book from its earliest stages to proofs with W. W. Norton and Lauren Davis for getting us to the finish line with Routledge. Thank you so much to John J. Lee, Virgo Lee, and David Thind, who allowed us to feature photos taken by and of their loved ones in this book; to Curtis Chin and Samip Mallick at SAADA for facilitating those communications; and to Elizabeth Clemens at the Walter P. Reuther Library at Wayne State University for her help with the Archives of Labor and Urban Affairs.

We are also grateful for the feedback and manuscript support received as we approached the finish line for this manuscript from Melissa Allen, Michael Brown, Sarah Park Dahlen, Anna Falkner,

Diana Kim, Hannah Kim, Todd Krause, Melanie M. McCormick, Acelynn Perkins, and Neil Shah.

Additionally, Noreen would like to thank Rosalie Ip, Phonshia Nie, Esther Chung Martin, and the Navarro teachers who first showed her the possibilities of teaching Asian American histories to young learners. Esther and Sohyun, I'm so grateful for you both—you have always understood why this work matters and you never cease to push my thinking in new ways. I'm so glad to have found such wonderful friendships and writing partnerships with you, and I hope this is just the beginning of our work together! Christine Her, Tina Shaw, Henny Orr, Mira Yusef, Hieu Pham, and Audri Lu: thank you for being such badass Asian American women and community leaders in Iowa. To my Iowa State AAPI crew—Harrison, Rachel, Rosie, and Soo: thanks for always being down for delicious food and venting! Much love and gratitude to my brilliant Coloradan Asian American educators and colleagues: Carla Cariño, Amy Okimoto, Ying Ong, Jeanette Scotti, Dan Taylor, Deepti Misri, Nishant Upadhyay, Azita Ranjbar, and Seema Sohi. To my emergent community in Michigan, including the Michigan State Asian Pacific American Studies faculty and students, Rising Voices, and MAPAAC, I look forward to the relationship building and work ahead. Shout out to Rebecca Linares and Stephanie Toliver for their unrelenting encouragement and enthusiasm for chisme. I don't know how I would have survived my time in Colorado without you! Last but not least, I want to thank my family, who make everything I do and write possible: Mohammad and Ruth Villamayor Naseem, Alex, Lucia, and Sofia. To Lolo Zosimo, the most famous educator in our family: I never got the chance to meet you, but I hope this book would make you proud.

Sohyun is profoundly appreciative of Noreen and Esther. Without you, this book and our future dream projects would not be a reality! My fabulous and fierce mama activist friends at Asian American Voices for Education—Weonhee Anne Shin, Ruth Youn, Theresa Alviar-Martin, Kym Lee, Terianne Wong, Vivian Liao, Mila Konomos, Lisa Chu, and Melody Yoo: thank you for learning and fighting together to bring change in Georgia! To my parents—서향하, 안이수, 양정숙, 권순국—and Jean: I am beyond thankful for your love and support. Lastly, to

Jacqueline and Terrie: I love you, and you are the reason why I write and teach.

Esther would like to thank Noreen for her mentorship and the opportunities she sought and opened up for all the Asian American graduate students who came after her, including myself. Sohyun, thank you for your constant encouragement and for the example you have always set as a Korean American scholar and a compassionate human being. Thank you also to Francis Tanglao Aguas, Deenesh Sohoni, and Jason Chen for your support and for inviting me into the work you all do for K–12 Asian American studies in Virginia. Gladys Krause and Kathryn Lanouette, I am so grateful to you both for showing me how amazing elementary education can be when the wonder of students is centered. To Jane Kim and Jeannie Jun, thank you for cheering me on through the finish. And finally, thank you 엄마, 아빠, Richard, and Lila, my family whose unconditional support and hope for me makes everything possible and full of joy.

• Introduction •

When those who have the power to name and to socially construct reality choose not to see you or hear you . . . when someone with the authority of a teacher, say, describes the world and you are not in it, there is a moment of psychic disequilibrium, as if you looked in the mirror and saw nothing. It takes some strength of soul—and not just individual strength, but collective understanding—to resist this void, this non-being, into which you are thrust, and to stand up, demanding to be seen and heard.

—Adrienne Rich, *Blood, Bread, and Poetry: Selected Prose*, 1979–1985

"Where are you from? No, where are you *really* from?" Most Asian Americans have been asked this question more times than they can count. People in the United States consume Japanese technology, Korean pop music and streaming films, wear clothes made in Bangladesh, India, and the Philippines, and enjoy a wide array of Asian origin cuisine. However, Asian Americans are still viewed as outsiders who are assumed to be recently-arrived immigrants and to speak languages other than English. This fundamental misperception of who Asian Americans are begins with young learners, often in school. This book aims to change these and other misconceptions and omissions about Asian Americans.

We are three Asian American teacher educators—that is, we are all former K–12 teachers (Noreen taught elementary students, Esther and Sohyun taught high schoolers) who now work in teacher preparation programs with the next generation of educators. We keep in touch with our former students, many of whom are now experienced teachers themselves, and work with teachers, school districts, and national organizations to offer professional development on a range of topics.

We are united by our Asian American identities as well as a commitment to support social studies educators in teaching Asian American histories. For Esther and Noreen, these were histories that they never learned in school when they were students. Those omissions often left them confused, with feelings of isolation. As for Sohyun, she sees the danger of exclusionary curriculum continuing today as her children struggle to find belonging and connection to the U.S. history taught in school. After conducting many professional development workshops about teaching Asian American histories, we knew it was time to come together to create a resource to support educators in this work.

In this book, we offer readers a thematic approach to teaching Asian American stories and histories. Most stories shared with young children, whether through popular media or trade books used in and outside of the classroom, tend to center white-presenting, cisgender, heterosexual, Protestant, abled English-speaking characters and families. In terms of historical narratives, traditional U.S. history follows the chronological approach, which allows learners to see how issues and events occur over time. One problem with this approach is the presentation of historical events as if they were disconnected. For example, students may not see the connection between the Spanish-American War of 1898 and Filipinx migration in the 1900s, or between U.S. wars in Korea and Vietnam and the migration of Koreans, Vietnamese, Lao, Hmong, and Cambodians to the United States from the 1950s onward.

Another challenge is that the substantial teaching of U.S. history with explicit connections and context is often reserved for intermediate grades and above. In addition, as teacher educators, we are painfully aware of the ever-decreasing amount of instructional time devoted to social studies in the elementary grades. In some schools, social studies teaching and learning may only take place every 4 or 6 weeks, making content even more disjointed and limited. We hope that the themes laid out in this book offer educators the flexibility they need to integrate Asian American content into elementary classrooms, in social studies and beyond.

WHO WE ARE

We write this book drawing from our expertise as experienced former teachers in K–12 settings, as current teacher educators, as researchers of social studies education, and as Asian American women. Yet even with our shared teacher and racial identities, we hold other unique identities and experiences that distinctly inform how we approach the topics covered in this book. In this section, we share a little about ourselves, from our own educational experiences to our work as teachers, so that you can better understand how and why the teaching of Asian America is so important to us individually and as a group.

Noreen

Noreen is the child of Asian immigrants. Her father was born in New Delhi just before Partition, one of the largest and most violent mass migrations that occurred after the independence of the Indian subcontinent and the subsequent creation of the majority-Muslim nation of Pakistan and the majority-Hindu nation of India. His family migrated to Karachi when he was a baby. As a young adult, he immigrated by himself to Houston, Texas in 1972 to pursue graduate school. Noreen's mother was born in the small town of Dolores in the Quezon province of the Philippines. After attending nursing school, she immigrated to Yazoo City, Mississippi in 1973. Noreen's parents immigrated as a result of the 1965 Immigration and Nationality Act, along with millions of other people from Asia, Latin America, and Africa. They met in Houston in 1978, where they were part of a vibrant immigrant community that included several other Pakistani-Filipina couples, and moved to San Antonio shortly after they were married in 1980.

Months later, Noreen's grandmother joined them in San Antonio to care for her while her parents worked full-time. Shortly afterward, her mother's youngest sisters immigrated to the United States and lived with them for a few years. As Noreen's father was the only person in his entire extended family to come to the U.S., her stateside family has been limited to her maternal Filipinx side. She grew up listening to English and Tagalog, and heard her father and his friends speak Urdu at weekend gatherings. Noreen was raised Muslim but also occasionally attended Catholic church with her mother's side of the family. At school, however, these varied cultural aspects were rarely present. Surrounded by Mexican American peers, she blended in physically with her brown skin and black hair but never heard her parents' languages or cultures mentioned in any meaningful way across her K–12 education in the 1980s and 1990s.

In her first undergraduate education class in 2001, Noreen learned about bilingual education. She was blown away by the notion that schools and teachers might center the languages and cultures of students in their curriculum and instruction. After this realization, Noreen quickly changed her major from generalist education to bilingual/bicultural education and added additional majors in Spanish and linguistics. She taught bilingual students in Austin, Texas for nine years before leaving the classroom to pursue a Ph.D. full-time after the birth of her second child.

Although Noreen initially intended to continue working with Latine immigrant students and families, she quickly realized that she knew far more about Mexican American culture and history than she did about her own Asian American origins. One day, at the age of 32, she discovered that the first Filipinos landed in Morro Bay, California in 1587. Despite spending nearly 30 years in classrooms, first as a student and then as a teacher, this fact had previously eluded her. Why hadn't she learned this? Why had she and her family always been viewed as outsiders, as foreigners, when her people landed in what would become the United States long before the Pilgrims and the so-called Founding Fathers? At that moment, Noreen decided she needed to immerse herself in Asian American histories. Her dissertation explored how Asian American elementary educators in Texas attempted to teach their students the Asian American histories that they were denied in schools. The teaching and learning of Asian American histories in K–12 settings has been her primary scholarly passion ever since.

Esther

Esther was born and raised in California, where her parents immigrated from South Korea. Like Noreen's parents, they immigrated shortly after the 1965 Immigration and Nationality Act. Esther's paternal family was originally from what is now known as North Korea, but escaped to the South during the Korean War, when her grandfather was jailed and tortured because he was a leader of the underground church resistance. Her mother's family was in China during that time and thereby escaped much of the devastation and poverty that resulted from the war. However, Esther's maternal grandfather was from the Northern area of Korea. After the U.S. and the USSR decided to split the Korean peninsula, he never saw much of his family again. Esther grew up with these stories and histories at home. She never learned about them in schools, except perhaps as a short paragraph or sentence in her high school U.S. history textbook.

As with many other Korean Americans in southern California, Esther's Korean identity was very much shaped by church. Church was where she made all her Korean American friends and took Korean language classes. In contrast, school was where she learned to feel shame about her race and culture, from being called "chink" by her schoolmates to hearing comments about smelly Korean food. When she began teaching high school history, she wanted to make sure that no one in her class would be made to feel shame about their cultures. This was also the first time she learned many Asian histories (often one or two days before she had to teach her students about them) in ways that did not make Asian countries sound backwards and inferior. But it was not until Esther's doctoral studies in Texas that she learned about Asian *American* histories. Studying these histories was the first time Esther felt her and her family's life and experiences connected directly to what she was learning in school. Her focus since then has been on purposeful and authentic representation of different identities in school curriculum.

Sohyun

Sohyun is a first-generation immigrant born and raised in South Korea. She loved learning about history as a kid and became a secondary social studies teacher. In 2003, she came to the University of Wisconsin-Madison for doctoral study. Her original goal was to go back and continue her teaching career in Korea, yet she eventually decided to stay with a newfound passion for advancing Asian American studies in K–12 schools as a curriculum scholar and teacher educator.

Growing up in 1980s South Korea, where 99.99% of its population was Korean ethnic, race hardly mattered to Sohyun. It was rather class and gender that shaped her and other Koreans' everyday lives. In fact, Sohyun never thought about herself as "Asian" and never met a person of another race until she came to the United States. Her initial ideas about other races exclusively came from Western (U.S.-made) movies and books that were popular in South Korea during her childhood, such as *MacGyver*, *Top Gun*, *Super Man*, *Tarzan*, *Little House on the Prairie*, *Cinderella*, *Beauty and the Beast*, and *Snow White*. Through these cultural products, she learned that the United States was the best country in the world; whites were real and good Americans; Blacks were inferior and dangerous; Native Americans were long-gone; and there was no structural racism, just a few racist people, in America.

These beliefs were proven wrong as soon as Sohyun arrived in the U.S. Her daily experiences as an international student from South Korea, as well as her doctoral study on U.S. social studies education, helped her build critical race knowledge. After Sohyun found a sheer lack of research on K–12 Asian American studies and the challenges of teaching Asian American histories, she decided to spend her professional career filling these gaps. Her passion got much stronger as she became a mother of Asian American children. Listening to her daughters' frustration with white-dominant social studies curriculum and their yearning to see themselves and other marginalized groups in school lessons was the impetus for Sohyun's research and practice centering on K–12 Asian American studies.

Coming Together

Our paths crossed in a couple different ways. We each arrived at the importance of teaching and learning Asian American histories later in life, largely through our second careers as teacher educators and educational researchers. Noreen and Esther met in graduate school at the University of Texas at Austin, where they were both part of the Social Studies Education program. As the only Asian American students in the program, they initially bonded over children's literature that

Noreen eagerly shared with Esther. What began as an informal interest in Asian American children's literature that was unlike anything either of them had read when they were young soon blossomed into a qualitative research project where Noreen and Esther conducted a detailed analysis of children's literature (Rodríguez & Kim, 2018). That project was the first of many collaborations between the two, most of which have been centered around Asian American children's literature and the use of primary sources (see Chapter 1 for more details) to teach in-depth Asian American histories to young learners (see Rodríguez & Kim, 2021; 2022).

While Esther and Noreen were still in graduate school, Sohyun was already an experienced professor and an active member of the College and University Faculty Assembly of the National Council for the Social Studies. Sohyun's scholarship was unique in that she was the first social studies researcher to engage Asian American critical race theory as a way to understand the absence of Asian Americans in state social studies standards (An, 2016; 2017). Her research was pivotal to Esther and Noreen's emerging scholarship. As there have been very few Asian American scholars in the College and University Faculty Assembly, the three of us found ourselves frequently on the same conference panels and presentations and in the same academic journal special issues. A rich mentorship and friendship were born, and after the beginning of the COVID-19 pandemic, Sohyun and Noreen began to collaborate on work aimed to increase awareness about anti-Asian violence.

They co-authored the National Council for the Social Studies's organizational current event response to anti-Asian violence as well as a chapter in *Post-Pandemic Social Studies: How Covid-19 Changed the World and How We Teach* (An & Rodríguez, 2021). In 2022, Sohyun and Noreen guest edited a special issue of *Social Studies and the Young Learner* focused on Asian American narratives and developed an Asian American Studies K–12 Framework sponsored by the nonprofit Stop AAPI Hate (see Appendix). Sohyun and Noreen continue to work together to conduct professional development workshops for teachers, but this book is the first time all three of us have been able to bring together our shared expertise. We are so grateful for this opportunity, and to *you* for reading the fruit of our labor!

While we do consider ourselves primarily experts in the teaching and research of social studies with a secondary focus on children's literature and literacy, we want to acknowledge that our knowledge of Asian American histories and experiences is not all-encompassing. Of course, there is no way to deeply understand the transnational relationships and unique histories of every Asian nation *and* its diaspora, but this is further complicated by the ways that the very definition of Asian American has shifted over time. We recognize that our training has privileged the "traditional" view of Asian America as including only East Asia, Southeast Asia, and South Asia, while problematically leaving out Central and West Asia. We will explore some of these tensions in Chapter 1, but want to make clear that we are continuing to learn and grow. We hope that you as a reader are engaging in this book as someone who is trying to improve their own knowledge and expertise in order to do better by your students. We want you to know that we are right alongside you on this path to recognize everyone's full humanity and histories through more inclusive and critical teaching.

UNDERSTANDING ASIAN AMERICA

Before one can teach Asian American histories, they must know where the term "Asian American" came from. Contrary to popular belief, it is not simply a racial category. Rather, the term was the creation of two college students—Emma Gee and Yuji Ichioka—who selected the phrase with great deliberation in 1968 (Maeda, 2012). Inspired by civil rights and Third World Liberation Front activists (more about them in Chapter 6), Gee and Ichioka wanted to create a coalition of University of California Berkeley students whose families were of Asian origin. At the time, this was mostly Chinese Americans, Japanese Americans, and Filipinx Americans. While these groups came from nations with their own distinct histories, cultures, languages, religions, and politics, in the United States they were often lumped together as "Orientals," an archaic term that positioned them as exotic Others. By naming their organization the Asian American Political Alliance, Gee and Ichioka sought to unify students who shared a common antiracist and anti-imperialist political orientation and faced similar types of racism and discrimination, regardless of their families' countries of origin.

The sociopolitical origins of this term remain important today. Although Asian Americans are an extraordinarily diverse group of people (and we will dive into this diversity shortly), they often remain racialized and misunderstood in similar ways. In particular, Asian Americans are typically considered to be either Chinese or Japanese, viewed as recent immigrants who are not expected to speak English, and believed to be quiet, submissive people who do well in school, stay out of trouble, and work hard. Many of these stereotypes have historical roots, while others reveal the impact of popular culture and media in influencing beliefs when a group is largely missing from the K–12 curriculum. In Chapter 2, we will explore the most common stereotypes in greater detail.

For now, we want to offer a quick overview. Asian Americans are the fastest growing ethnoracial group in the United States and number over 22 million. Asian Americans make up over 6% of the U.S. population and are projected to reach 46 million by 2060. Six origin groups make up 85% of the Asian American population: Chinese (24%), Indian (21%), Filipinx (19%), Korean (19%), Vietnamese (10%), and Japanese (7%). Nearly half of Asian Americans live in the Western United States, with California serving as home to 30% of them. The South is home to 24% of Asian America, followed by 19% in the Northeast, and 12% in the Midwest. About six out of every 10 Asian Americans (57%) were born outside of the United States and have a median age of 45, the same as the nation's overall immigrant population. U.S.-born Asian Americans have a median age of 19, much younger than the rest of the population, and 95% of them are proficient in English, compared to 57% of foreign-born Asian Americans (Budiman & Ruiz, 2021).

These statistics are just a small starting point. The Pew Research Center (Budiman & Ruiz, 2021) has detailed statistics about Asian Americans that explore everything from rates of homeownership to annual income and educational attainment. However, as we will explain in Chapter 2, their data does not include West and Central Asians.

We will touch on various aspects of Asian American identities, experiences, and histories throughout this book, but also encourage you to

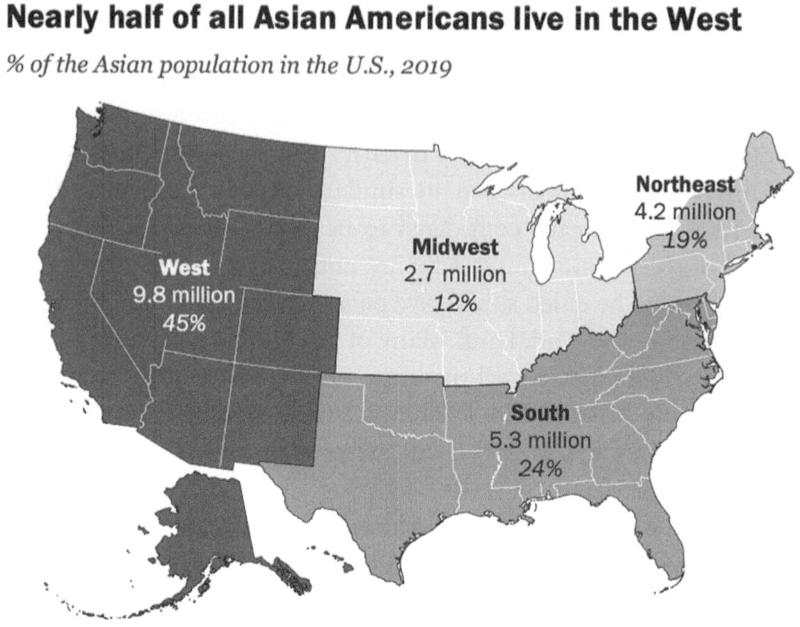

FIGURE I.1 Key facts about Asian Americans, a diverse and growing population: nearly half of all Asian Americans live in the West. PEW RESEARCH CENTER, WASHINGTON, D.C., 2021, APRIL 29 (HTTPS://WWW.PEWRESEARCH.ORG/FACT-TANK/2021/04/29/KEY-FACTS-ABOUT-ASIAN-AMERICANS).

learn more beyond this text. Our favorite recommendations for Asian American history are Ronald Takaki's *Strangers from a Distant Shore* (1998), Erika Lee's *The Making of Asian America* (2015), and Catherine Ceniza Choy's *Asian American Histories of the United States* (2022). These books can help you understand the different groups that came to the United States from Asia and the wide range of reasons they left their homelands.

ASIAN AMERICANS IN ELEMENTARY SCHOOL CURRICULUM

Think back to your own schooling experiences—do you remember learning about Asian Americans at any point? Research shows that Asian Americans have been virtually absent from the U.S. history curriculum. When they are present, they are generally depicted either as exotic Others, as dangerous foreigners, or as a successful, hard-working, compliant minority—representations we'll explore throughout this book with a particular focus and with lists of book recommendations in Chapter 2. These curricular omissions and misrepresentations are not inconsequential. When textbooks and school lessons exclude or misrepresent Asian Americans as perpetually foreign, insignificant, or dangerous, they send the message that Asian Americans are not and should not be valued, cared for, or respected.

When this message spreads uninterrupted by teachers, it enacts a kind of psychological violence on Asian American students by suggesting that they have no value in their own country, which Lamar Johnson and Nathaniel Bryan (2016) describe as "spirit murder" (p.164), a form of dehumanization. Furthermore, these dehumanizing messages may leave Asian Americans vulnerable to physical attacks from people who take up the oppressive narrative that Asian Americans are undesirable, foreign, inassimilable, and/or dangerous to the nation. Meanwhile, by promoting the idea that anyone can make it in America if they are as smart and hard-working as Asian Americans, the curricular message of Asian Americans as a model minority is also dangerous. This portrayal pits Asian Americans against other communities of color, denies demands for change, and ultimately maintains white supremacy.

While social studies is an ideal place to teach Asian American histories, the instructional time dedicated to social studies teaching and learning has declined steadily since the No Child Left Behind Act of 2001. Yet most state social studies standards are far more comprehensive than even the most experienced teacher can manage to cover, leaving educators with too much to cover in too little time. Since social studies teaching is rarely a regular part of daily elementary school instruction except in grades/states where it is tested, administrators often don't care what teachers choose to include or how they teach it, and many teachers rely on familiar content that requires little planning. While there is nothing wrong with using lessons that you know to be of solid quality and strong interest to students, we urge you to challenge yourself to teach Asian American content. We hope that this book helps you imagine ways to make such teaching possible in your context. In Chapter 1, we will explore ways to teach about Asian America across all content areas, and will offer recommendations for children's literature, other media, and more throughout the book.

One common approach to the teaching of Asian America that we urge you to move away from (if you haven't already) is known as "food, fun, and festivals." This means only teaching about Asians and Asian Americans through food, holidays, and arts/crafts projects. These approaches can be problematic because they often occur with little context and lack nuance or complexity, which can lead to assumptions about an entire culture and can position groups as distinct from what is considered "American" and "normal" (Rodríguez & Swalwell, 2022).

A quick Pinterest or Teachers Pay Teachers search demonstrates how many of the activities associated with Asian cultures do just this, often relying on superficial content with cheesy, and sometimes outright stereotypical, clip art. Rather than rely on materials developed by cultural outsiders, consider prioritizing the voices and perspectives of cultural *insiders*. At the same time, remember that there is no singular way to celebrate or do *anything*, so exposing students to multiple perspectives and ways of being is important. Lunar New Year is celebrated differently in Chinese, Korean, Vietnamese, Filipinx, Japanese, Malaysian, Thai, and Indonesian cultures, *and* that may also look different in American contexts. What happens in San Francisco's Chinatown may not be the same as what takes place in Chicago, Philadelphia, or Atlanta. Always remember to take into account local contexts, including the Asian American communities where you are.

Finally, don't save Asian American content for Asian Pacific American History and Heritage Month in May. Teach it *all year long* because Asian Americans exist all year long! This is true for all heritage months. While we appreciate the sentiment in highlighting stories that have long been marginalized in the curriculum, we worry that centering heritage months means that students are exposed to more diverse narratives only during certain months of the year. This approach doesn't truly diversify the curriculum. Heritage month celebrations can be an opportunity to center groups, ethnicities, and cultures that are typically excluded, but shouldn't be the only time this happens.

For Esther and Noreen, who were educated in U.S. public and private schools, to be able to see themselves, their families, and their communities in the school curriculum would have done *so much* for their self-esteem and cultural identities. Unfortunately, in most schools nothing has really changed, as Sohyun's children rarely find connections to what their schools in Georgia teach about America and American culture. Literacy scholar Rudine Sims Bishop (1990) used the metaphor of windows and mirrors to explain this. Books that serve as mirrors reflect our own lives and experiences as a form of self-affirmation, while books that allow us to view perspectives and worlds different from our own can serve as windows. For many, if not most, Asian American children in the United States, schools feature far more "window" texts than "mirror" texts.

Unfortunately, this is true for many other groups: Latine, Indigenous, Black, multiracial, and multiethnic children; adopted and foster children; LGBTQ+ children; children who speak languages other than English; undocumented youth; disabled children; and those who follow faiths other than Protestant Christianity. For decades, few resources were available for educators who wanted to bring more diverse and inclusive texts into their classrooms. Today, however, we have more options than ever before. We will share many of our favorite textual mirrors and windows of the Asian American experience with you in this book, and we hope they will become a part of your classroom collection. We don't want any children to feel the exclusion that we have felt and witnessed in our own families, but we have to make clear why, where, and how this happens in order to address this problem with both intention and care.

WHY THIS MATTERS NOW

Whether and how we teach Asian American history is not an academic debate. It is a life-and-death issue. Since the COVID-19 pandemic began, there has been a surge of anti-Asian violence. In thousands of reported cases, people of Asian descent were insulted, spat on, yelled at, beaten, and faced other bodily harm by being baselessly accused as the cause of the pandemic (Yellow Horse et al., 2022). We have experienced these harms, too. Our children were called "coronavirus" or "China virus" at school. At grocery stores and in the parks, people have yelled to us, "Go back to China!" and "Stay home, you sickly people!"

Then, on March 16, 2021, a 21-year-old white man traveled to three different locations in metro Atlanta and shot eight people to death. Six of the victims were Asian immigrant women, making it an outright hate crime against people of Asian heritage. One witness remembered that the murderer said, "I am going to kill all Asians." Yet a white police spokesperson justified the white terror, stating that the murderer simply had a "bad day" (Kim, 2021).

As Susan Cridland-Hughes and LaGarrett King (2015) poignantly stated, while violence on unarmed Black and Indigenous bodies, and bodies of people of color occurs on the streets, the *idea* of this violence begins in the classroom. If we are sincere in our commitment to stop racism and violence against communities of color and Indigenous Peoples, we cannot continue to teach Eurocentric history that excludes or misrepresents people of color and Indigenous Peoples as inferior, insignificant, unworthy, and dangerous. We hope that our book contributes to antiracist education by offering rigorous and engaging ways to bring Asian American histories and narratives into the teaching and learning of the United States.

A FEW NOTES ABOUT LANGUAGE, NAMING, AND CAPITALIZATION

Language matters. Words can honor and uplift or demean and humiliate. Sometimes this occurs on purpose, and sometimes it is accidental. Writing this book with educators in mind, we want to be transparent about our decisions regarding phrasing that is essential to Asian American topics. First and foremost, you will notice that we do *not* use a hyphen in "Asian American." Historically, hyphenated identities have suggested dual loyalties—that is, a Thai-American would be considered just as loyal to Thailand as they would be to the United States. However, white people self-identify as Americans while non-white, "other" Americans have been assigned hyphenated racial identities.

Journalist Frances Kai-Hwa Wang (2021) explained, "Every time we call ourselves Asian American, we are making a powerful political statement that we are American, and we belong here. Note there is no hyphen" (para. 7). While you may still occasionally see the hyphen used in print, the Chicago Manual of Style dropped it in 2010 and the Associated Press Stylebook used by journalists around the globe stopped using the hyphen in 2019. We follow this model and will only hyphenate "Asian-American" when the term is used by others in quotes.

A second shift that has also been made by journalists and publishers in recent years is in regard to racial identities. When referring to racialized communities, we capitalize the first letter, such as Black and Brown. However, we are also mindful of the ways that language can indicate power or oppression. Drawing from the work of legal scholar Neil Gotanda (1991), whose thinking was deeply influenced by fellow legal scholar Kimberlé Crenshaw, we recognize that the term "white" has historically and contemporarily signaled racial domination. In contrast, Gotanda notes that "Black" is a liberating term with deep political and social meaning. So, while we capitalize Black, we do not capitalize white. We also use Indigenous Peoples, with both first letters capitalized, to indicate respect and recognition to tribal sovereignty and the multitude of nations that are included in this term. Another linguistic choice we've made that reflects cultural shifts in society is in regard to gender. Throughout this book, we will use an "e" and "x" to be as inclusive as possible when we utilize terms that otherwise gender a group of individuals, such as Latine (instead of Latina or Latino) or Filipinx (instead of Filipina or Filipino). In cases where we are specifically talking about a person or group that is strictly of a particular known gender, we will indicate that through linguistic choices, like Filipina or Latino.

The third point we want to make about language is that we will only use italics for emphasis, to denote the titles of books, films, and other forms of media, and when using terms related to scientific classifications. We will *not* use italics as a way to indicate words or phrases in languages other than English. This has long been a method that normalizes the English language while marking other languages as nonstandard. As bi/multilingual speakers, we choose to honor and normalize all languages, so when you see words in Korean, Urdu, Tagalog, or Arabic in this book, they will be written without italics. In this vein, we write Hawaiʻi with a diacritical mark called the okina that is a consonant in the Hawaiian language. The okina looks like a single open quote mark or reversed apostrophe and indicates what linguists call a glottal stop—a brief pause, like when one says "uh oh"—that impacts pronunciation.

Finally, we avoid language that is euphemistic (i.e., strategically changes the meaning of something so that it sounds less "bad") or rooted in oppression. For example, as we will explain in Chapter 4, we use the word incarceration, *not* internment, to describe what happened to 120,000 Japanese Americans who were forced to leave their homes on the West Coast to live in isolated prison camps. We also avoid the term "mixed race" due to its origins in racial purity, and instead privilege "multiracial." However, as language is ever-evolving, by the time this book is published, there may be some terms that we have used that may be considered offensive in some way. We apologize for any errors we have made and encourage you to reach out to us so that we can do better in the future. If you'd like to learn more about conscious language that promotes equity, we highly recommend the Conscious Style Guide (https://consciousstyleguide.com).

OVERVIEW OF THE BOOK

We have organized this book thematically rather than chronologically, given how common thematic instruction is in elementary schools. However, within many of our chapters, we unfold histories chronologically as there are important developments that occur over time, especially as laws and policies change. The Introduction has familiarized you with us and our reasons for writing this book. Chapter 1 lays out pedagogical considerations for teaching about Asian America, across content areas and in terms of resource selection. The remaining chapters are thematic and offer specific teaching strategies for each theme.

Chapter 2 explores the complexity of Asian American identity and common stereotypes of the past and present. We offer recommendations for children's literature to address each stereotype and share how reading the chapter book *Front Desk* by Kelly Yang can support students in understanding a wide array of issues relevant to Asian Americans. Chapter 3 outlines major moments in Asian immigration and Asian American migration. In this and subsequent chapters, we highlight historical artifacts and recommend children's literature and other media that can support the teaching of these concepts.

Chapter 4 dives into the topic of citizenship, considering how Asian Americans have specifically been denied access to naturalization and who is typically understood as "citizen" in the United States on the basis of race and religion. Chapter 5 is about war and displacement with a focus on the Philippine-American, Korean, and Vietnam Wars. The chapter describes ways for upper elementary teachers to examine how U.S. wars in Asia led to Asian migration to the United States, so that students can challenge militarism and understand war and subsequent migration with a critical lens.

Chapter 6 describes examples of Asian American activism and resistance, from struggles toward women's suffrage and cross-racial solidarity to labor and LGBTQ+ rights in the past and present. Finally, Chapter 7 grapples with contentious issues that often cause divides within Asian American communities. Part of understanding the complexity of Asian America is remembering that Asian Americans are not a monolithic group and do not share the same beliefs; in some cases, such as the examples explored in this chapter, people may be on opposite sides of an issue.

Each of these chapters offers suggestions for guided class discussions, recommended children's literature, and ideas for broader units of instruction across content areas. While several primary sources and graphic organizers are included in the text, we encourage readers to visit our website (www.teachingasianamerica.com) for more visual resources and lesson plans. The Appendix includes the Stop AAPI Hate Asian American Studies K–12 Framework developed by Sohyun and Noreen; a list of online archives of primary sources related to Asian American content; additional children's literature recommendations; and answers to frequently asked questions.

1

Pedagogical Overview

Early childhood centers and elementary schools are often the sites of young learners' earliest experiences exploring difference, whether related to personality, class, gender, race, ethnicity, language, or religion. Some of these differences arise informally, as kids compare their shoes or weekend activities on the playground or in the cafeteria. Other differences are presented formally by teachers, from making charts about food preferences and hair color to reading levels and math ability groups.

While race and ethnicity have become topics of heated discussion in terms of whether these essential aspects of one's identity should be taught in classrooms, they inevitably emerge in students' conversations. In particular, children of color often hear racial comments (and slurs) for the first time when they are young—and many of these initial comments come from their peers. When Sohyun's youngest daughter was five years old, she didn't want to draw herself because she didn't like her "flat nose," which she described as "not pretty" because it was unlike the noses of her mostly white friends. When Noreen's eldest daughter was three years old, she asked her parents why she didn't have "clear hair" like her friends, who were blonde. Noreen's daughter had jet black hair, just like her mother and father, and even though she was still in preschool, she noticed that she did not look like her peers.

Young people ask questions about race and ethnicity because *they want to understand race and ethnicity.* And even if children don't share

DOI: 10.4324/9781032662695-1

aloud the questions they are wrestling with, they are still taking in information and trying to understand how these ideas matter in our world. This book aims to support educators in teaching young children about race and ethnicity, with particular attention to Asian Americans. Contrary to popular politicized rhetoric, talking about race and ethnicity is *not* inherently racist; if done as part of building student understanding and empathy, it can be a powerful way to foster community and friendship. Ultimately, ensuring that young people understand and respect racial and ethnic differences is good for our democracy and its future. However, the structure of a typical school day and the curricular constraints faced by many educators can make it difficult to squeeze this content into the classroom regularly and in meaningful ways.

The advice we offer in the chapters that follow recognizes that social studies, the content area that specifically attends to cultures, the movement of people over time, and their impact on society, is rarely taught with regularity in elementary classrooms. Since the passage of the No Child Left Behind Act in 2001, elementary educators have increasingly focused on teaching math and reading skills that are measured by school district and state assessments. As these assessments become more frequent and high stakes, content areas like science and social studies, which are not assessed in early grades, fall to the wayside. We understand this reality and offer ways to integrate Asian American content across disciplines. Because we know language arts instruction happens every single day in elementary classrooms, we especially emphasize ways to teach Asian American narratives through children's literature and language arts activities.

However, as social studies educators, we also want to encourage readers to bring social studies learning back to the classroom. In the next section, we offer some content-area-specific suggestions to consider as you read the rest of the book, beginning with social studies. Whenever possible, we encourage educators to integrate across disciplines and content areas and to collaborate with other colleagues, such as special education experts on campus as well as music, arts, and physical education teachers. In addition, educators should be intentional about including community members who may have ethnicity-specific expertise. We also describe what it means to *critically* engage students in conversations and with texts about ethnoracial groups, and why it is important to center Asian American voices and experiences.

CONTENT AREA APPLICATIONS

Social Studies

Social studies includes the disciplines of history, geography, economics, civics, government, sociology, psychology, and anthropology (Rodríguez & Swalwell, 2022). It's a content area well-suited to teach students about different ethnoracial groups in the United States and how they are part of our diverse democracy. In classrooms, however, it's often reduced to superficial historical narratives that focus on a small group of heroes and a selection of holidays. While we recognize that in some schools educators are explicitly told *not* to teach social studies regularly, when we consider how deeply embedded it is in the everyday lives of young people, we find it hard to abide by such an ill-informed directive. Basic aspects of socialization, like showing respect and care for others, building community, and demonstrating civic responsibility, are fundamentally tied to social studies. Contrary to popular belief, social studies isn't just history—we should never forget that the *social* part of social studies is precisely what makes it essential for our students.

Increasingly, teachers rely less and less on textbooks. Textbooks are notoriously dense and boring, and districts have begun replacing them with online curriculum or consumables for individual students. But their replacements often repeat the missteps of the textbooks that many educators grew up with. These texts have been criticized as superficial, Eurocentric, male-dominated narratives told from an omniscient voice presumed to be neutral, in which women, Indigenous Peoples, and people of color make minimal appearances that are relegated to sidebars and supplementary worksheets (Cornbleth & Waugh, 2012; Sleeter & Grant, 2017).

These narratives highlight U.S. exceptionalism while minimizing histories of oppression. Consider how the Civil Rights Movement is often reduced to Rosa Parks refusing to leave her bus seat and Martin Luther King Jr. giving a great speech condensed to a single line that becomes reframed to assert that one's race doesn't matter. Spoiler: The rest of the speech argues otherwise, and the line in question is almost always presented out of content. Rather than giving students opportunities to discuss how much violence activists like Parks and King faced and why—as well as how we continue to struggle with racism today—mainstream texts and learning standards offer a simpler, apolitical, and inaccurate version of events (Busey & Walker, 2017).

It's not just textbooks and standards that take this watered-down approach to historical narratives. Children's literature does it, too. Historical artifacts can add nuance to children's literature, textbooks, documentaries, and videos. In the section about language arts, we will explore some strategies that educators can use to take a more critical approach to read alouds and book clubs. But first, we want to make clear how using primary sources (historical artifacts that we will describe in greater detail shortly) alongside secondary sources (including children's literature, encyclopedias, and websites) can pack a powerful punch in helping students interpret social studies in dynamic, meaningful ways (Rodríguez, 2022; Salinas et al., 2012).

The simplest definition of primary sources is that they are firsthand accounts. While photographs, letters, and journal entries are some of the most common examples, primary sources can also include legal documents, political cartoons, interviews, and newspaper articles, as long as they are created by people expressing how they perceived an event at the time that it occurred. In contrast, secondary sources are secondhand accounts by people who did not experience the event themselves. Secondary sources, especially those written for children, may leave out details that can offer important insight and nuance into historical events. Using primary sources before, during, and after read alouds can give students opportunities to ask questions, consider multiple perspectives, and launch into further research (Rodríguez et al., 2022).

For example, primary sources can be used as an introductory activity at the start of a unit. To begin her unit about Japanese American incarceration during World War II, second grade teacher Rosalie Ip engaged students with a "picture flood": she printed photographs of War Relocation Authority (WRA) prison camps from the Library of Congress (https://www.loc.gov/classroom-materials/japanese-american-internment/) and spread them across students' desks. She urged her students to walk around the room and think aloud as they observed the photos. As they looked and wondered aloud to themselves and their peers, Ip and her student teacher jotted students' questions and comments on sticky notes. The next day, as Ip's students gathered together on the carpet, she began by reviewing the questions they posed. The sticky notes were posted on the easel beside her chair at the edge of the carpet, where students could easily refer to them.

She encouraged students to think about their questions as she read aloud *The Bracelet* (1996) by Yoshiko Uchida. As several of the illustrations in the book were similar to the photographs that students had viewed the day before, the children made many visual connections. Some murmured to themselves while others loudly exclaimed their observations, but all were deeply engaged.

The use of and discussion around primary sources continued after they finished reading *The Bracelet*. They analyzed a collection of primary sources from the local Taniguchi family, who had been imprisoned in a WRA camp at Crystal City, Texas. After learning about the patriarch Isamu, who had been taken from his family (similar to the characters in *The Bracelet*), students made many connections to the new set of photographs.

Months later, Ip was reading a different book with her students. She chose the chapter book *Sylvia and Aki* (2013) by Winifred Conkling as her final read aloud of the academic year, reading one chapter a day. Like *The Bracelet*, portions of *Sylvia and Aki* took place in a prison camp during World War II. As she read about the horrible conditions at the camp in *Sylvia and Aki*, she also shared photographs of the camp in Poston, Arizona, supplementing her historical fiction read aloud with primary sources so students could see real images of families and the barracks they lived in. Conkling's writing was vivid and detailed—indeed, many students were frightened as the narrator described scorpions and snakes coming up through the floorboards—but being able to see the crowded barracks and the desolate desert landscape in photographs made the text truly come to life.

These examples illustrate how primary sources can add tremendous depth and spark rich conversations among young learners before, during, and after read alouds. Primary sources can also be used as a form of assessment: for a formative assessment at the end of a lesson, students can write a caption in their own words on a sticky note or respond to open-ended questions about a primary source. For a summative assessment at the end of a unit, educators can offer students a selection of sources and they can choose a handful to describe and sequence or create slide decks that summarize a historical event.

But how do you find primary sources for events that are lesser known? Unfortunately, the most well-known national archives, like the Library of Congress and National Archives, have slim pickings when it comes to Asian American content. Fortunately, there is the Smithsonian Institute's Asian Pacific American Center and a range of community archives and museums that offer open-access primary sources. Most of these, however, are specific to particular nationalities and ethnic groups. The Museum of Chinese in America and Wing Luke Museum have impressive collections, as does the ever-growing South Asian American Digital Archive. For resources related to Japanese American incarceration, Densho and the Japanese American Citizens League have wide collections, while the Go for Broke National Education Center highlights Japanese American World War II Veterans. The Welga Digital Archive hosted by the Bulosan Center for Filipino Studies at the University of California Davis features primary sources related to the Filipinx American experience. A treasure trove of primary sources centered on local Southeast Asian American communities has been collected and digitized by the University of California at Irvine and the University of Massachusetts Lowell. Websites for these and other archives can be found in the Appendix.

The last thing we want to note about social studies teaching and learning is the role of inquiry. When the Common Core standards were developed, they did not include social studies, so the National Council for the Social Studies and its partner organizations created the Civic, College, and Career Readiness (C3) Framework to offer a national set of social studies standards. The C3 Framework, and many of the curriculum packages that have been created by other groups since its development, is deeply rooted in inquiry, which is most simply defined as wrestling with a problem or question. The C3 Framework consists of four steps:

1. Developing questions that students will try to answer by the end of the unit
2. Applying disciplinary concepts and tools to help students answer the questions they developed
3. Gathering and evaluating sources to develop claims and use evidence in response to the questions they developed
4. Communicating and critiquing conclusions students make and taking informed action

True inquiry gives students opportunities to develop their own questions, rather than a teacher imposing or presuming questions that students want to know the answers to. Of course, in a world of pre-planned curriculum, many inquiry lessons have a canned set of questions and in some cases, those are perfectly fine ways to launch student learning. However, you can still find ways to build in students' interests and questions. When students have time and space to develop and pursue questions that matter *to them*, their engagement becomes infectious, so if you have the opportunity to try it out, we highly recommend it!

Language Arts

Reading and writing are two of the most important skills that are taught and learned in elementary grades. The No Child Left Behind Act was the start of an era in which these skills became constantly assessed and scrutinized by individuals other than teachers, students, and their families, whether through beginning-, middle-, and end-of-year diagnostics or in high-stakes standardized tests. In many schools, this shift toward the constant monitoring and reporting of literacy skills occurred alongside a decline in educators' ability to choose texts they featured in their classrooms, which was often the result of districts purchasing literacy curriculum that includes basal readers or spotlighted texts. Unlike social studies, however, the vital nature of literacy assures that reading and writing are *always* a part of the daily schedule and may allow some flexibility in terms of text selection.

Nonfiction reading and writing is a common literacy focus, especially through the use of biographies. Such biography units are an excellent opportunity to highlight Asian American experiences and figures, from the first Chinese American actress Anna May Wong (Yoo, 2009) and Chinese American women pilots Hazel Ying Lee (Leung, 2021) and Maggie Gee (Moss, 2009), to Korean Americans like Olympic medal-winner Sammy Lee (Yoo, 2005) and chef Roy Choi (Martin & Lee, 2015), Japanese Americans such as artist Gyo Fujikawa (Maclear, 2019) and chef Niki Nakayama (Michalak & Florence, 2021), as well as Afghan American pilot Shaesta Waiz (Pimm, 2020) and Thai American politician Tammy Duckworth (Soontornvat, 2022). You can find these and more biographies in the inset box; please note that this list is *very* East Asian heavy, so we have included a few biographical collections that present a broader range of Asian ethnicities.

RECOMMENDED ASIAN AMERICAN BIOGRAPHICAL PICTUREBOOKS

- *Asian American Women in Science: An Asian American History Book for Kids* by Tina Cho
- *A Boy Named Isamu* by James Yang
- *Building Zaha: The Story of Architect Zaha Hadid* by Victoria Tentler-Krylov
- *Chef Roy Choi and the Street Food Remix* by Jacqueline Briggs Martin and June Jo Lee, illustrated by Man One
- *Dumpling Dreams: How Joyce Chen Brought the Dumpling from Beijing to Cambridge* by Carrie Clickard, illustrated by Katy Wu
- *Fall Down Seven Times, Stand Up Eight: Patsy Takemoto Mink and the Fight for Title IX* by Jen Bryant
- *The Fearless Flights of Hazel Ying Lee* by Julie Leung, illustrated by Julie Kwon
- *Fly, Girl, Fly!: Shaesta Waiz Soars around the World* by Nancy Roe Pimm, illustrated by Alexandra Bye
- *Fred Korematsu Speaks Up* by Laura Atkins & Stan Yogi, illustrated by Yutaka Houlette
- *It Began with a Page* by Kyo Maclear, illustrated by Julie Morstad

- *Journey for Justice: The Life of Larry Itliong* by Dawn B. Mabalon and Gayle Romasanta, illustrated by Andre Sibayan
- *Kamala Harris: Rooted in Justice* by Nikki Grimes, illustrated by Laura Freeman
- *A Life Made by Hand: The Story of Ruth Asawa* by Andrea D'Aquino
- *A Life of Service: The Story of Senator Tammy Duckworth* by Christina Soontornvat, illustrated by Dow Phumiruk
- *Loujain Dreams of Sunflowers* by Lina AlHathloul and Uma Mishra-Newbery, illustrated by Rebecca Green
- *Maya Lin: Artist-Architect of Light and Lines* by Jeanne Walker Harvey, illustrated by Dow Phumiruk
- *Mountain Chef: How One Man Lost His Groceries, Changed His Plans, and Helped Cook Up the National Park Service* by Annette Bay Pimentel, illustrated by Rich Lo
- *Niki Nakayama: A Chef's Tale in 13 Bites* by Jamie Michalak & Debbi Michiko Florence, illustrated by Yuko Jones
- *Paper Son* by Julie Leung, illustrated by Chris Sasaki
- *Playing at the Border: A Story of Yo-Yo Ma* by Joanna Ho, illustrated by Teresa Martinez
- *Shapes, Lines, and Light: My Grandfather's American Journey* by Katie Yamasaki
- *She Persisted: Patsy Mink* by Tae Keller
- *Shining Star: The Anna May Wong Story* by Paula Yoo, illustrated by Lin Wang
- *Sixteen Years in Sixty Seconds: The Sammy Lee Story* by Paula Yoo, illustrated by Dom Lee
- *Sky High: The True Story of Maggie Gee* by Marissa Moss, illustrated by Carl Angel
- *Stories of South Asian Super Girls* by Raj Kaur Khaira
- *We Are Here: 30 Inspiring Asian Americans and Pacific Islanders Who Have Shaped the United States* by Naomi Hirahara, illustrated by Illi Ferandez
- *Yes We Will: Asian Americans Who Shaped This Country* by Kelly Yang, illustrated by N. H. Ali et al.

When using picturebooks about Asian American figures or histories, it is important to consider that most students may have little background knowledge or context about Asian Americans. A valuable resource for children and adults to address this problem is peritext. Peritext includes all the parts of the book that surround the main content, such as the title page, dedication, table of contents, glossary, timeline, and source notes (Gross, 2019). If a book is about a time period or historical event that students have not learned about before, its peritext can offer important background information. Often, reading peritextual features like Author's Notes occurs *after* a read aloud of the main text. However, if educators *begin* with the peritext, they can contextualize the events that unfold during the read aloud and offer insight into how the author is connected to this particular story. Moreover, the background information that students learn may provoke questions that can be answered by the main text and can spark connections to their own lives and prior knowledge.

While read alouds can focus on historical moments or contemporary issues, they can also highlight books that serve as mentor texts for student work, such as writing. For example, fourth grade teacher Amy Okimoto spotlighted the books *Eyes That Kiss in the Corners* (Ho, 2021) and *Watercress* (Wang, 2021) with her students as they began a unit on memoir writing. Okimoto wanted students to reflect on their connections to family members and later conduct family interviews. *Eyes That Kiss in the Corners* (Ho, 2021) offered a range of examples for them to connect personal experiences to broader histories. Okimoto noted the book's mention of tea and the Chinese revolution: "I think there is such an opportunity to tie picturebooks to real-life experiences, and I feel like picturebooks can open the door to a topic that allows students to become engaged and interested. Then . . . that can be a springboard to real history . . . Even though history seems like this big magical thing, it really is real-life people experiencing real-life things" (personal communication, June 29, 2022). Okimoto considers such an approach to be one way to make history more tangible and accessible, as it allows students to realize that the narratives they craft are a way to share their family's histories and, in turn, for other people to connect with them.

For Okimoto, *Watercress* (Wang, 2021) is an excellent mentor text for highlighting small moments due to the author's vibrant memories of childhood told through lush but concise language. In the book, the daughter refuses to eat watercress, embarrassed that the family harvested it from a ditch, so her mother shares a story about her family's struggles with poverty and hunger to illustrate the importance of eating the food that is available. "Even with young students," Okimoto recounted, "It is a story that evokes emotions . . . to bring out that idea of how often we as kids neglect to understand the significance of a moment. We [Okimoto and her fourth graders] talk about foods that we eat, foods that might be from your family that maybe other people don't like." She shared the story of an Ethiopian student who responded to the text by talking about injera, a fermented flatbread made from teff flour. Despite injera being viewed as strange and uncommon in suburban Colorado, this food was a part of him and his culture and therefore was important for others to know about. Okimoto loves how the small but powerful details and emotions in *Watercress* fully immerse the reader in a specific moment in time.

You may be wondering how educators like Okimoto find powerful texts focusing on Asian American narratives such as *Eyes That Kiss in the Corners* and *Watercress.* Okimoto relies on Twitter, where she follows Asian American authors and other educators. Social media was the birthplace of the movement #WeNeedDiverseBooks, in which youth literature authors came together to demand changes to the lack of ethnoracial diversity in the publishing industry. By following the social media of publishers committed to the development of more ethnoracially diverse texts, you can learn about new and upcoming releases, including but not limited to those written by and about Asian Americans. We recommend following the social media accounts for Lee & Low, Kokila (a Penguin Random House imprint), Salaam Reads (a Simon & Schuster imprint), Saffron Press, and W. W. Norton.

Make sure to follow the authors and illustrators you love to learn about who *they* are reading and enjoying in the realm of youth literature! We also appreciate the book lists available at the Social Justice Books website (https://socialjusticebooks.org/booklists) as well as the lists and award-winners highlighted by the Asian Pacific American

Librarian Association (https://www.apalaweb.org), although the latter is not specifically Asian American and honors many books that take place in Asia and the Pacific Islands. Remember not to conflate these distinct experiences and contexts! Questions to guide you in selecting high-quality children's literature can be found in the Appendix.

Mathematics

Mathematics may not seem like a space where Asian American content might fit in. However, we view the teaching of Asian American narratives and histories as part of a larger effort to teach for social justice that isn't limited to social studies or language arts but is woven across all content areas. As math education scholar Cathery Yeh reminds us, "Mathematics is a human activity tied to languages, histories, lands and culture" (Dingle & Yeh, 2021, para. 27). Educators can leverage mathematical concepts to explore and understand data about populations, such as changes to immigration over time and nation-based quotas, to analyze tables, graphs, and charts to better understand segregation, statistics related to educational attainment and income, and much more.

Educators Gloria Gallardo's and Cathery Yeh's (2022) lesson " 'Tu lucha es mi lucha': Mathematics for Movement Building" highlights how math can be deeply integrated with literacy and social studies through a focus on the United Farm Workers labor union. Their lesson begins with students drawing an image of a farmworker, then writing three adjectives to describe the person they have drawn. Next, students discuss and categorize their adjectives, considering the role of one's perspective in how they understand others before a read aloud of *Journey for Justice: The Life of Larry Itliong* (Mabalon & Romasanta, 2018). As students move through the book, Gallardo and Yeh recommend stopping at pivotal moments when Larry Itliong, a Filipino farmworker and organizer, notes his wages. By using base-10 blocks, place value mats, and/or coins, students can represent and compare his wages at different jobs, including when workers protested for greater wages and when employers threatened to cut their earnings. Approaches like this make lessons about place value and money much more powerful and interesting than decontextualized worksheets with arbitrary amounts for students to compose and label.

Science

A social justice approach to science also offers opportunities to include Asian American stories and figures. Many scientific innovations were created by Asian Americans; for example, the development of California's rich farmland was largely due to the irrigation technology implemented by Asian immigrants like the Japanese. In the 1880s, Chinese American orchard foreman Ah Bing cared for modified cherry trees in Oregon, and the Bing cherry was named in his honor. In 1920, Korean American agricultural entrepreneur Hyong-sun Kim and his employee Anderson invented the nectarine by crossing a peach and a plum. Moving into the contemporary era, *Queen of Physics: How Wu Chien Shiung Helped Unlock the Secrets of the Atom* (Robeson, 2019) is a picturebook about a Chinese woman physicist who did important research on beta decay.

When teaching about bacteria, educators can illustrate how early Chinese immigrants who worked on the railroads stayed healthier than their white counterparts due to their diet. Chinese workers boiled water to make hot tea and ate vegetables like bamboo shoots and mushrooms, which prevented them from falling victim to waterborne diseases and scurvy (Osumi, 2006). Seasonal plant growth can be explored through the migratory movements of Filipino and Mexican American farm laborers, who followed harvests across the United States. When learning about space exploration, include the story of Ellison Onizuka, the first Asian American astronaut! Many other incredible scientists can be found in the pages of Tina Cho's *Asian American Women in Science: An Asian American History Book for Kids* (2022). If you can connect human stories and experiences to science, you can find Asian American examples!

Physical Education and the Arts (Music, Visual Art, Dance, Media)

Asian American content can be a part of all subject areas, including the arts and physical education! In some parts of the United States, the traditional Filipino dance of tinikling has long been featured in physical fitness curriculum. But simply including Asian American cultural or historical content isn't enough—it's important to ensure that context is also a part of instruction. If we take the example of tinikling, in which two long poles of bamboo are moved in rhythm while dancers move their feet in and out of the poles, we can consider how the dance is named after a bird called the tikling that swiftly avoids bamboo traps in rice fields. Video streaming sites offer opportunities to share traditional dances as well as modern versions that incorporate contemporary music. We need to share examples of how art forms evolve based on their context and who is performing, as well as how one cultural tradition can be taken up by another to create new forms and styles.

The Smithsonian American Art Museum's website (https://americanart.si.edu/art/highlights/asian-american) features a curated Asian American collection and includes online galleries with past and current exhibits for student exploration. Several picturebook biographies listed earlier in this chapter bring attention to Asian American artists like Ruth Asawa, Gyo Fujikawa, and Isamu Noguchi (who has an online gallery at the Smithsonian American Art Museum), as well as the first famous Chinese American actress Wong Liu Tsong, better known by her stage name Anna May Wong (see Chapter 4). Wong's story is a powerful example of how innovators in specific fields may suffer for their "uniqueness"—in her case, her Asian Americanness limited the roles she was able to play *even when the characters were Asian!* Wong's story can be presented alongside contemporary barrier-breaking artists and athletes like Misty Copeland, the first Black woman to be promoted to principal dancer in the history of American Ballet Theater; Naomi Osaka, the first Asian American woman to hold the top ranking in singles tennis; and Sunisa "Suni" Lee, the first Hmong American Olympian.

Many Asian American musicians can be found across popular culture, but their contributions often go unrecognized. Yo-Yo Ma is one of the most famous Asian Americans in classical music, and Asian Americans abound in contemporary pop music, from Filipinx Americans like Olivia Rodrigo, H.E.R., Ruby Ibarra, and Bruno Mars, to the Korean American rock band Run River North and indie singer-songwriter Michelle Zauner, better known as Japanese Breakfast. While we are thrilled that Korean pop (a.k.a. K-Pop) has achieved tremendous popularity in the United States, don't conflate K-Pop, which comes *from Asia*, with music like that of Run River North, which emerged from *Asian American* cultures and musicians.

INTEGRATION ACROSS CONTENT AREAS

Given the disproportionate amount of instructional time dedicated to language arts in recent decades, many elementary educators squeeze social studies and science content in through language arts activities like read alouds and nonfiction reading and writing. However, simply selecting a social studies topic doesn't make a lesson focused on social studies if all the questions and activities remain focused on literary concepts, such as character development, sequence of events, and summarizing. Education researcher Elizabeth Hinde (2015) notes three ways that curriculum is typically integrated in elementary classrooms:

TABLE 1.1 Common Manifestations of Curriculum Integration in Elementary Classrooms

Fractured Social Studies Integration	Stealthy Integration	Healthy Integration
Small chunks of content area information related to the weekly reading or language arts activities are presented to students without much depth. Social studies content has no connection to children's lives or to other areas of the curriculum. The purpose of social studies is mainly to enhance reading/language arts and is not focused on preparing students for effective citizenship. Does not inspire disciplinary modes of thinking because the content is disjointed.	Disguises social studies content as language arts lessons. Covertly teaches social studies content in order to satisfy mandates to spend most of the daily instructional time on language arts activities. Teacher chooses reading/language arts materials with rich spatial or historical content, but focuses on reading/language arts skills. Reading/language arts are the center of the curriculum. Social studies has no pedagogy of its own. Does not inspire disciplinary modes of thinking because content is disguised as something else.	The connection of social studies to children's lives and other content areas is explicit and clear to students. Reading/language arts are recognized as tools for helping children come to an understanding of the world (and how to communicate that understanding) and are not considered the purpose of schooling. Children and their knowledge of the content are the center of the curriculum. Reading/language arts activities are focused on developing disciplinary frames of mind in students.

From Hinde, E. R. (2015). The theoretical foundations of curriculum integration and its application in social studies instruction. In L. Bennett & E. R. Hinde (Eds.), *Becoming integrated thinkers: Case studies in elementary social studies* (pp. 21-29). National Council for the Social Studies. Reprinted with permission.

Unsurprisingly, we recommend *healthy* integration where the social studies content is deeply contextualized *and* connected to students' lives and communities.

We also believe that elementary teaching and learning has many opportunities for rich integration beyond social studies and language arts. As noted above in the sections on math and science, having a justice-oriented curriculum allows students opportunities to examine societal issues more deeply across disciplines. They can read a non-fiction text, summarize and make inferences about what they learned (reading skills!), gather more information from data organized in charts and graphs (math!), then consider the impact on the environment (science!) and on different communities (social studies!) in order to compose a persuasive piece (writing!), or create an illustrated poster (arts!) or animation (technology!) that informs the public about what they have learned. We know that many elementary schools require daily schedules which separate content areas, but we urge educators to fight for more interdisciplinary approaches that address *all* content areas in more authentic and inquiry-based ways. In the chapters that follow, we will point out moments in which specific content areas can be addressed to teach Asian American topics but encourage interdisciplinary integration whenever possible to maximize student engagement and provide richer learning experiences.

CRITICAL INSTRUCTION INSTEAD OF MULTICULTURAL APPROACHES

We hope the recommendations we offer in this book move *away* from multicultural approaches of the past and *toward* critical instruction that considers issues of power, so that Asian American voices, experiences, and histories are centered rather than completely ignored, sidelined, or spoken for by others. While the term "multicultural" evokes greater representation and diversity, many of the multicultural education efforts developed in recent decades often rely on stereotypical depictions of culture that are meant to be palatable to white audiences but may be grossly inauthentic. This results in what is known as the "food, fun, and festivals" approach or, alternatively, what some people refer to as the 5 F's: food, festivals, famous people, fashion, and flags.

No matter which of these approaches are used, these are aspects of culture that are often exoticized and appropriated by cultural outsiders while still distinguishing Asian culture(s) as different and weird from what is viewed as normal in U.S. society.

In contrast, critical instruction means that you as an educator need to think deeply about what you are going to teach when it comes to introducing an unfamiliar culture or history to your students and how you might need to be thoughtful in your approach. The questions in the accompanying box offer a few considerations that we urge educators to sit with as you embark on teaching about topics that may be new to *you*, but perhaps are well known to students and members of the school and/or local communities.

CONSIDERATIONS WHEN TEACHING CULTURAL OR HISTORICAL TOPICS THAT ARE NEW TO YOU

- Do students and their families have knowledge and experiences that you should learn from first?
- What are the various perspectives that you should consider?
- How can you make sure you are pronouncing names and words correctly?
- How can you make sure that you are recognizing diversity within this culture or different voices within this history? What voices are still being left out?
- What resources are you privileging and who created them?

Do you know a cultural insider who would be willing to help you vet those resources for authenticity and accuracy? The idea of lifting up stories of marginalized people that are created by people who belong to those communities went viral with #OwnVoices. This hashtag was created by young adult author Corinne Duyvis in 2015 to consider which voices and stories might need to be uplifted in terms of accuracy and authenticity when it comes to groups who are rarely represented in books. Given the stereotypical and inaccurate representations of Asians found in "classic" texts like *The Five Chinese Brothers* (Bishop, 1938) and *Tikki Tikki Tembo* (Mosel, 1968) that sadly remain in circulation, we hope readers will amplify #OwnVoices books written by and about Asian Americans that tell authentic stories from a place of love.

Avoid relying on dated and racist texts written by outsiders to Asian and Asian American cultures who ultimately exoticize Asians and Asian Americans and thereby misinform students. These books, alongside some beloved but problematic texts by Dr. Seuss mentioned in Chapter 2, may have been childhood favorites—that's okay! We're not trying to ruin your childhood memories of books that were meaningful in your development! We are, however, thinking about the ways those same books alienated Asian American children who had no other literary options that reflected people who looked like them. There are so many more alternatives available today that can be used instead, and we spotlight many of those titles throughout our book.

Recently, Sohyun and Noreen collaborated with Asian American studies and education scholars across the country to develop an Asian American Studies K–12 Framework to support this work in classrooms. The framework focuses on several essential concepts and subconcepts, which you can find in the following list. It also includes guiding questions for educators and students, as well as teaching considerations (many of which we explore here and in the chapters that follow) and a glossary (see the framework summary and website in Appendix):

- **Identity**
  - Exploration of Self
  - Stereotypes and Discrimination
- **Power and Oppression**
  - Imperialism, War, and Migration
  - Citizenship and Racialization
- **Community and Solidarity**
  - Resistance and Solidarity
  - Contention and Complexity
- **Reclamation and Joy**
  - Reclaiming Histories
  - Creative Expression

As you begin to brainstorm instructional activities and lessons related to Asian America, this framework may serve as a useful resource for the topics covered in this book. Importantly, the framework centers experiences and stories told by Asian Americans themselves and encourages a deep exploration of identity before learning about issues related to race, ethnicity, stereotypes, and discrimination. While power and oppression are undeniably a part of the Asian American experience, educators should also be intentional about emphasizing resistance and examples of solidarity with other groups. Finally, educators must also address how Asian Americans have reclaimed their histories and found joy in spite of their struggles.

INCLUSION OF CURRENT EVENTS AND REAL-WORLD EXAMPLES

Much of this text necessarily focuses on Asian American histories and common stereotypes that we hope you can disrupt with your students. The nature of book publishing means that some of the events included at the time this book was written may not be current whenever you start reading it. While we have created a website to supplement this text, we urge readers to pay attention to local, state, and national news and note when and where Asian American connections can be made. In Chapter 6, we include the names of several organizations that we encourage you to follow on social media so you can stay abreast of the latest issues relevant to Asian American communities.

LOCAL CONNECTIONS

In the section on social studies at the beginning of this chapter, we mentioned how second grade teacher Rosalie Ip connected her lessons about Japanese American incarceration to her Texas context by sharing the story of Isamu Taniguchi. Taniguchi was imprisoned in a camp in Crystal City, Texas, then stayed in Texas after his release, resuming his farming career in the Rio Grande Valley before retiring in Austin where his son was a prominent architect. During his retirement, Taniguchi built a traditional Zen garden adjacent to Zilker Park, one of the largest public spaces in Austin.

Using primary sources from a recent exhibit at the Austin History Center, Ip shared Taniguchi's story with her students, who were able to make connections between Japanese American incarceration and the community in which they lived. While they may not have known anyone Japanese American or anybody who was imprisoned in a World War II camp, they *did* know Zilker Park and often drove by or walked on the famous Hike and Bike Trail around Lady Bird Lake designed by Taniguchi's architect son, Alan. After sharing this story, all of Ip's students knew why this garden had been renamed the Isamu Taniguchi Japanese Garden and understood the long-lasting impact of Japanese American incarceration on a local family. This classroom vignette is a vivid example of how you can connect your lessons to local Asian American communities and histories.

EMBRACE A LEARNING STANCE

We end this chapter by asking you to adopt a learning stance as you proceed through this text. Some of what you read might be familiar while other sections may be brand-new content. We know it's a *lot* to take in. We learned most of this ourselves when we were adults, long after we started teaching. Reimagining the way you teach social studies, language arts, math, science, and the arts by including the content that follows will be a *process.* You will likely have missteps, misspeak, mispronounce something, or get names or terms mixed up. We've all been there. If you make a mistake, own it. Let your students know that you are learning, too, and that you are trying to do new things in order to better represent the diverse democracy we live in. Tell them that you want them to learn *as kids* stuff that you only recently learned as an adult! Encourage students to take risks, whether it's reading a new genre, trying a different kind of food, or pronouncing a word that might look intimidating. This is how we learn and grow!

Indeed, we the authors are still learning and growing. As we mentioned in the Introduction, our training and research related to Asian American narratives and studies has been mostly limited to East, Southeast, and South Asia. Due to their ancestry, Sohyun and Esther have much deeper knowledge of Korean and East Asian history. Due to her familial origins, Noreen knows South Asian and Filipinx histories best, but *none of us* are scholars of Asian history. Even within these groups and regions, we still have lots to learn, particularly about ethnic and religious communities that we do not belong to. And when it comes to Central and West Asia, we don't pretend to be experts in these areas. We have a lot of growing and reading to do ourselves. We rely on other folks who know much more than we do, and we want to remind you that there is nothing wrong with asking others to help you build your knowledge. There's no way any one person can know it all, and you don't know what you don't know.

By the time you finish this book, you will not be an expert on all things Asian American. It's simply not possible. But you will hopefully know a lot more than you did when you started reading, and will know how you can learn even more. We offer this book as a starting point and way to center Asian American voices, experiences, and histories that have for too long been ignored. Our advice and recommendations are based on scholarly expertise as well as on our shared experiences as Asian Americans, students, and teachers. Our approaches are not the only way to do this work, but they *are* grounded in peer-reviewed social studies and educational research. We believe that any good teacher knows how to modify lessons and instructional ideas to best fit the students they teach in their particular context. Take our recommendations and make them work for young people in *your* community. Now, let's dive in!

2

Identity and Stereotypes

Who *is* an Asian American? This chapter breaks down who does and does not fall under the umbrella of this term. We also explore how it emerged, changed, and has been misunderstood in the past and present. Next, we address the importance of names, as traditional Asian names are often mispronounced, mocked, and even replaced by peers and teachers. We also identify common stereotypes associated with Asian Americans, including perceptions of Asian food as stinky/weird, the model minority trope, forever foreigner, "Yellow Peril," "Dusky Peril," and alien threat/terrorist. We describe how elementary educators can use children's literature and other media to examine these stereotypes in popular culture. Lastly, we illustrate how a read aloud of *Front Desk* (2019) by Kelly Yang (an ideal chapter book for grades 3–5) can help you explore many complexities of Asian American identity and stereotypes in the classroom.

ASIAN AMERICAN IDENTITY

As we described in our Introduction, the term "Asian American" was coined in 1968 by two activist college students who wanted to bring together Japanese, Chinese, and Filipinx American students with shared political goals. Before Emma Gee and Yuji Ichioka created this term, people of Asian descent were typically described by their specific ethnicity (e.g., Korean American). If people spoke broadly about

DOI: 10.4324/9781032662695-2

people of Asian descent, the racist and colonial term "Oriental" was commonly used. In the decades since Gee and Ichioka gave us a homegrown alternative, it has been taken up by the U.S. Census and other organizations as a racial category found on government forms, surveys, and other documents. Like any term used to refer to an immense social group, this concept can be both useful *and* ineffective in describing the histories, experiences, and perspectives of an incredibly large and diverse group of people who speak different languages and belong to various cultures, ethnicities, religions, and socioeconomic classes.

While a deep dive into the individual ethnicities that make up Asia (and Asian America) is beyond the scope of this book, we want to make sure that readers know who is included under the Asian American umbrella. Let's do a quick geography review: Asia is the world's largest and most populous continent, spanning the Eastern *and* Western hemispheres. Asia shares continental landmass with both Europe and Africa, which can be confusing in terms of the borders between continents. Most geographers consider the Ural Mountains to be the dividing line between Europe and Asia, while the Suez Canal is widely understood as the border between Africa and Asia.

This means that the country of Russia is spread across both Europe and Asia. While most of Russia's landmass is located in Asia, over three-fourths of its population lives on the European side. The nation's capital Moscow (where the Russian empire began) is on the European side and is home to 12 million people. The Asian portion of Russia, located to the east of the Ural Mountains, is Siberia, known for its inhospitable freezing weather. Like most places with extreme climates, it is sparsely populated, and most Siberians live along the southern border. Thus, given Russia's demographic concentration and historical roots in Europe, Russians who immigrate to the United States are generally *not* considered Asian Americans.

With that understanding of Russia out of the way, let's consider the rest of the Asian continent. Asia is composed of five regions: Central Asia, East Asia, Southeast Asia, South Asia, and West Asia. Yet Asian Americans are most often conflated with East Asians/East Asian Americans. We want to disrupt this misperception right now and make clear that there are historical reasons for this misunderstanding. We need to take a more expansive view of who is considered Asian American.

Before 1965, Asian Americans made up less than 1% of the U.S. population. Chapter 3 will trace the history of early immigrants from Asia to the United States, but you may already know that the Chinese were the first major group of Asians to settle in the United States in the 1800s. While Punjabis, Koreans, and Filipinxs began to immigrate at the turn of the century, the largest group of Asian immigrants after the Chinese were Japanese. Due to the U.S. colonization of the Philippines in 1898, Filipinxs had unique status as U.S. nationals which allowed them to migrate freely between the Philippines and U.S., so they comprised the third-largest group of Asian immigrants. So, by the time Emma Gee and Yuji Ichioka created the term Asian American, Japanese Americans were 41% of the Asian American population, Chinese Americans constituted 30%, and Filipinx Americans made up 24% (Takaki, 1998). The first century of Asian immigration was largely composed of individuals from East Asia, although this changed significantly after 1965, as you will learn in the next chapter.

East Asia includes the nations of China, Japan, Mongolia, North Korea, South Korea, Taiwan, and Tibet. Southeast Asia consists of Brunei, Burma, Cambodia, East Timor, Indonesia, Laos, Malaysia, the Philippines, Singapore, Thailand, and Vietnam. South Asia is made up of Bangladesh, Bhutan, India, the Maldives, Nepal, Pakistan, and Sri Lanka. In 1997, the U.S. Office of Management and Budget (OMB) revised its racial and ethnic classifications and separated the "Asian or Pacific Islander" category into "Asian" and "Native Hawaiian or Other Pacific Islander." OMB (1997) defined Asian as, "A person having origins in any of the original peoples of the Far East, Southeast Asia, or the Indian subcontinent including, for example, Cambodia, China, India, Japan, Korea, Malaysia, Pakistan, the Philippine Islands, Thailand, and Vietnam" (para. 56). This definition excluded people from Central and West Asia, and requests that the OMB add a separate ethnic category for Arabs/Middle Easterners were ignored. Since the OMB dictates the ethnoracial classifications included in federal data, this shift had important implications for who was and was not considered Asian.

So where do Central and West Asians fit in? This is a complicated topic due to the complex and contested histories of these regions, and West Asia in particular. West Asia includes Afghanistan, Armenia, Iran, Iraq, Israel, Palestine, Syria, and Yemen. Central Asia consists of

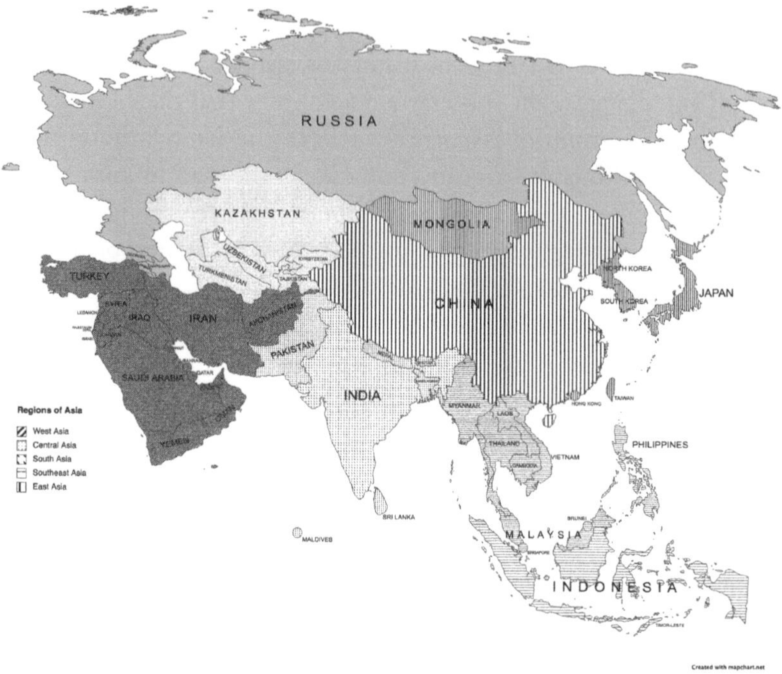

FIGURE 2.1 Regions of Asia. CREATED BY NOREEN NASEEM RODRÍGUEZ WITH MAPCHART (WWW.MAPCHART.NET).

Tajikistan, Uzbekistan, Kazakhstan, Turkmenistan, and Kyrgyzstan. Immigrants from Central and West Asia, such as Iranians and Armenians, have been racially classified as white. Historically, this allowed them to acquire U.S. citizenship on the basis of race, while East and South Asians were denied citizenship for the same reason. The access to whiteness historically afforded to Central and West Asians is a major reason why they have not typically been categorized as Asian despite their geographical origins. In Chapter 4, we will dig into how East, Southeast, and South Asian Americans were *denied* claims to whiteness and therefore access to U.S. citizenship.

You may have heard West Asia referred to by another name—the Middle East. This name was coined by the British foreign service at the end of the 19th century and was initially used to refer to the area *east* of what was known as the Near East (the Balkans and Ottoman

Empire) and west of India, including Afghanistan and Persia (modern-day Iran) (TeachMideast, n. d.). The *Far* East was what we now know as East Asia. All of these terms come from the perspective of Western Europe, namely the British. Whenever a name for a place comes from people who are not *of* that place, we should take pause before using it. Why not refer to a place by the name that the people *who are from there* use? Why prioritize the nomenclature of the colonizer? This has been the subject of intense debate, especially since many people who live in West Asia have come to use the name "Middle East" to describe their region due to this term's pervasiveness.

The Middle East spans westward from Afghanistan across Northern Africa from the Persian Gulf to the Mediterranean Sea, bounded by the Black and Caspian Seas in the north and the Sahara Desert and Indian Ocean in the south. Some historians and other scholars have argued that this region would better be described as the Middle East/North Africa (MENA). Ethnically, many of those who reside in this region identify as Arab and are Arabic-speaking, with the exception of Iran (where Persian is the national language) and Israel (where Hebrew and Arabic are the national languages). Sometimes Pakistan is mistakenly included, although—due to the political and cultural history of South Asia and the fact that Pakistan's official language is Urdu—it should not be. Similarly, Afghanistan is sometimes considered part of South Asia and other times categorized as West Asia/the Middle East. The national languages of Afghanistan are Pashto and Dari. However, after the U.S.-led invasion of Afghanistan, it has been more often associated with the Middle East for political and religious reasons. Ultimately, what we refer to as West Asia is a contested region that educators and scholars have yet to agree on, so we would be remiss to not address its presence and importance as part of the Asian continent.

Sociologists Jennifer Lee and Karthick Ramakrishnan (2020) analyzed results of the 2016 National Asian American Survey relying on OMB data, which meant operating from the definition of Asian American that does *not* include West and Central Asians. They found that the majority of people surveyed defined Asians or Asian Americans as Chinese, Japanese, and Korean. Slightly fewer survey respondents also included Filipinxs, and less than half included Indians and Pakistanis.

In particular, respondents who were *not* Asian or Asian American were even less likely to consider Indians and Pakistanis to be Asian.

These results echo long-standing complaints from South Asian Americans about their exclusion from Asian American histories, politics, and narratives. However, South Asians *do* racially self-identify as Asian, despite the fact that other Asian groups may not see them as such. These findings are particularly concerning because the East Asian American population dropped from 43% to 36% since 2000, while the South Asian American population increased from 19% to 27%. Despite shifting demographics, Asian Americans continue to be equated with only *East* Asian Americans. We hope that now, after understanding how exclusionary and inaccurate this misconception is, you can work to interrupt it among the students and educators you work with.

Now that we've covered *who* is Asian, we want to make crystal clear how diverse Asians are. Asians are not racialized in Asia as they are in the United States, although colorism (the differential treatment of someone based on their skin color) is an unjust colonial byproduct that continues to exist in many Asian societies. Every Asian nation has tremendous diversity in terms of economic and education levels. Many countries have multiple ethnicities, languages, cultures, and religions that exist within their boundaries; some ethnic groups, like the Hmong, have migrated over time so that they are not bound to a single nation-state. Asian nations have Indigenous Peoples, and many have histories of colonization and imperialism—both from European powers and Asian empires—that have impacted how religion and language have spread and combined in unexpected ways. It is also important to consider the dimensions of gender and sexuality. For example, there is a wide range of gender norms that exist across the continent.

Importantly, many Asian nations have had women as heads of state and government, from Prime Ministers Sirimavo Bandaranaike of Sri Lanka (1960–1965, 1970–1977, 1994–2000), Benazir Bhutto of Pakistan (1988–1990, 1993–1996), Indira Gandhi of India (1966–1977, 1980–1984), Sheikh Hasina of Bangladesh (1996–2001, 2009–present), Golda Meir of Israel (1969–1974), Yingluck Shinawatra of Thailand (2011–2014), and Khaleda Zia of Bangladesh (1991–1996, 2001–2006), to Presidents Corazon Aquino (1986–1992) and Gloria Macapagal

Arroyo (2001–2010) of the Philippines, Bidya Devi Bhandari of Nepal (2015–present), Park Geun-hye of South Korea (2013–2017), Tsai Ing-wen of Taiwan (2016–present), Megawati Sukarnoputri of Indonesia (2001–2004), and Halimah Yacob of Singapore (2017–present). This list, which is, notably, not exhaustive, disrupts perceptions of Asian nations as socially "backwards" and conservative in terms of gender roles in comparison to popular beliefs around the United States' progressive politics. How many women have been President of the United States?

These facts are a good reminder that knowing a single Korean, Bangladeshi, Tai Dam, Indonesian, or Iraqi and their personal story will never allow anyone to fully understand the experiences of the *people* of an Asian nation or ethnicity. Whenever possible, avoid presenting a single version of events or experiences to describe what it means to be any "kind" of Asian. Just as there is no one specific way to be or look American, there is no one specific way to be or look Asian. Additionally, we have to consider ancestors and family members of any person residing in the U.S.: the wide range of reasons they had for leaving their homelands, their journeys, and the diversity of experiences they had upon arriving in the United States.

Some Asian American families have lived in the United States for five or six generations, while others live transnationally, going back and forth between and across continents. Some Asian Americans are part of diasporic movements, such as South Asians who lived in Europe, the Caribbean, or Africa prior to arriving in the United States; some are refugees who fled to camps in nearby Asian nations and/or were hosted on other continents prior to stateside resettlement; transnational adoptees; or they are Filipinxs who immigrated and worked in Australia or the Middle East before their U.S. arrival. Some may be U.S.-born with no experience outside of North America, while many arrived in the United States as adults with decades of experiences and young children.

On top of that, Asian Americans can be multiracial and/or multiethnic. Noreen's maternal family is Filipinx with members of Chinese and Spanish descent; her paternal family is Pakistani, but due to the history of Partition, her ancestors are Indian. There are countless unique Asian American stories, and we hope this book launches you into learning about many more than you knew before.

UNDERSTANDING THE IMPORTANCE OF ASIAN NAMES

Names hold tremendous importance in many cultures. They can be a way to honor ancestors, convey religious meanings, and/or carry forward histories that might otherwise be lost. Therefore, one's name is often an important part of one's identity. Yet many students who do not have European or Biblical names are often teased and subjected to constant mispronunciation; in some cases, teachers and/or peers will impose a *different* name on them to use and respond to at school. Can you imagine how it must feel to be told that your name, lovingly given to you by your family, is "too hard" or "difficult" for someone to bother learning? Unfortunately, this happens all too often to Asian Americans. It also has been a historic problem for enslaved Africans whose names were replaced by their enslavers, among Native Americans and Latines in assimilationist school settings, and among Black Americans whose names reclaim their African roots.

Education scholars Rita Kohli and Daniel Solórzano (2012) note that comments about the difficulty or length of non-European students' names are actually racial slights or microaggressions. Even if such comments are unintentionally hurtful, they nonetheless cause harm and ultimately present students as Others due to their race, language, or culture. Kohli and Solórzano (2012) conducted interviews with 49 individuals, many of whom shared stories of humiliation, shame, and embarrassment related to how their teachers and peers responded to their names. One participant from their study shared this powerful and heartbreaking story about a primary grade teacher:

> The teacher called someone whose name is Fidel, "Fiddle, Fiddle," and the student did not respond because that's not his name. You're not going to respond to your name if you don't recognize it. And then she berated him, yelled at him like, "Why aren't you answering me? Why aren't you answering me?" and of course imagine how confused [he was]. It was clear that [he was thinking] . . . "This teacher is yelling at me because I'm doing something wrong. I don't know what I'm doing, but I'm being bad." (Kohli & Solórzano, 2012, p. 454)

We don't want any student to feel this way. We hope that by emphasizing both how important it is to learn to correctly pronounce students' names *and* how harmful it can be if you don't, we can prevent future generations of students from dealing with the demeaning and painful naming practices that we and many others have faced in school.

SELECTING ASIAN AMERICAN CHILDREN'S LITERATURE

In the year 2000, Asian American children's literature was extremely limited. The few books that were widely used in schools were often written by cultural outsiders and mostly focused on East Asian American and recently arrived immigrant experiences. Today, the world of Asian American children's literature is far more expansive and diverse, with many texts written by individuals who hold the same cultural, ethnic, religious, linguistic, and immigrant experiences as the characters featured in them. Consequently, we recommend that you consider the role of the author's identity in the telling of Asian American stories and encourage you to look for recently published books rather than texts with older publication dates.

Authors and illustrators who are well acquainted with the cultures they are representing often include important culturally-specific details in both the written and visual text. This is in contrast to books written by cultural outsiders, who have historically included inaccurate and inauthentic details in their stories. When looking for children's literature about cultural and ethnic groups that you are unfamiliar with, spend some time online to determine how members of those groups perceive books that may represent them. We have a collection of our favorite pieces of children's literature available on www.teachingasianamerica.com.

In primary grades, many educators begin the school year with a book (or multiple books) about names. When Noreen began teaching first grade in 2005, there was not a huge selection of books to choose from, and Kevin Henkes's (1991) picturebook *Chrysanthemum* was an old standard. In recent years, many more books that explore names in a wide range of ways have been published that offer opportunities to share culturally-specific stories. Although *Chrysanthemum* remains delightful, students need opportunities to learn about names of Asian origin with human protagonists. Animals doing humanlike actions make for cute stories, but young learners also need examples of human ethnoracially diverse protagonists with whom they can relate. In addition to whole-class read alouds, you can ask students to record their names on the first day of school so that you and their peers can listen to names *exactly* as students pronounce them and practice them as needed. This could even be a center during the first weeks of school! It takes effort and a little extra time, but for something this important, it is absolutely worth it.

RECOMMENDED CHILDREN'S LITERATURE TO HONOR ASIAN NAMES

- *Always Anjali* by Sheetal Sheth, illustrated by Jessica Blank
- *The Many Meanings of Meilan* by Andrea Wang
- *My Name is Bana* by Bana Alabed, illustrated by Nez Riaz
- *My Name is Bilal* by Asma Mobin-Uddin
- *My Name is Saajin Singh* by Kuljinder Kaur Brar, illustrated by Samrath Kaur
- *Teach Us Your Name* by Huda Essa, illustrated by Diana Cojocaru
- *Thao* by Thao Lam
- *That's Not My Name* by Anoosha Syed
- *Your Name is a Song* by Jamilah Thompkins-Bigelow, illustrated by Luisa Uribe

STEREOTYPES OF ASIAN AMERICANS

Now that you know who Asian Americans are, we want to explore common stereotypes that many people have about them. We will provide some historical background (we can't help it, we're social studies educators!) as well as ideas for tackling these stereotypes when they emerge from students at school. There are also inset boxes that list recommended children's literature. While not all of these stereotypes may surface in your classroom context or in students' conversations, we want you to be able to reference how and why they came to be in the event that they do arise. We aim to equip you with ideas for confronting them so that you're prepared if they appear unexpectedly.

Asian Food as Stinky and Weird

When Noreen's eldest daughter was in preschool, she brought one of her favorite treats for snack: a packet of seaweed. But after her classmates complained about the smell and how weird it looked, she refused to bring it to school again, even though she loved to eat it at home. Many immigrant and second-generation children have similar experiences in school, which have become known as "lunchbox moments." They bring food lovingly prepared at home to school. Once their meal or snack emerges from the lunch box or paper bag, their peers express disdain or distaste. "Ew, what's that?", "That smells gross!", and "Weird, that doesn't look like people food!" are some common reactions.

These kinds of interactions position foods typically associated with Asian, Latine, and African cultures as "weird" or "strange" compared to mainstream European foods, which are understood as "normal" and "American." If the goal of a classroom/campus is to cultivate a culture of mutual respect, educators should be attentive to ways that students (*and* adults!) might insult or demean someone's food. Some educators have taken up slogans like "Don't yuck my yum!" to encourage a positive attitude toward foods that may be enjoyed by some students but not by others. While it's not necessary to insist that everyone like everything, it *is* important to let students know that, just because *they* don't like something, this doesn't mean it's reasonable to insult someone who *does* enjoy it. And being unfamiliar with a particular food doesn't make it weird. When students view unfamiliar foods as strange or gross, educators can present these situations as opportunities to try new things and learn about other cultures. While we are framing this as a student issue, we want to recognize that plenty of adults are close-minded when it comes to food, too—those lunchbox moments continue to occur in the teacher's lounge and at school potlucks!

Making parallels across cultures and food traditions can help explain why certain foods and ingredients are common to some groups of people but not others. This practice supports the understanding of widespread styles of food preparation that simply use different ingredients. For example, the process of fermentation has occurred in nearly every culture for millennia as a way to preserve food and create new and dynamic tastes and textures. Fermented foods are "foods or beverages made through controlled microbial growth and enzymatic conversions" (Marco et al., 2017, p. 94), and include everything from yeast-based items, like bread and beer, to yogurt, cheese, sausage, miso, and olives. Yet, while pickles and sauerkraut, a cabbage-based dish of German origin, may be considered normal all-American fare easily found in restaurants, some people balk at the thought of kimchi, a Korean fermented dish often made with cabbage, radishes, or cucumbers. In Korea, kimchi is a staple side dish; however, Germans settled in the United States generations before most Korean immigrants arrived en masse, which allowed German foods more time to integrate into American culture. As many grocery stores from coast to coast have kimchi available today, we need to recognize that what constitutes "American" food is ever-changing and should take the time to explain this clearly to students.

As the United States' population has diversified, so too have culinary options. While Chinese food and sushi have been ubiquitous for several decades, one can also find Thai restaurants in Williamsburg, Virginia; Lao and Cambodian meals in Des Moines, Iowa; and Afghan kabobs in Denver, Colorado. Moreover, as multiracial and multiethnic families grow, we are witnessing creative and delicious combinations emerge. As a self-described Pakipina, Noreen was excited to see a Pakistani-Filipino restaurant open in the town of Ankeny when she lived in Iowa. A fast-food Indian restaurant chain in Texas serves "naaninis" (panini-style sandwiches made with a folded piece of naan) and in Los Angeles, kimchi burritos and Korean barbeque tacos have been a staple on many menus, as detailed in *Chef Roy Choi and the Street Food Remix* (Martin & Lee, 2017)!

Several picturebooks offer educators opportunities to plan structured conversations about Asian foods, such as *The Invisible Boy* (Ludwig, 2013), *The Day You Begin* (Woodson, 2018), and *Lunch from Home* (Stein, 2022). In the box below, we offer books that spotlight specific Asian foods that are culturally specific but have parallels to other culinary traditions. For example, *Bilal Cooks Daal* (Saeed, 2019) is about a typical South Asian lentil dish served with rice. Lentils are a staple in many cultures but may be unfamiliar to some students. If possible, families could contribute different preparations of lentils (or any other dish!) and students could conduct taste tests. Rather than simply judging food as "good" or "bad," students could engage their senses and descriptive language to describe textures, smells, and flavors. They could also consider the science behind food preparation—lentils are actually dangerous to consume unless they are cooked!—and explore how food preparation varies from place to place, and how cooking technology has evolved over time.

RECOMMENDED CHILDREN'S LITERATURE TO HONOR ASIAN FOODS

- *Amy Wu and the Perfect Bao* by Kat Zhang, illustrated by Charlene Chua
- *Bee-Bim Bop!* By Linda Sue Park, illustrated by Ho Baek Lee
- *Bilal Cooks Daal* by Aisha Saeed, illustrated by Aneesha Syed
- *Cora Cooks Pancit* by Dorina K. Lazo Gilmore, illustrated by Kristi Valiant
- *Dim Sum for Everyone!* by Grace Lin
- *Dumpling Soup* by Jama Kim Rattigan, illustrated by Lillian Hsu
- *Dumplings for Lili* by Melissa Iwai
- *Hot, Hot Roti for Dada-gi* by F. Zia, illustrated by Ken Min
- *Hot Pot Night* by Vincent Chen
- *I Love Boba* by Katrina Liu, illustrated by Dhidit Prayoga
- *Jasmine Toguchi, Mochi Queen* by Debbie Michiko Florence
- *Kimchi, Kimchi Every Day* by Erica Kim
- *Let's Go Yum Cha: A Dim Sum Adventure!* by Alister Felix, illustrated by Yenna Mariana
- *Measuring Up* by Lily LaMotte, illustrated by Ann Xu
- *P is for Poppadoms! An Indian Alphabet Book* by Kabir Sehgal and Surishtha Sehgal, illustrated by Hazel Ito
- *Tofu Takes Time* by Helen H. Wu, illustrated by Julie Jarema

- *Tomatoes for Neela* by Padma Lakshmi, illustrated by Juana Martinez-Neal
- *Watercress* by Andrea Wang, illustrated by Jason Chin
- *The Whole World Inside Nan's Soup* by Hunter Liguore, illustrated by Vikki Zhang

The Model Minority

Asian American youth are often considered to be ideal students who exhibit good behavior and excel academically. This stereotype, while seemingly positive, has insidious roots. First, one must recognize that immigration from Asia was almost entirely banned from 1917 until 1952 (see Chapter 3 for details). The Immigration and Nationality Act of 1965 allowed large-scale immigration from Asia to the United States for the first time; however, there was a notable preference for immigrants who were considered highly skilled professionals. That is, people who held graduate degrees and worked in high-demand sectors, such as medicine, engineering, and technology, were more likely to get visas to the United States. Thus, when Asian immigrants began to arrive in large groups in the late 1960s, many of these new arrivals were disproportionately highly educated and largely English-speaking.

Although their visa and residency status often meant that these workers received less pay than their U.S.-born counterparts, professional Asian immigrants nonetheless were able to earn wages that quickly positioned them as middle class. Research shows that highly educated parents invest time, money, and other resources in supporting their children's academic success. As individuals who have received college and even graduate degrees, they are familiar with the postsecondary admissions process, understand the factors that boost young people's chances of getting into the college or university of their choice, and often have the financial means to ensure their children's participation in tutoring, test preparation, and extracurricular opportunities in addition to saving money for college tuition (Hill et al., 2004; Lee & Bowen, 2006; Perna & Titus, 2005; Stanton-Salazar, 2011; Yosso, 2005).

An immigration system that prefers highly educated workers is not the only reason why Asian Americans are considered the model minority. A second cause is rooted in social shifts during the Cold War and anti-Blackness in the midst of the Civil Rights Movement. As the struggles for Black civil rights intensified in the 1950s and 1960s, Assistant Secretary of Labor Daniel Moynihan published what became known as the Moynihan report in 1965. While the intention may have been to draw attention to racial inequality in the United States, the report actually pointed away from the long history of enslavement, Jim Crow, and other racist laws and policies. Instead, Moynihan wrote that the fundamental problem of economic and social inequality was rooted in non-traditional or "broken" family structures of low income Black communities. This racist narrative persists even today.

Although not mentioned in the report, Asian Americans—specifically Chinese and Japanese families—were soon held up as the model example proving that, in contrast to Black families, racial inequalities could be overcome by people of color in the United States. This image of Asian American families and their children's academic success in popular publications like *U.S. News and World Report* and on the cover of *Time Magazine* was promoted on purpose as the United States government struggled to improve their international image during the violence of the Civil Rights Movement and the Cold War.

This strategy of pitting communities of color against one another has concealed at least three realities: anti-Black racism, the diversity of Asian Americans, and the ever-present stereotype of Asian and Asian American peoples as a foreign threat to America. Although accepted and sometimes embraced in many communities, the stereotype of Asian Americans as a model minority not only becomes a tool to discipline Black and Latine communities ("They succeeded, why can't you?"), but also erases the struggles and experiences of many Asian Americans.

In fact, Asian American communities are characterized by some of the widest disparities in education level and income. The average income for South Asian and some East Asian families is higher than the national U.S. average, while the average income of several

Southeast Asian ethnicities is the lowest in the country. For example, 78% of Taiwanese Americans and 75% of Indian Americans have bachelor's degrees, compared to 20% of Cambodian Americans and 16% of Lao Americans (Lee & Ramakrishnan, 2020). Further, there is a noted underrepresentation of Asian Americans in utilizing special education, mental health, and social services. In contrast, visibility for Asian Americans is consistently heightened when they are perceived as national threats. Often grouped together with Asians, Asian Americans become "foreigners" and "Others" who are falsely or preemptively accused of stealing jobs, committing acts of terrorism, of spying or stealing scientific research on behalf of their ancestral nation-state, or more recently (yet also historically), of spreading disease.

So how would you explain all this to children? You can begin by reminding them that *any* group of people will be diverse in a number of ways, and use your own classroom as an example. Would it be accurate to say that *every* student in your classroom is the same? Some students are athletic, while others are artistic, and some are both. Some students might speak more than one language, some excel at math and some struggle with it. Some have extraordinary imaginations that they can express through creative writing, while others are more skilled at building structures out of found materials. One's race or ethnicity does not determine these abilities, just as their gender or religion does not determine them. And if young people can understand that, then they will understand how silly it is to think that we would use blanket statements like "model minority" to describe a group that is linked primarily by their origin from a massive continent. Students should be aware of how and why this stereotype emerged, and then have opportunities to consider who benefits from it and who is harmed.

There's the old stereotype that people with eyeglasses somehow "look smart" or might be nerdy, but what eyeglasses truly indicate is a need for visual support. In some cases, people use them as a fashion accessory! The adage "You can't judge a book by its cover" is particularly useful in this case—students shouldn't make assumptions about someone based on their race or ethnicity, and that includes assumptions about one's intellect or language abilities. It's as simple as that, and once they know it, they can spread the word to others!

RECOMMENDED CHILDREN'S LITERATURE TO DISRUPT THE MODEL MINORITY STEREOTYPE

- *The Best At It* by Maulik Pancholy
- *Front Desk* by Kelly Yang
- *Hana Hashimoto, Sixth Violin* by Chieri Uegaki
- *Stargazing* by Jen Wang
- *Zayd Saleem, Chasing the Dream: Power Forward, On Point, Bounce Back* by Hena Khan, illustrated by Sally Wern Comport

"Yellow Peril" and "Dusky Peril"

Unlike the contemporary model minority stereotype, which became pervasive in the last 40 years, the idea that Asian immigrants are a "Yellow Peril" or "Dusky Peril" has a much longer history. "Yellow Peril" is a term frequently associated with East Asian immigrants that became popular in the 1800s, while "Dusky Peril" specifically refers to South Asian immigrants who arrived in the early 1900s. In both cases, "peril" invokes "a potential 'at your own risk' danger of injury or death" (Tchen & Yeats, 2014, p. 11), conjuring feelings of fear and alarm. In the paragraphs that follow, we'll take you on a quick trip through history and across continents to explore how these stereotypes were used to stoke xenophobic fears in the past and how they have reemerged in popular media and discourse in recent decades.

Let's travel back to the 1700s, when Swedish botanist, taxonomer, and physician Carl Linnaeus divided humankind into four "species" based on both geography and color, progressing from white to Black (Keevak, 2011). Initially, Linnaeus categorized the group we now refer to as Asians as *Asiaticus fuscus.* The Latin word "fuscus" can be translated as "brown" or "swarthy." But in its 10th edition, published in 1758–1759, Linnaeus' taxonomy expanded exponentially with many changes to his initial classifications, including the renaming of Asians as *Asiaticus luridus.* "Luridus" can be translated as "yellow," "sallow," "pallid," and "ghastly" (Keevak, 2011, p. 45) and was often used pejoratively, similar to the English word "lurid."

German physician, anatomist, and noted scientific racist Johann Friedrich Blumenbach was unhappy with Linnaeus' geographically-based categories. After studying his extensive collection of human skulls (the largest such collection at the time), Blumenbach determined that there were five human varieties rather than Linnaeus' four; he dubbed South Pacific Islanders and Indians "Malay" and called East Asians "Mongolians." Despite these new categories, in the third edition of his book *De generis humani varietate nativa* published in 1795, Blumenbach refers to a Chinese botanist named Whang as the "yellow man from the East" (p. 65). Notwithstanding shifts in science and language, the use of the word "yellow" to describe East Asians and East Asian Americans persists today (Keevak, 2011).

German Kaiser Wilhelm II is believed to have coined the term "Yellow Peril" when he claimed to have dreamt about Buddha on a dragon thunderstorm that approached Europe (Tchen & Yeats, 2014). In 1895, he commissioned artist Hermann Knackfuss to illustrate his dream, which represented the Asian threat against white Christian Europe. Fittingly, the lithograph was titled "Peoples of Europe, Defend Your Holiest Possessions," and you can view this image on our website (www.teachingasianamerica.com). In the 1800s, Chinese immigrants began to arrive in the United States. As we explore in Chapter 3, these immigrants—who were overwhelmingly young men—were perceived as paganistic heathens (because they were not Christian), diseased opium addicts, dangerous and shifty villains, and overall undesirable degenerates. These deplorable characteristics, alongside the rapidly increasing numbers of Chinese immigrants due to heavy recruitment by American businesses, led to depictions of them in popular newspapers like *Harper's Weekly*, *Puck*, and *The San Francisco Illustrated Wasp* as invading hordes to be feared and stopped.

Thus, "Yellow Peril" became shorthand for the threat that the Chinese newcomers allegedly posed to white Americans. For white male workers the menace was economic, as Chinese were not allowed to join labor unions and were exploited for their willingness to work for lesser wages. The danger to white women was of a sexual nature; due to their distinct dress, long braided hair, and work in restaurants and laundries, Chinese men were considered feminine and sexually deviant. Either way, views of Chinese immigrants as fundamentally unassimilable and threatening to (white) American life became widespread and eventually led to their exclusion in 1882. Despite the steady decrease of Chinese immigrants after the Chinese Exclusion Act was passed, Yellow Peril imagery continued in newspaper caricatures that depicted Chinese men with slanted eyes and bright yellow skin.

The most famous Yellow Peril character is Dr. Fu Manchu, the villain in crime novels published by British author Sax Rohmer beginning in 1913. Dr. Fu Manchu bears a resemblance to Ming the Merciless, a villain in the Flash Gordon comic strips of the late 1930s. Similar representations were used to vilify Japanese during World War II, as exemplified by the buck-toothed and slanted eye figures found in the political cartoons illustrated by Theodore Geisel, also known as beloved children's author Dr. Seuss (see Figure 2.2).

In fact, Geisel's egregiously racist depictions of Asians, Blacks, and Arabs were not limited to the texts for adult audiences—his book *And*

FIGURE 2.2 "Waiting for the Signal from Home . . . " DR. SEUSS POLITICAL CARTOONS, 1942, FEBRUARY 13. SPECIAL COLLECTION & ARCHIVES, UC SAN DIEGO LIBRARY.

to Think That I Saw It on Mulberry Street (1938) includes images so racist that his estate ceased publication and licensing of it and five other books with problematic illustrations (Dr. Seuss Enterprises, 2021). Similar images continued in popular media for decades afterward, such as the character of Mr. Yunioshi in the classic 1961 film *Breakfast at Tiffany's*.

The phrase "Dusky Peril" was part of a headline in an issue of the *Puget Sound American* from 1906 that asked, "Have we a Dusky Peril?" with the subheadline, "Hindu hordes invading the state" (see Figure 2.3). Similar to the language used against Chinese immigrants in the previous century, the article describes "more than a dozen swarthy sons of Hindustan" and warns that these "worshippers of Brahma, Buddha, and other strange deities of India may soon press the soil of Washington" (para. 1). The article later details the threat of these laborers (who were actually Sikhs, not Hindus) to the economic advancement of white laborers and describes them as "diseased" and "undesirable" (yet also "remarkably fine-looking"—racism is weird) (para. 15). In this way, the same fear-mongering prejudice used against Chinese immigrants in California in the late 1800s was recycled against the South Asian immigrants in Washington state decades afterward.

Over a century later, these stereotypes returned. In 2001, after the 9/11 terrorist attack on the World Trade Center and Pentagon, South Asian Americans were viewed as undesirable and threatening, which we will explore later in this chapter. In 2020, after the COVID-19 pandemic began in the United States, then-President Trump as well as some conservative politicians and members of the media referred to the coronavirus as the "Chinese virus," "Wuhan virus," and "kung flu"—all terms that associated the virus with East Asia and an unwanted invasion (An & Rodríguez, 2021). This anti-Asian rhetoric occurred as hate crimes and violence against Asian Americans surged. The nonprofit Stop AAPI Hate received 10,905 reports of hate incidents against Asian Americans and Pacific Islanders between March 19, 2020 and December 31, 2021 (Yellow Horse et al., 2022). These hate incidents ranged from verbal harassment to physical assaults. Nearly half of these incidents took place in public spaces, over 60% were reported by women, and Chinese Americans were the largest ethnic group who reported them.

THE SUNDAY PUGET SOUND AMERICAN BELLINGHAM, WASH. SEPTEMBER 16, 1906

HAVE WE A DUSKY PERIL

HINDU HORDES INVADING THE STATE

BELLINGHAM workmen are becoming excited over the arrival of East Indians in numbers across the Canadian border, and fear that the dusky Asiatics with their turbans will prove a worse menace to the working classes than the "Yellow Peril" that has so long threatened the Pacific Coast.

Keep the Hindus Out, Says Writer

FIGURE 2.3 "Have We a Dusky Peril? AN ARTICLE FROM PUGET SOUND AMERICAN DESCRIBING RECENT "HINDU" IMMIGRATION TO BELLINGHAM, WASHINGTON, 1906, SEPTEMBER 16. SOUTH ASIAN AMERICAN DIGITAL ARCHIVE (HTTPS://WWW.SAADA.ORG/ITEM/20111215-549).

While we do not expect you to detail this long history with your students, we do think it is important for you to know that the images of East Asians as the Yellow Peril and South Asians as the Dusky Peril are long-standing and have unfortunately made a comeback. Therefore, it is vital that adults intervene when these demeaning and insulting stereotypes emerge at school. Children likely don't know their insidious roots, but they can definitely perpetuate harmful stereotypes if they are not supported to understand why pulling one's eyelids sideways is offensive and why it's wrong to say that East Asians speak "ching chong." Esther and Noreen vividly remember these things happening at school when they were young with no teacher intervention. If you know better, do better. Here's how.

The folktale *The Five Chinese Brothers* (Bishop, 1938) features incredibly stereotypical illustrations that echo the Chinese caricatures of the 1800s, yet it is still in publication and widely available in school and public libraries. Although the five titular characters are quintuplets whose identical appearances make their feats in the book so impressive, in the scene with the townspeople, *everyone* looks the same and shares slanted eyes and bright yellow skin. Engaging in critical literacy skills, students can easily identify and explain how these particular images are grossly stereotypical and offensive. Then they can be on the lookout for illustrations that perpetuate such stereotypes (see Dahlen, 2022, 37:48) and make sure to avoid racist representations in their own artwork.

Students can also learn about how words formerly used as insults can be reclaimed to demonstrate one's power. An excellent example of this reclamation, which we detail in Chapter 6, is the Yellow Power Movement (also known as the Asian American Movement) inspired by the Civil Rights Movement of the 1950s and 1960s. Just be careful with this topic: you don't want students to think it is okay for them to use racial slurs in ways that continue to harm and insult others.

RECOMMENDED CHILDREN'S LITERATURE TO DISRUPT THE YELLOW PERIL AND DUSKY PERIL STEREOTYPES

- *American Born Chinese* by Gene Luen Yang
- *Brown is Beautiful* by Supriya Kelkar, illustrated by Noor Sofi
- *Coolies* by Yin, illustrated by Chris Soentpiet
- *Eyes That Kiss in the Corners* by Joanna Ho, illustrated by Dung Ho
- *Eyes That Speak to the Stars* by Joanna Ho, illustrated by Dung Ho
- *Gibberish* by Young Vo
- *Our Skin: A First Conversation about Race* by Megan Madison, Jessica Ralli and Isabel Roxas
- *What I See: Anti-Asian Racism from the Eyes of a Child* by Christine T. Leung, illustrated by Su En Tan
- *You are Life* by Bao Phi, illustrated by Hannah Li

Forever Foreigner

Asian Americans (and Latines) experience a distinct kind of racialized marginalization due to nativism and perceptions of foreignness (Ancheta, 2006). Nativism is a concept that first emerged in the mid-1850s with the creation of the Know Nothing political party. This group virulently opposed Catholic immigration, particularly from Ireland, and viewed it as a threat to U.S.-born Protestants. Never mind that most of those Protestants were themselves immigrants and not who we might consider Native or Indigenous, but we'll get into Asian settler colonialism in Chapter 7. For now, it's important to understand that nativism is a perspective that considers certain people as entitled to being in a place—in this case, white Protestants of European descent in the United States—while others are seen as *not* belonging and to be excluded at all costs. Nativism adopts an "us vs. them" mentality that is often leveraged against communities of color, those who adhere to faiths other than Christianity, and other groups that are viewed as undesirable or threatening to the dominant group.

With this in mind, scholar Mia Tuan (1998) argued, "Despite many Asian-Americans being longtime daughters and sons of this nation, some with lineages extending back to the 1800s, many people continually view and treat them as outsiders or foreigners within their own country" (p. 2). Tuan (1998) used the term "forever foreigners" to refer to this stereotypical and misguided idea that all Asian Americans are recently-arrived immigrants who do not know English and do not understand American customs. As we noted at the beginning of the Introduction, the forever foreigner stereotype rears its ugly head when Asian Americans are asked where they are from—because the presumption is that they couldn't possibly be from *here*. Being a forever foreigner is inferred when an Asian American is complimented on the quality of their English or their lack of an accent. By the way, everyone has an accent of some kind, and, due to British colonialism, English was imposed upon many Asian nations. While it may no longer be a required language, English is still taught in schools across the Asian continent and many young Asians are bi- or multilingual: they speak English as well as the languages of their homeland.

The forever foreigner stereotype works off the nativist assumption that being an American means that you are white, likely Christian, and born in the United States. It is reinforced by school curriculum, trade books, and popular media that center white families and characters who speak American English and attend church on Sundays. As schools are more segregated now than ever before, if those are the only examples of American life that students are surrounded by, then that is what they understand to be normal, and anything different seems weird and literally foreign.

As we mentioned earlier with the model minority stereotype, the long history of nativism isn't necessarily relevant to young learners, but you can certainly find examples of it emerging in children's conversations. Particularly if you are a white teacher who has never been asked where you are from or been told how good the quality of your English is, we hope that you will now be alerted to the assumptions that undergird such questions. So, if they come up in your classroom, you can call a time-out and have a conversation with your students about why they would direct those questions and comments only to certain individuals. This can lead to important conversations about stereotypes and prejudices—conversations that can ultimately disrupt such thinking.

RECOMMENDED CHILDREN'S LITERATURE TO DISRUPT THE FOREVER FOREIGNER STEREOTYPE

- *All Are Welcome* by Alexandra Penfold, illustrated by Suzanne Kaufman
- *Going Home, Coming Home* by Truong Tran, illustrated by Ann Phong
- *Grandmother's Visit* by Betty Quan, illustrated by Carmen Mok
- *Where Are You From?* by Yamile Saied Mendez, illustrated by Jaime Kim
- *What I Am* by Divya Srinivasan
- *Where Three Oceans Meet* by Rajani LaRocca, illustrated by Archana Sreenivasan

Terrorist Threats

While the Dusky Peril established South Asian men as an invading threat in Washington state in the early 1900s, the Gulf War (1990–1991) and 9/11 (2001) terrorist attacks had far more widespread and long-lasting repercussions for South Asian and Arab Americans. These two events specifically positioned Muslims as violent extremists, despite the facts that Iraq invaded a *Muslim* nation (Kuwait) and that *every* religion has its share of zealots who adopt extremist interpretations that do not represent mainstream followers.

There are 1.9 million Muslims across the globe (making up a quarter of the world's population) who prescribe to several different sects of Islam. Some of these sects encourage modest forms of dress while others follow more significantly conservative guidelines. Of course, individuals interpret religious doctrines differently, so Muslims wear a wide range of clothing and are not necessarily immediately identifiable based on their appearance. Religion is, after all, about spiritual beliefs, and not everyone wears outward religious markers. However, the image of Osama bin Laden after the 9/11 attacks—clad in a turban, wearing long flowy robes, and with a thick, unruly beard—became *the* image associated with Islamic terrorism.

ORIENTALISM

Like the Yellow Peril, contemporary Islamophobia has historical roots in an idea that scholar Edward Said (pronounced sa-EED) called "Orientalism." Orientalism is a European viewpoint that sees the East (Asia) in opposition to the West (Europe), with Westerners as civilized Christians and Easterners as exotic, barbaric, Oriental Others. The West is considered the center of modernity, and the East/Orient is understood as a threat to democracy and freedom, creating what Samuel Huntington (1996) described as a "clash of civilizations."

Contemporary Islamophobia is a revival of Orientalism, where Islam is viewed as a foreign, Eastern religion that threatens a Christian United States. This is a flawed concept for many reasons, but it is worth noting that Muslims have lived in the "West" before the founding of the United

States; furthermore, the U.S. has no official religion. In fact, Thomas Jefferson specifically used the example of civil rights for Muslims and Jews in his arguments against a national religion and had a copy of the Qur'an, the holy book of Islam, in his library.

Turbans are not especially common headwear among Muslim men, although some followers of Shia Islam (the second largest branch, followed by 10–15% of all Muslims) and Sufism (a mystical practice of Islam) may wear them. They are more commonly worn by Sikhs (both men and women) and some Hindu men. Yet, because the name and image of bin Laden became synonymous with Islamic terrorism, in the days, months, and years that followed 9/11, Muslims *and those perceived as Muslim*—namely Sikhs and Hindus—faced tremendous physical and verbal harassment, including violence. The first known hate crime purportedly in response to the 9/11 attacks was the murder of Balbir Singh Sodhi, a turban-wearing Sikh, who was shot outside of the gas station he owned while planting flowers on September 15, 2001. Days earlier, his killer told a restaurant waiter, "I'm going to go out and shoot some towel-heads" (Kaur, 2016). After his arrest, the killer yelled "I am a patriot!" and "I stand for America!"

This violence was not limited to adult men who wore turbans. Sikh, Hindu, and Muslim children faced an alarming amount of bullying in schools, from being called "terrorist" and "Osama" to experiencing physical assaults, in addition to social ostracism from their peers *and* school staff (Bajaj et al., 2016; Britto, 2001). Women wearing hijab (Islamic head coverings) have also been harassed and assaulted. In a particularly horrific example, a white supremacist entered a Sikh gurdwara (place of worship) in Oak Creek, Wisconsin in August 2012 and killed six Sikhs. Personal property and places of worship were defaced and covered with racial slurs and religious insults, while individuals and organizations were subjected to abuses from federal agencies including but not limited to secret evidence collection, denials of due process, racial profiling, detentions, illegal wiretapping, and other forms of surveillance (South Asian Americans Leading Together, 2014).

These examples illustrate just a small sampling of the ways that Islamophobia has become pervasive in U.S. society. But it isn't *simply* a fear or phobia. Recent political rhetoric and a frightening number of acts of violence against Muslims and those perceived as Muslim demonstrate that Islamophobia as it exists today (indeed, since 9/11) is better described as a hatred of Islam, which manifests through hate speech, bullying, and violence that is viewed as justified. And it's not just adults who believe this. In Noreen's final year of teaching fifth grade, one of her students gave a presentation to the class about Malcolm X and the Nation of Islam. He had clearly conflated the Nation of Islam with the broader religion of Islam, so Noreen took several minutes to explain the differences between the two. After she concluded, another student commented, "Oh, I thought all Muslims were terrorists" (Rodríguez, 2017, p. 130). He was *12*.

Scholars James Hoot, Tunde Szecsi, and Samira Moosa (2003) interviewed Muslim parents, children, and teachers in New York and found a shared desire for direct teacher intervention when teasing of Muslim children is observed. While these Muslim community members recognized that teachers who lack knowledge and resources about Islam might opt to ignore such teasing, the researchers argued, "Ignoring religious differences and allowing such behaviors, however, neither avoids controversy nor encourages the development of dispositions for tolerance among children" (p. 88). Educators have a responsibility to defend the fundamental right of religious freedom *and* students' dignity when it comes to subscribing to religions that their peers may not be familiar with or misunderstand. Below are some resources to support educators in building basic knowledge about Islam.

GUIDES ABOUT ISLAM AND COUNTERING ISLAMOPHOBIA FOR ELEMENTARY TEACHERS

- *In the Face of Xenophobia: Lessons to Address Bullying of South Asian American Youth* by Monisha Bajaj, Ameena Ghaffar-Kucher & Karishma Desai (available online)
- *Muslims in Story: Expanding Multicultural Understanding Through Children's and Young Adult Literature* by Gauri Manglik and Sadaf Siddique

- *Patriot Acts: Narratives of Post-9/11 Injustice* edited by Alia Malek
- *Teaching Against Islamophobia* edited by Joe L. Kincheloe, Shirley R. Steinberg, and Christopher D. Stonebanks
- "Understanding Islam in the U.S. Classroom: A Guide for Elementary School Teachers" by Kazi I. Hossain in *Multicultural Education* (available online)
- *We Too Sing America* by Deepa Iyer

Over 20 years after 9/11, the trope of Muslims (and those perceived as Muslims) as terrorists persists. Luckily, several groups have created free curriculum and educational resources so that teachers can address this stereotype directly. The University of Pennsylvania Graduate School of Education created the Teaching Beyond September 11th curriculum project, which spans from 2001 to 2021. While this particular resource is targeted toward high school and college students, there are some materials that can be adapted for fourth and fifth graders. Noreen created modules about the representation of Muslim women and Muslims broadly in popular culture that include analysis of political cartoons and clips from streaming and network television shows. Education scholars Monisha Bajaj, Ameena Ghaffar-Kucher, and Karishma Desai (2013) have developed lessons (available online) to address the bullying of South Asian American youth. The Sikh Coalition's website includes school toolkits for educators and parents as well as book recommendations.

RECOMMENDED CHILDREN'S LITERATURE TO DISRUPT THE TERRORIST THREAT STEREOTYPE

- *American Desi* by Jyoti Rajan Gopal, illustrated by Supriya Kelkar
- *Amina's Voice* and *Amina's Song* by Hena Khan
- *Amira's Picture Day* by Reem Faruqi, illustrated by Fahmida Azim
- *Bindu's Bindis* by Supriya Kelkar
- *Count Me In* by Varsha Bajaj
- *Hair Twins* by Raakhee Mirchandani, illustrated by Holly Hatam
- *In My Mosque* by M. O. Yuksel, illustrated by Hatem Aly

- *Lailah's Lunchbox: A Ramadan Story* by Reem Faruqi, illustrated by Lea Lyon
- *The Many Colors of Harpreet Singh* by Supriya Kelkar, illustrated by Alea Marley
- *Mommy's Khimar* by Jamilah Thompkins-Bigelow, illustrated by Ebony Glenn
- *Muslim Girls Rise* by Saira Mir, illustrated by Aaliya Jaleel
- *My Religion and Me: We are Sikhs* by Philip Blake
- *Once Upon an Eid: Stories of Hope and Joy by 15 Muslim Voices* edited by S. K. Ali and Aisha Saeed
- *Our Favorite Day of the Year* by A. E. Ali, illustrated by Rahele Jomepour Bell
- *Planet Omar: Accidental Trouble Magnet* by Zanib Mian, illustrated by Nasaya Mafaridik
- *The Proudest Blue: A Story of Hijab and Family* by Ibtihaj Muhammad with S. K. Ali, illustrated by Hatem Aly
- *Salam Alaikum: A Message of Peace* by Harris J, illustrated by Ward Jenkins
- *Under My Hijab* by Hena Khan, illustrated by Aaliya Jaleel
- *Yasmin* series by Saadia Faruqi, illustrated by Hatem Aly
- *Yo Soy Muslim* by Mark Gonzales, illustrated by Mehrdokt Amini
- *Yusuf Azeem is Not a Hero* by Saadia Faruqi

BRINGING IT ALL TOGETHER WITH KELLY YANG'S *FRONT DESK*

While each stereotype addressed here has its own list of recommended children's literature, we close this chapter by offering read aloud suggestions for an award-winning middle grades book that addresses many of these stereotypes in sensitive and engaging ways: *Front Desk* by Kelly Yang. *Front Desk* is the story of Mia, a ten-year-old Chinese immigrant whose parents manage the Calivista Motel. Fourth grade teacher Ying Ong read this book aloud with her students and began by reviewing terms like "prejudice," "discrimination," and "racism." Ong described how students may be quick to declare things as racist without recognizing that everyone has prejudices. Consequently, throughout the book, she asks students if particular examples constitute personal prejudice, discrimination due to prejudice-based exclusion or mistreatment, and/or if policies or laws were responsible for limiting people's access to things, therefore serving as examples of institutionalized racism. As these conversations should be ongoing and frequently structured around examples in the text, students can begin to make connections to what they observe in school and in the world around them.

Front Desk exposes students to the differences between first- and second-generation immigrants through the eyes of its young protagonist Mia Tang, who is learning English and struggles socially in school while experiencing culture clashes with her traditional Chinese parents. At the same time, she feels completely different from Jason, the U.S.-born child of the motel owner whose middle-class family experiences American society very differently from Mia's working class family. Mia befriends a Mexican American girl named Lupe who exposes her to other cultural ways of being, and Mia also becomes friendly with long-term residents at the hotel, including an older Black gentleman named Hank. Ong notes that an important and unique aspect of *Front Desk* is how it challenges anti-Blackness by making plain how others view Hank as a criminal on the basis of his skin color. Mia also wrestles with her Asian American identity, resisting her mother's pressure for her to focus on math and instead embracing her developing love of writing and English and thereby disrupting stereotypes of Asian Americans as intrinsically gifted in school, particularly in math and science.

Front Desk is the first book in a five-part series that has become beloved by many readers. The second book in the series, *Three Keys* (Yang, 2020), deals with undocumented immigration—an issue that tends to be associated only with Latine communities but is also deeply relevant to many Asian American communities. The book describes the passage of Proposition 187 in California in 1994, a xenophobic piece of legislation that sought to ban undocumented immigrants from utilizing major state public services, and *Three Keys* draws readers' attention to housing insecurity and immigrant detention and deportation.

The third book, *Room to Dream* (2021), explores gentrification and the Tang family's visit back home to China. *Key Player* (2022), the fourth book, centers on sports and the challenges the Tangs face when they pursue home ownership. *Top Story* (2023) is the final book in the series where Mia attends journalism camp and learns about the history of San Francisco's Chinatown. Ultimately, the characters are beautifully developed and complex young people who all students can relate to in some way. Each book has a tantalizing cliffhanger that ensures readers are hooked and ready to dive into the next book. We love this series because it brings so many complex aspects of Asian American life to the forefront in genuinely interesting and realistic ways that children can easily understand. Discussion guides for the books are available online; see the Appendix for guiding questions to promote student engagement.

IDENTITY AND STEREOTYPES MATTER

This chapter walked you through the most common stereotypes about Asian Americans in U.S. society. We hope that the recommended book lists and strategies for discussing these stereotypes with young learners will give you the confidence you need to tackle conversations about racial prejudice, which can be difficult and uncomfortable when you don't know the history behind them. Moreover, we hope that you have the courage to do this work and support your students in disrupting these stereotypes when they encounter them. This is how we care for our shared communities and create a more inclusive and respectful society!

3

Im/Migration

In most elementary schools, the teaching of immigration is limited to Ellis Island and the European immigrants who passed through that station from 1892 to 1954. By limiting the history of U.S. immigration solely to this particular immigration station that closed nearly 70 years ago, students are taught a distorted view of immigration history without any explanation for our nation's contemporary diversity. Similarly, migration within the United States is largely framed around the movement of white settlers in centuries past, such as Westward Expansion. This chapter offers readers an overview of key moments of Asian immigration to the United States with instructional recommendations.

EARLY CHINESE IMMIGRATION

The first substantial group of Asian immigrants who arrived in the United States were the Chinese along the West Coast in the 1800s. After numerous wars, internal rebellions, and natural disasters, rural families in China's Pearl River Delta struggled economically in the early to mid-1800s. When gold was discovered in California in 1848, word spread quickly, including across the ocean! California became known as Gam Saan—"Gold Mountain"—and young men eager to seek their fortunes and support their families in China made the trek abroad,

DOI: 10.4324/9781032662695-3

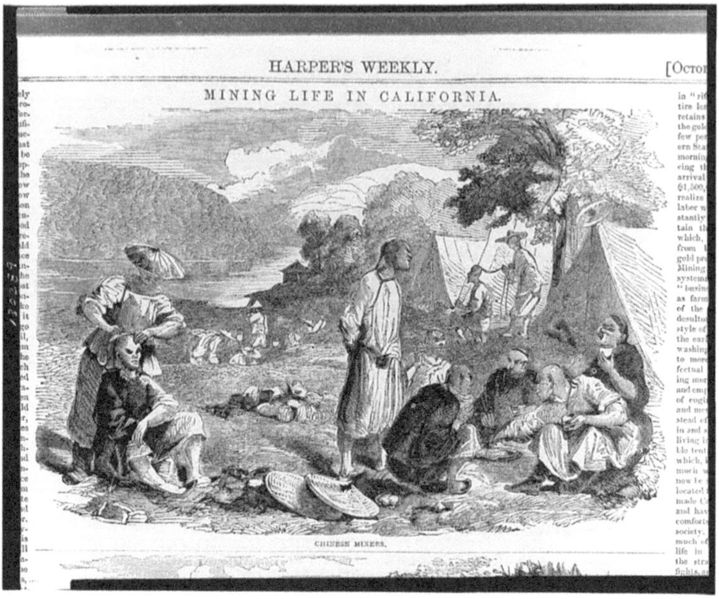

FIGURE 3.1 Mining Life in California—Chinese Miners: Wood engraving of Chinese miners in California. *HARPER'S WEEKLY*, CALIFORNIA, 1857. LIBRARY OF CONGRESS (HTTPS://WWW.LOC.GOV/ITEM/2001700332).

sometimes relying on credit to pay for their voyage. These immigrants were known as "sojourners," meaning they intended to work for a short time then return home rather than settle permanently in the United States. By 1855, 24,000 Chinese were working in California mines. As gold quickly ran out by the late 1850s, these sojourners began to look for work on the railroads, and railroad companies also began directly recruiting Chinese immigrants in 1864 to complete the Transcontinental Railroad.

Approximately 90% of the Central Pacific Railroad Company's workforce from 1864 to 1869 were Chinese; indeed, these workers were largely responsible for the completion of the Transcontinental Railroad. They worked in the California mountains from sunrise to sunset, six days a week. Chinese workers drank copious amounts of tea and soup; as these required the boiling of water, Chinese workers had far fewer incidences of dysentery and other waterborne illnesses and were much healthier than white workers. However, Chinese workers were grossly underpaid in comparison to their Irish counterparts (who held skilled occupations and supervised the Chinese rather than serving as line workers) and had to perform dangerous tasks, such as laying dynamite and tracks in the middle of blizzards. They even worked and lived underneath the snow; during the winter of 1867–68, there were more than 40 storms with snowdrifts over 45 feet tall. Chinese workers constructed chimneys, air shafts, and snow tunnels in order to continue boring through the mountain's granite during blizzards (Chang, 2019; Hsu, 2000).

Because Chinese workers were denied membership to labor unions due to their race, contractors and employers were able to exploit them with no recourse. For example, according to an 1866 payroll sheet, the total pay that Chinese men received for working on the Summit Tunnel (the first railroad tunnel to pass through the Sierra Nevada mountains) ranged from $3.96 for six days work to $25 for 30 days work. Most European workers on the payroll sheet received between $60 and $90 for the same periods of time respectively. Additionally, daily fees for housing were deducted from the wages of many Chinese workers, while no deductions were made from European workers' wages (Chang, 2019). An exploration of these stark differences in wages and deductions with students can easily demonstrate how employers took advantage of Chinese workers, many of whom did not have the language skills to contest such inequities. Students can use the statistics in the table below to calculate the wages that could be earned by different workers over the same time span.

TABLE 3.1 Railroad Worker Wage Comparisons

White carpenter's daily pay: $4 White foremen's daily pay: $3.75 (board included)	Chinese laborer's daily pay: $2.25–$2.75 (board not included, $0.40–$1.25 deducted a day)
White wood chopper's monthly pay: $40 (board included)	Chinese wood chopper's monthly pay: $30 (board not included, and higher fees charged when working in high elevations)

These numbers come from *Ghosts of Gold Mountain* (2019) by Gordon H. Chang.

After years of grueling work mostly done by underpaid and mistreated Chinese men, the Central Pacific Railroad was connected with the Union Pacific Railroad on May 10, 1869 at Promontory Summit in Utah. The completion of the first Transcontinental Railroad was celebrated through the driving of a commemorative golden spike. The photograph shown in Figure 3.2 is found in many U.S. history textbooks and is known as the "champagne photo" or "East and West Shaking Hands." It is easy to notice that the people responsible for most of the rail line's construction—the Chinese—are missing from this famous image. After discussing the contributions and mistreatment of Chinese railroad workers, students should be quick to note their absence in the photo. Ultimately, the Chinese are rarely credited for their incredible accomplishments in building the Transcontinental Railroad. About one in 10 Chinese workers died in the process, yet after the railroad's completion, a Sacramento parade only recognized Irish workers. Not until 1969, when plaques were installed in Sacramento and Promontory Summit, were Chinese laborers formally recognized for their efforts. In 2014, Chinese Railroad Workers were at long last inducted into the Department of Labor's Hall of Honor.

After railroad work was completed, Chinese immigrants sought work in other industries. Thousands moved to San Francisco, where they worked in factories and started their own businesses. Others moved elsewhere in search of work, heading to the fields for agricultural labor or across the country to the northeast and south along the Mississippi Delta. Creating their own stores, laundries, and restaurants was especially popular; these businesses did not require a great deal of capital nor equipment and were ideal for workers who could not read or speak English. Moreover, Chinese were facing increased hostility and discrimination, so self-employment was an ideal option for those who had the interest and ability.

By 1870, there were 63,000 Chinese in the U.S., with 48,510 living in California. Just 20 years earlier, in 1850, there had been only 450 Chinese in California! (Lee, 2019). Chinese workers stood out visually in their traditional blue cotton tunics, loose-fitting pants, blue stockings, wooden-soled shoes, cone-shaped hats, and long braided hair. The queue hairstyle—which included shaving the area above the temples

FIGURE 3.2 Completion of the First Transcontinental Railroad: The ceremony for the driving of the golden spike at Promontory Summit, Utah on May 10, 1869. Notice the absence of Chinese workers. PHOTOGRAPH BY ANDREW J. RUSSELL, 1869. LIBRARY OF CONGRESS (HTTPS://WWW.LOC.GOV/ITEM/CPS26858).

and forehead, growing out the rest of the hair, and wearing it in a braid as shown in Figure 3.3—was required by men as a sign of loyalty to the Qing dynasty in the 19th century. To shave off one's queue could result in death back in China, because it would have implied treason. Since Chinese sojourners intended to return home, it was vital that they leave it intact while working in the United States.

As white residents in California began to feel threatened by the growing numbers of Chinese, particularly in cities like San Francisco where they congregated and formed the first Chinatown, the queue became the subject of a law that put Chinese in a dangerous predicament. In 1873, San Francisco passed the Queue Ordinance, which required that all prisoners' heads be shaved. At the time, San Francisco jails were overcrowded due to another law which was meant to prevent

FIGURE 3.3 Elderly Chinese American man with queue. PHOTOGRAPH TAKEN BEFORE 1910 IN CHINATOWN OF SAN FRANCISCO. CALIFORNIA HISTORICAL SOCIETY, WIKIMEDIA COMMONS (HTTPS://COMMONS.WIKIMEDIA.ORG/WIKI/FILE:ELDERLY_CHINESE_AMERICAN_MAN_WITH_QUEUE.JPG).

unsafe housing conditions while also aiming to displace Chinese in the city. Chinese had limited housing options and were frequently forced to share crowded rooms and apartments. The Cubic Air Ordinance (see the box on p. 61) made too many people sharing a living space a misdemeanor, resulting in a fine, imprisonment, or both. As a result, many Chinese had to serve prison time, which also meant they were forced to shave their hair.

Ironically, laws like these created in an effort to encourage Chinese to leave the country often resulted in them being unable to return home. Comparing these and other laws featured on pages 61 and 62 is an excellent exercise for students to understand the multiple approaches taken by white communities and legislators against the Chinese, despite the recruitment of these immigrants for jobs that Americans did not desire.

ANTI-CHINESE TAXES, RULINGS, AND LEGISLATION

A shocking number of laws and provisions were passed in San Francisco and later statewide in California in efforts to discourage Chinese from settling in the United States. Here are some of the most important examples:

- **Foreign Miner's License Tax (1852):** Every foreign miner who did not desire to become a citizen had to pay a monthly tax of $3. Chinese were ineligible to become citizens whether they desired to or not—see Chapter 4. This tax was not uniformly collected, and Chinese were frequently forced to pay more than they owed.
- ***People v. Hall* (1854):** After a white man was convicted based on the testimony of three Chinese witnesses, this court decision resulted in Chinese witnesses becoming unable to testify against whites in court.
- **California School Law (1860):** According to this law, "Negroes, Mongolians and Indians shall not be admitted into the public schools."
- **Cubic Air Ordinance (1870):** Each person living in a residence was required to have 500 cubic feet of air. This ordinance was targeted at Chinese living in overcrowded apartments, who often did not pay the resulting fines and were then jailed.
- **Queue ("Pig Tail") Ordinance (1871):** All prisoners in city jail were required to have their heads shaved down to one inch.
- **The Page Act (1875):** The recruitment of laborers from China, Japan, or any Asian country not brought to the U.S. of their own free will or who were brought for immoral purposes, like prostitution, was prohibited. This was largely used to prevent Chinese women from immigrating.
- **Chinese Exclusion Act (1882):** The entry of Chinese laborers (described as skilled, unskilled, and employed in mining) to the United States was banned. Diplomats, government officers, and their servants were exempt, as were teachers, students, travelers, and merchants.
- **Scott Act (1888):** The exempt status of returning laborers was abolished to better enforce exclusion laws.

- **Geary Act (1892):** Chinese Exclusion laws were renewed for ten years with additional provisions, such as requiring Chinese people to carry a Certificate of Residence. Any Chinese resident caught without their certificate was subject to detention and deportation.

Anti-Chinese sentiment culminated in 1882 with the passage of the Chinese Exclusion Act. This is usually the first major piece of Asian American history that is taught to students across K–12 classrooms, but it is often taught in ways that are misleading or incomplete. In Chapter 2, we mentioned the Know Nothing party—a nativist political group that was active in the 1850s and opposed Irish immigration. The Know Nothing members also targeted the Chinese, describing them as "an evil of great present magnitude" (Lee, 2019, p. 76), accusing them of carrying infectious diseases, posing sexual danger to the country, and as we have detailed earlier, threatening the livelihood of white laborers.

An organizing committee of Know Nothings sent a delegation of nearly 20,000 people to Washington, D.C. to lobby for legislation restricting Chinese in the United States. The central argument against the Chinese was based on what historian Erika Lee (2019) describes as "a new kind of American national identity" (p. 78) that considered *all* European immigrants to be *true* Americans, despite privileging Northern and Western Europeans in previous years. The anti-Chinese campaign was incredibly successful, and the Chinese Exclusion Act became the first law to establish federal control over immigration while legalizing xenophobia.

Importantly, and contrary to popular belief, the Chinese Exclusion Act did *not* completely ban Chinese immigration to the United States. It simply banned skilled and unskilled laborers and miners and denied naturalized citizenship to Chinese who already lived in the United States (see Chapter 4). Chinese officials, teachers, students, tourists, and merchants were still allowed entry. Interestingly, although the Chinese population in the U.S. certainly grew exponentially in a short period of time, Chinese only made up 0.002% of the population in 1880 (Lee, 2003).

While there are no known firsthand accounts from these early Chinese immigrants, there are some excellent pieces of children's literature that describe their experiences. Most of these texts are chapter books for middle grades (ages 8–12) which offer detailed descriptions that pair well with the primary sources included in this section. For example, *Chinese Immigrants in America: An Interactive History Adventure* is a "YouChoose" book that may remind educators of a certain age of the "Choose Your Own Adventure" books popular decades ago. Additional resources can be found at the interactive Chinese Railroad Workers in North America Project website (http://web.stanford.edu/group/chineserailroad/cgi-bin/website). While most of the lesson plans provided on the website are for secondary students (a constant challenge for elementary folks and a part of our reasoning for writing this book!), the primary sources found in the lesson plans and PowerPoints are ideal for use with younger students.

RECOMMENDED CHILDREN'S LITERATURE ABOUT EARLY CHINESE IMMIGRANTS

- *Chinese Immigrants in America: An Interactive History Adventure* by Kelley Hunsicker
- *Coolies* by Yin, illustrated by Chris Soentpiet
- *Dragonwings* by Laurence Yep
- *Escape to Gold Mountain* by David H. T. Wong
- *Lily and the Great Quake: A San Francisco Earthquake Survival Story* by Veeda Bybee
- *Mountain Chef: How One Man Lost His Groceries, Changed His Plans, and Helped Cook Up the National Park Service* by Annette Bay Pimentel, illustrated by Rich Lo
- *Prairie Lotus* by Linda Sue Park
- *Staking a Claim: The Journal of Wong Ming-Chung* by Laurence Yep
- *Sugar* by Jewell Parker Rhodes
- *Tales from Gold Mountain* by Paul Yee, illustrated by Simon Ng
- *Ten Mile Day and the Building of the Transcontinental Railroad* by Mary Ann Fraser
- *Tracks* by Diane Lee Wilson

DISCUSSION QUESTIONS ABOUT EARLY CHINESE IMMIGRANTS

- Why do you think so many young Chinese men left their families behind to come to the United States, a place with a different language and culture?
- What do you think life was like for Chinese immigrants in the 1800s?
- Which groups did not want Chinese workers to stay in the U.S.? What were their reasons for wanting them to leave? How did these people benefit from the exclusion of Chinese workers?
- How did Chinese workers, who were so far from their families and homes, create communities in the United States? What are some examples of their influence on American culture that we can see today?

ANGEL ISLAND IMMIGRATION STATION

When the teaching of immigration in elementary grades only focuses on Ellis Island and its mostly European immigrants, students don't get the opportunity to learn about immigration to the United States from other continents. Teaching about the Angel Island Immigration Station, located on the West Coast in the San Francisco Bay, allows students to better understand our nation's rich diversity *and* its complicated past related to Chinese immigrants. San Francisco was the largest point of entry for Chinese and other Asian immigrants in the United States, processing one million people on their way into or out of the nation between 1910 and 1940. Half of these immigrants went through the Angel Island Immigration Station, which opened on January 21, 1910.

The history of Angel Island is directly related to Chinese Exclusion. After the Exclusion Act passed, immigration officials were required to carefully review the documents of all Chinese arrivals. This required passengers to be detained somewhere after disembarking from their ships. Initially, other ships were used for detention and processing, followed by a converted shed, but it soon became clear that a more permanent and sanitary space was needed. Thus, the greatest distinction between Ellis and Angel Islands is that the former was meant to welcome immigrants to the United States while the latter was designed specifically to exclude them—at least the ones who were Chinese.

This distinction is illustrated by the fact that 70% of the immigrants who arrived at Angel Island were detained in the island's segregated barracks. Of the approximately 300,000 people who were detained between 1910 and 1940, one-third are believed to have been Chinese (Lee & Yung, 2010). Detainees were segregated by gender, race, and ethnicity, with Asian immigrants subjected to more invasive health examinations (see Figure 3.4) and more intensive interrogations. For comparison, the Ellis Island detention rates were 10% for legal reasons and 10% for medical treatment. In contrast, 60% of immigrants passing through Angel Island were detained for up to three days. The remaining 10% of Angel Island detainees experienced longer stays that averaged two weeks. Kong Din Quong, a Chinese man, had the longest known detention of 756 days; Kong's father held U.S. native status, but Kong's admission was denied on legal grounds. Unable to successfully appeal the decision, Kong was deported after spending 25 months in detention on Angel Island (Lee, 2015).

The lengthy detentions experienced by immigrants resulted in intense feelings of isolation and anger, and several people carved poems expressing their feelings into the barrack walls. Some of these poems have been preserved (see the sidebar for resources to teach about these poems). As historians Erika Lee and Judy Yung (2010) noted, "Angel Island was both an entry point for immigrants seeking better lives in America and a last stop on a forced journey out of the country" (p. 9).

Part of the rationale behind these detentions was that they constituted a response to a system of false immigration claims that developed in the years before the Angel Island Immigration Station opened. In 1906, the San Francisco earthquake and fire destroyed all of the city's birth records. This created an opportunity for members of the exempt Chinese classes —who were still allowed to legally immigrate to the U.S.—to make a profit off of immigrants belonging to the excluded classes by claiming family members who didn't exist. Chinese who

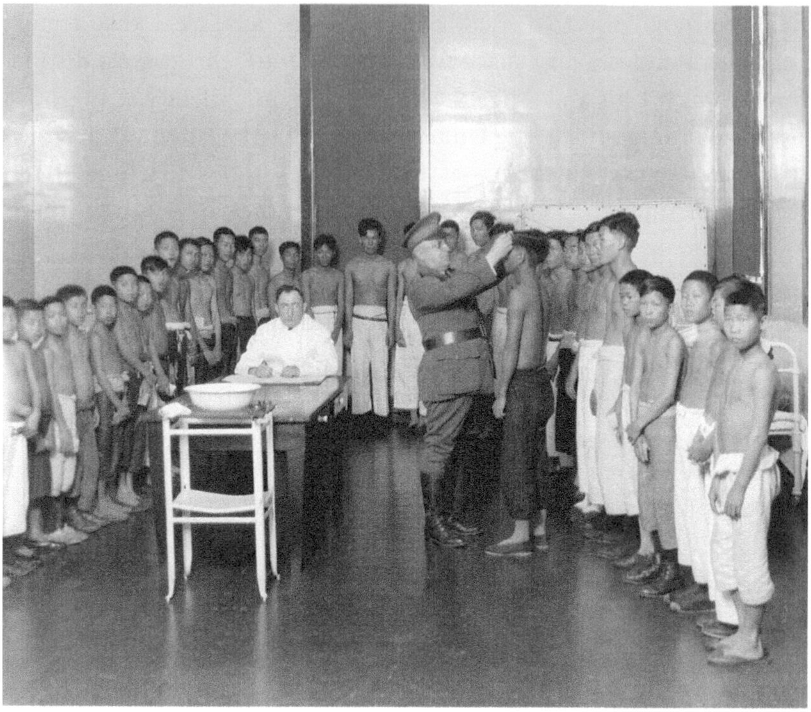

FIGURE 3.4 Intensive physical examination of aliens, Angel Island, California Immigration Hospital. NATIONAL ARCHIVES.

held fake identification papers were known as "paper sons" or "paper daughters."

But simply possessing false documentation was not enough to guarantee admission to the country. By the time the Angel Island Immigration Station opened, immigration officials were on the lookout for paper sons and daughters and adjusted their interrogation procedures accordingly. One of the most famous paper sons was artist Tyrus Wong, best known for the illustrative style found throughout the Disney film *Bambi*. The 2015 documentary *Tyrus* includes an interview where Wong describes the interrogation procedures that he and many others faced at Angel Island. Several of the books listed on page 68 also detail these lengthy interviews as well as some of the strategies young people used to be able to get through them successfully.

ANGEL ISLAND POETRY

Some detainees on Angel Island expressed their frustration and anger through poems. Over 200 poems have been preserved, mostly in Chinese but also in Russian, English, Japanese, and other languages. The Angel Island Immigration Station Foundation website features these poems in an online exhibition titled "Voices of Resilience," which includes audio recordings, translations, and biographies of authors. Poem audio in Mandarin and Cantonese can also be found at Pacific Link (https://www.kqed.org/w/pacificlink/home.html), and images of poems are featured in the adult-level book *Island: Poetry and History of Chinese Immigrants on Angel Island, 1910–1940* by Him Mark Lai, Genny Lim, and Judy Yung.

While this section focused mostly on the Chinese who passed through Angel Island, immigrants from Japan, Korea, South Asia, Russia, Mexico, and the Philippines were also processed at the station in large numbers. The Angel Island Immigration Station Foundation website (https://www.aiisf.org) includes several virtual galleries that allow online visitors to take 3D tours of the detention barracks. An impressive array of primary sources and educator resources such as lesson plans are also available. The Immigrant Voices section of the website allows students to dive deeply into the stories of individuals who immigrated through Angel Island, many of which are written by the immigrants' descendants or Angel Island researchers. There are also several historical fiction picturebooks and nonfiction books to support the teaching of this often-ignored immigration station. The breadth of resources now available about Angel Island work well in comparison/contrast to the many Ellis Island activities that exist. However, don't feel compelled to only teach about Angel Island as it relates to Ellis Island—its history is unique and important and can stand on its own!

RECOMMENDED CHILDREN'S LITERATURE ABOUT ANGEL ISLAND

- *Angel Island* by Russell Freedman
- *The Dragon's Child* by Laurence Yep with Kathleen Yep
- *Kai's Journey to Gold Mountain* by Katrina Currier
- *Landed* by Milly Lee, illustrated by Yangsook Choi
- *Li on Angel Island* by Veeda Bybee, illustrated by Andrea Rossetto
- *Paper Son: The Inspiring Journey of Tyrus Wong, Immigrant and Artist* by Julie Leung, illustrated by Chris Sasaki
- *Paper Son: Lee's Journey to America* by Helen Foster James & Virginia Shin-Loh, illustrated by Wilson Ong

RECOMMENDED ADULT TEXTS ABOUT ANGEL ISLAND

- *Angel Island: Immigrant Gateway to America* by Erika Lee and Judy Yung
- *Attachments: Faces and Stories from America's Gates* from the National Archives
- *Island: Poetry and History of Chinese Immigrants on Angel Island, 1910–1940* by Him Mark Lai, Genny Lim, and Judy Yung

DISCUSSION QUESTIONS ABOUT ANGEL ISLAND

- Why do countries have immigration stations? What is their purpose and why might islands be good locations for such places?
- Why do you think some immigrants were willing to break immigration rules by becoming "paper sons" or "paper daughters"?
- Some immigrants were children traveling alone. What do you think that experience would feel like? What are some of the challenges they might have faced?
- The Angel Island Immigration Station Foundation website has a list of sample interrogation questions in the Curriculum Guides section. Do you think you could answer these questions about your own family/place where you live? Try it out with a partner!

FROM EXCLUSION TO SELECTIVE INCLUSION OF ASIAN IMMIGRANTS

After Chinese laborers were banned by the 1882 Chinese Exclusion Act, Japanese began to arrive in the United States in greater numbers. As Japanese laborers replaced Chinese workers, the white working class launched an anti-Japanese movement that resulted in the Gentlemen's Agreement of 1907–1908. In the Agreement, Japan agreed to not issue passports for Japanese laborers wishing to work in the Continental United States. In return, U.S. President Theodore Roosevelt agreed to urge the city of San Francisco to allow Japanese American children to attend white schools (more details in Chapter 7).

Next, anti-Asian nativist groups targeted South Asians, vilifying them as the "Hindoo invasion," "tide of turbans," and a "horde of fanatics" (Takaki, 1998, pp. 295–298). In response, Congress passed the Immigration Act of 1917, which created an "Asiatic barred zone" that prohibited immigration from almost all of Asia. The Immigration Act of 1924 further restricted the number of immigrants allowed from each country. White Anglo-Saxon immigrants (such as British and Germans) were given the highest annual quota, while southern (Italians, Greeks) and eastern Europeans (Russians) received a far lower cap. These numbers were still far higher than the quotas for Asian nations, which allowed only 100 individuals *per year* per national origin to immigrate (Ngai, 2014). Together, immigration legislation in 1917 and 1924 effectively slammed America's gates shut to Asian immigrants.

This closed door began to slowly open for Asian immigrants during World War II. For the first time since the passage of the Chinese Exclusion Act, the U.S. needed a wartime alliance with China. This military-inspired change of heart shifted the image of Chinese from dangerous foreigners who stole jobs from white Americans to brave resistors fighting against the Japanese empire alongside the United States. This led Congress to finally repeal the Chinese Exclusion Act in 1943 after 60 years of legal exclusion. Similarly, U.S. alliances with India and the Philippines ended Filipinx and Indian exclusion in 1946 (Wu, 2019). It's important to recognize that the impetus for these immigration changes was not due to changes in American society or an interest in diversifying racial demographics. It was about fostering goodwill for necessary war alliances, plain and simple.

The Cold War and the Civil Rights Movement of the 1960s brought further change for similarly strategic reasons. The U.S. was in a battle with the communist USSR to prove that democracy and capitalism were the best government and economic systems. One way for the U.S. to prove this was to gain as many allies as possible to stop the influence of the communist USSR from spreading to other countries. The U.S. also wanted to attract scientists and engineers (especially from Asia) who would help them build the best space technology and weapons (Hsu, 2015). However, it was difficult for the United States to maintain its image of superiority over the Soviets when news of discrimination and the disenfranchisement of people of color at home were making global headlines (Wu, 2019). The Civil Rights Movement also pushed the U.S. government to address inequities in immigration policies (Wu, 2014), leading Congress to pass the Immigration and Nationality Act of 1965 (also known as the Hart–Celler Act), which abolished the racist quota system established in 1924. The new law applied an equal immigration cap on *all* countries, with preferences given first to family reunification (75%), then economic employment (20%), and finally to refugees (5%).

Interestingly, President Lyndon B. Johnson (1965) stated,

> This bill that we will sign today is not a revolutionary bill. It does not affect the lives of millions. It will not reshape the structure of our daily lives, or really add importantly to either our wealth or our power. Yet it is still one of the most important acts of this Congress and of this administration. For it does repair a very deep and painful flaw in the fabric of American justice. It corrects a cruel and enduring wrong in the conduct of the American Nation. (p. 1038)

While he was right about the act correcting long-standing injustices in immigration, Johnson couldn't have been more wrong about the act's impact! Since the passage of the 1965 Immigration Act, the Asian American population rapidly grew from 500,000 in 1960 to nearly

20 million in 2020. Many Asians immigrated through the "economic preferences" category, which prioritized highly educated individuals—especially in STEM fields—as the U.S. continued to compete with the Soviets during the Cold War.

As discussed in Chapter 2, this immigration pattern contributed to the perception of Asians and Asian Americans as the model minority. The H-1B visa program (see Tables 3.2, 3.3, and 3.4), which was introduced in 1990 and allows U.S. employers to hire foreign workers for specialty jobs requiring a bachelor's degree, also contributed to the model minority myth, as many Asian professionals were recruited through the program. In 2020, China and India accounted for more than 85% of all H-1B visas grantees. H-1B visas can lead to lawful permanent residence and eventually citizenship, although this pathway is controlled by employers and immigration authorities.

The history of Asian immigration to the U.S. debunks the popular myth of America as a nation of immigrants that welcomes everyone regardless of race or other social identities. It reveals how racism as well as political and economic interests have shaped immigration policies, determining who is allowed to immigrate and who is not. To engage students in the study of Asian immigration, you can use a graph of U.S. immigration by decade and continent (Figure 3.5) and challenge

TABLE 3.2 Approved H-1B Visas by Level of Education, 2021

Level of Education	Approximate Number of Years in School	Number of H-1B Visa Petitions Approved in 2021	Percentage of All Beneficiaries
Less than a bachelor's degree	< 17	289	0.1
Bachelor's degree	17	137,050	33.7
Master's degree	18–20	230,326	56.6
Doctorate degree	21–24	27,752	6.8
Professional degree	N/A	11,623	2.8
Unknown	N/A	31	0

Characteristics of H-1B Specialty Occupation Workers: Fiscal Year 2021 Annual Report to Congress October 1, 2020–September 30, 2021. *U.S. Citizenship and Immigration Services.*

TABLE 3.3 Approved H-1B Visas by Occupational Category, 2021

Occupational Category	Number H-1B Visa Petitions Approved in 2021
Computer-related occupations	280,032
Occupation in architecture, engineering, and surveying	38,863
Occupation in administrative specializations	20,730
Occupations in education	16,226
Occupations in medicine and health	14,070
Occupations in mathematics and physical sciences	11,849
Occupations in life sciences	6,759
Managers and officials	5,098
Miscellaneous professional and technical, and managerial occupations	4,140
Occupations in social sciences	3,665
Occupations in art	1,887
Occupations in law and jurisprudence	1,585
Occupations in writing	334
Miscellaneous	237
Occupations in museum, library, and archival sciences	155
Occupations in entertainment and recreation	122
Occupations in religion and theology	47
Sale promotion occupations	3
Occupation unknown	1269

Characteristics of H-1B Specialty Occupation Workers: Fiscal Year 2021 Annual Report to Congress October 1, 2020–September 30, 2021. *U.S. Citizenship and Immigration Services.*

young people to think about possible causes behind the immigration patterns they observe. Then briefly explain the history of exclusion and selective inclusion of Asian immigration and facilitate a class discussion about the political and economic interests behind immigration policies.

Once students have an understanding of how immigration access shifted over time, share data like the pie charts on Scholastic's immi-

TABLE 3.4 H-1B Approved Petitions by Place of Birth, Top 10 Countries, 2021

Place of Birth	Number H-1B Visa Petitions Approved in 2021	Percentage of All Beneficiaries
India	301,616	74.1
China	50,328	12.4
Canada	3,836	0.9
South Korea	3,481	0.9
Philippines	2,786	0.7
Mexico	2,611	0.6
Taiwan	2,604	0.6
Brazil	1,986	0.5
Pakistan	1,880	0.5
Nepal	1,584	0.4

Characteristics of H-1B Specialty Occupation Workers: Fiscal Year 2021 Annual Report to Congress October 1, 2020–September 30, 2021. *U.S. Citizenship and Immigration Services.*

gration website (http://teacher.scholastic.com/activities/immigration/index.htm) that show immigration by continent in 50-year increments. What information is hidden when data is shown in this way versus by decade? Many other organizations and websites have interactive maps that students can explore and compare to determine the best formats to demonstrate different kinds of demographic information.

As we move toward contemporary immigration, consider how you might update classic immigration units. Conducting interviews with immigrants remains a solid activity (although prep students accordingly to make sure they aren't describing activities, customs, or clothing as weird or strange!), but there's more that you can do. For example, rather than having students do the traditional but not very interesting activity where they draw what they would pack in a suitcase if they had to move to a different country, consider asking them to learn about immigrant communities in the local area or across the state.

In Sohyun's home state of Georgia, a dizzying array of ethnic enclaves exist in and around Atlanta. Using technology, students can

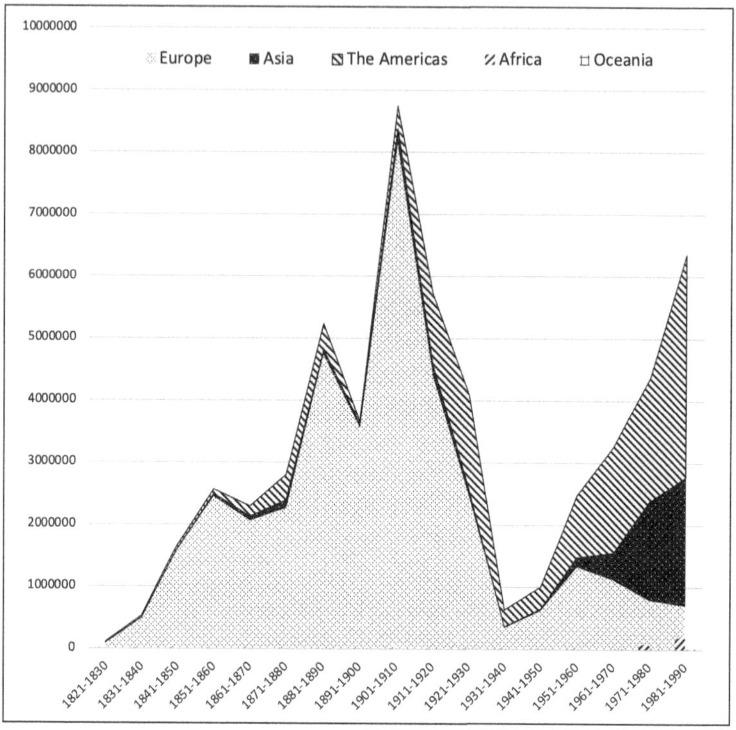

FIGURE 3.5 U.S. Immigration by continent and decade, 1821–1990. CREATED BY SOHYUN AN BASED ON DATA FROM U.S. DEPARTMENT OF HOMELAND SECURITY (HTTPS://WWW.DHS.GOV/IMMIGRATION-STATISTICS/YEARBOOK)

locate restaurants and grocery stores where an immigrant from a particular culture might be able to find the foods and ingredients needed to make a dish from their homeland. When a student conducting an interview learns what the interviewee's favorite dish is, they could search for the items needed to prepare it or find a restaurant that makes it. They could also learn which community organizations might support the transition to a new country. If students use maps to indicate the journey from an interviewee's place of origin to where they immigrated, consider using different color lines or strings to indicate multiple migrations and/or to note which laws impacted their family's ability to immigrate. Also consider expanding the range of people who students interview to go beyond first-generation immigrants. This allows students to learn more about different generations and how their immigrant journeys changed over time!

The books included in this box are about Asian immigration that occurred after the closure of the Angel Island Immigration Station in 1940 through the present. There are many books that we did not have space to name, so consider this list an assorted starter pack that includes stories about the cultural clashes experienced between first- and second-generation immigrant children and their families; immigrants who arrive in rural and suburban spaces where they are the only Asians in town; recently-arrived immigrants describing their elementary and middle school experiences; and friendships between U.S.-born Asian Americans and recently-arrived immigrants from Asia.

RECOMMENDED CHILDREN'S LITERATURE ABOUT ASIAN IMMIGRATION, 1920–2020

- *American as Paneer Pie* by Supriya Kelkar
- *Any Day with You* by Mae Respicio
- *Front Desk* series (*Front Desk; Three Keys; Room to Dream; Key Player; Top Story)* by Kelly Yang
- *Golden Girl* by Reem Faruqi
- *Hana Is My Name* by Belle Yang
- *I Was Their American Dream* by Malaka Gharib
- *In the Beautiful Country* by Jane Kuo
- *The Land of Forgotten Girls* by Erin Entrada Kelly
- *Maizy Chen's Last Chance* by Lisa Yee
- *The Many Meanings of Meilan* by Andrea Wang
- *Measuring Up* by Lily LaMotte, illustrated by Ann Xu
- *More to the Story* by Hena Khan
- *Red, White, and Whole* by Rajani LaRocca
- *Stargazing* by Jen Wang
- *Step Up to the Plate Maria Singh* by Uma Krishnaswami
- *The Turtle of Oman* by Naomi Shihab Nye

DISCUSSION QUESTIONS ABOUT ASIAN IMMIGRATION, 1920–2020

- What do you know about <insert Asian country of origin>? What do you know about the state that the main character lives in? What are some challenges that immigrants from <insert Asian country of origin> might face in this area? What are some things that might be easy to adjust to or that feel familiar?
- What are some ways that you and your family are similar to the characters in this book? What are some ways that you and your family are different?
- How does the main character describe the immigrant experience (their own and/or of their family/friends)? How does this compare to what you expected to learn/read?
- What did you learn about the culture of <insert Asian country of origin> from this book? What are some ways that the characters combine that culture with what is commonly known as "American" culture?
- What does being American mean to the characters in this story?

ASIAN REFUGEES

While many Asians entered America as immigrants, some arrived as refugees. Most notably, Southeast Asian Americans represent the largest refugee community ever to be resettled in the United States after being forcefully displaced by the U.S. wars in Vietnam, Laos, and Cambodia (see Chapter 5 for more details). When the U.S. withdrew from the region in 1975 after a decade of war and military intervention, communist governments came to power in Vietnam, Laos, and Cambodia. Those who supported and aided U.S. military actions during the Vietnam War or who suffered from the new communist regimes began to flee. Among the countless people displaced by the Vietnam War and its aftermath, 1,250,000 arrived in the U.S. between 1975 and 1994 (Espiritu, 2014).

The American public's reactions to the refugees were mixed. A poll taken in 1979 showed about 30% of Americans approved of accepting

Vietnam War refugees, whereas 62% disapproved, fearing that the refugees from Asia would become economic and cultural threats (DeSilver, 2015). In order to encourage assimilation and prevent the formation of ethnic ghettos, the U.S. government dispersed Southeast Asian refugees across the country (Lee, 2015). Many refugees, however, soon relocated to areas where they could find fellow Asians and supportive ethnic networks. Vietnamese refugees created large ethnic communities in Los Angeles, Orange, and San Diego counties in southern California, in the cities of San Francisco, Oakland, and San Jose in Northern California, and in Houston, Texas. Cambodian refugees built communities in Long Beach, California, Lowell, Massachusetts, and the Bronx in New York City. Hmong refugees largely settled in rural areas in California, Wisconsin, and Minnesota (Lee, 2015).

As you might imagine, resettling and adjusting to U.S society as war refugees was not easy. Many Southeast Asian refugee families struggled with poverty, racism, and war trauma (Espiritu, 2014). Some refugee youth dropped out of school and joined gangs as they suffered from the same systematic marginalization as many other youth of color: failing schools, poverty, racial profiling, over-policing, and mass incarceration (Tang, 2015). For Southeast Asian refugee youth who have not naturalized, this school-to-prison pipeline extends to deportation. In other words, for noncitizen refugees with criminal records, deportation is mandatory due to harsh policies (Hing, 2005). Southeast Asian American communities have been mobilizing to fight against mass deportations over the past two decades.

As refugee flows from Vietnam, Laos, and Cambodia ceased, the largest Asian refugee groups in recent years have been from Bhutan and Burma (or Myanmar). Most refugees from Bhutan are Nepali-speaking Lhotshampa, an ethnic religious minority who fled Bhutan due to political repression and violence during the 1990s. After nearly two decades living in refugee camps in Nepal, this community was allowed to resettle in the U.S. beginning in 2007. Similarly, most refugees from Burma came from rural regions where several ethnic and religious minority groups, such as Karen, Chin, and Rohingya, faced oppression and violence from the military government. After being displaced in neighboring countries, including Bangladesh, India, Malaysia, and Thailand, some of these refugees were permitted to resettle in the U.S. In 2011, refugees from Burma and Bhutan made up the vast majority (56%) of refugees resettled in the United States (Trieu & Vang, 2015).

Afghans are the most recent Asian community to arrive in the U.S. as refugees. After two decades of U.S. war and military intervention in Afghanistan, which began in response to the September 11, 2001 terrorist attacks, the United States finally withdrew from Afghanistan on August 30, 2021. The withdrawal left tens of thousands of Afghan citizens scrambling as a resurgent Taliban moved into the city of Kabul. Despite the United States' responsibility in generating the refugee crisis through lengthy war and military actions (Vine, 2020), anti-Muslim groups opposed accepting the refugees, framing Afghan refugees as a cultural and national security threat (Kieffer, 2021). Given the persistent hate and discrimination against Arab and Muslim Americans in the U.S. (see Chapter 2), Afghan refugees may struggle when resettling in the U.S.

To bring these complex stories of Asian refugees into the classroom, you can use children's literature (for read alouds, book clubs, and individual book study) and guide students to think about the larger forces behind the refugee crises as well as the struggles and resilience of refugees. There is an ample selection of children's literature on Southeast Asian and Syrian refugees. However, few books for young readers exist about recent refugees from Burma, Bhutan, Afghanistan, or other places in Asia. In these cases, you can use news stories or oral histories from websites such as the Immigration History Research Center at the University of Minnesota (https://cla.umn.edu/ihrc) and the United Nations High Commissioner for Refugees (https://www.unhcr.org/en-us/teaching-about-refugees.html).

When using children's books, news, or oral histories, be careful not to present refugees as helpless victims in need of rescue without agency or resilience. And definitely do *not* ask students to weigh the pros and cons of refugee resettlement—asking children to consider whether or not a person deserves the chance to live without the threat of danger is a dehumanizing exercise. While there are political considerations for such conversations, young learners would be arguing for legislative proposals without sufficient context and understanding of complex issues.

That is an incomplete instructional goal beyond the scope of elementary social studies.

Instead, compare the refugee experience in a welcoming environment to a hostile one. Guide students to identify and critique racism and discrimination as well as linguistic and economic challenges that refugees may experience when resettling and adjusting to the U.S. society. What might life be like for a young student who was successful at school in their homeland but finds it difficult to communicate in writing *and* orally in a new place, surrounded by people who do not understand their culture nor experiences? Particularly in the case of Southeast Asian and South Asian refugees, encourage students to think about the complex roles that the U.S. played in generating the refugee crisis in the first place. For example, prompt them to think about how U.S. wars in the region may have contributed to displacement, scarce resources, and physical destruction of homes and businesses. Such interrogation is critical to avoid reproducing the popular myth of the U.S. exclusively as a benevolent rescuer of desperate refugees (see Chapter 5).

RECOMMENDED CHILDREN'S LITERATURE ABOUT ASIAN REFUGEES

- *Adrift at Sea* by Marsha Forchuk Skrypuch with Tuan Ho, illustrated by Brian Deines
- *Dia's Story Cloth* by Dia Cha, illustrated by Chue and Nhia Thao Cha
- *A Different Pond* by Bao Phi, illustrated by Thi Bui
- *Escape from Aleppo* by N. H. Senzai
- *Grandfather's Story Cloth* by Linda Gerdner and Sarah Langford, illustrated by Stuart Loughridge
- *Half Spoon of Rice: A Survival Story of the Cambodian Genocide* by Icy Smith, illustrated by Sopaul Nhem
- *Homeland: My Father Dreams of Palestine* by Hannah Moushabeck, illustrated by Reem Madooh
- *Inside Out and Back Again* by Thanhha Lai
- *Other Words for Home* by Jasmine Warga
- *Mai Ya's Long Journey* by Sheila Cohen

- *The Most Beautiful Thing* by Kao Kalia Yang, illustrated by Khoa Le
- *Refugees and Migrants* by Ceri Roberts and Hanane Kai
- *Stepping Stones: A Refugee Family's Journey* by Margriet Ruurs, artwork by Nizar Ali Badr
- *When Everything Was Everything* by Saymoukda Duangphouxay Vongsay, illustrated by Cory Nakamura Lin
- *Wishes* by Mượn Thị Văn, illustrated by Victo Ngai
- *Yang Warriors* by Kao Kalia Yang

DISCUSSION QUESTIONS FOR CHILDREN'S LITERATURE ABOUT ASIAN REFUGEES

- Who are refugees? How are refugees different from immigrants?
- Where did the main character come from? What happened to the main character and their family and country?
- Who is responsible for the refugee crisis in the book?
- What role did the U.S. play in the refugee crisis in the book?
- What struggle(s) did the main character face in coming to the United States? How did they adjust to U.S. school and culture? What actions did the main character take to address the challenges?
- What small steps can we take in our school and in our community to help respond to refugee crises?
- What big steps might our local, state, and government leaders need to take in response to refugee crises?

IM/MIGRATION MATTERS

While it may not be possible to teach all of the Asian American immigration and refugee histories described in this chapter in a single academic year, we encourage you to add whatever you can to your existing curriculum. An activity that allows you to explore a range of immigration stories beyond traditional Ellis Island and European narratives is to create a timeline that will allow you and your students to track the movements of various groups over time. This can be a digital timeline or a physical one that spans the length of the classroom. One approach that is ideal for fourth and fifth grades is to color-code different types of information along the timeline, such as world events (e.g., wars and conflicts that cause people to leave a specific place), legislation that allows or prohibits entry to specific nations (e.g., Chinese Exclusion Act of 1882; Immigration Act of 1917; Immigration and Nationality Act of 1965), as well as specific events, court cases, and historical figures (e.g., completion of the Transcontinental Railroad; Wong Kim Ark; Takao Ozawa; Bhagat Singh Thind) that represent important moments and societal shifts.

Noreen took such an approach with her fifth grade classroom and made each moment on the timeline interactive. Folding a piece of construction paper in half, she pasted a primary source on the top and students wrote a description of the event/person/legislation on notebook paper that was glued underneath the fold. From afar, the timeline had images and labels on it. Up close, students and visitors could interact with the timeline by lifting the primary source flap to view the detailed, student-created information beneath.

However you choose to incorporate Asian American immigration and refugee narratives into your curriculum, please forefront the voices and experiences of those who have actually participated in those narratives. For too long, social studies curriculum and popular trade books about these topics have been told by cultural outsiders whose renditions focus on achieving the American dream. These accounts often omit the nightmarish struggles with discrimination and injustice that many people face after arriving in their new home and that are particularly applicable to the Asian American experience historically and contemporarily. Leaving your homeland for a new place involves struggle *and* achievement; it is important to support your students in understanding both of these realities.

4

Citizenship

Schools have long been considered the places where our nation's citizens develop. In the early grades, citizenship is often defined as patriotism and individual responsibility. In this chapter, we expand these ideas to include teaching about historical and legal citizenship. The experiences of many Asians in America as well as of Asian Americans expose historical and current tensions of how citizenship is understood and applied inequitably in the United States. They also reveal alternative ideas of citizenship in the classroom and society, specifically, identities and communities across and beyond borders. We begin by discussing pathways to legal citizenship and how Asian Americans used the court system to argue for their place in the United States. Next, we focus on how not all citizens are treated equally based on their race and religion by exploring Japanese American incarceration, the Dusky Peril, and Islamophobia.

DEFINING CITIZENSHIP

"A good citizen cleans up after themselves." "A good citizen takes turns." How many times have we heard these phrases in classrooms, or used them ourselves when speaking to our students? For Esther, being a good citizen in elementary school meant getting an "O" for outstanding under the "citizenship" category on her report cards. In reality, she often received an "S" for satisfactory at best, and usually an "N" for

DOI: 10.4324/9781032662695-4

"needs improvement," since citizenship at her school was tied to doing homework, a responsibility she rarely fulfilled. These ideas of citizenship in elementary classrooms can be important in guiding students to consider how we choose to live responsibly and interact with each other in ways that do the least harm to ourselves and others. But to stop there means that we give little credit to the intellectual and civic capacities of young people, not simply as "future citizens" but as *active* citizens in the communities that they belong to.

Narrowly defining "good" citizenship fails to adequately prepare students to think critically and independently as they make decisions about which rules and laws should be followed and which should be changed to improve the conditions in schools *and* in our society. Citizenship in classrooms is too often tied to following rules rather than questioning *which* rules we should follow, which ones we actually *need,* and why.

In elementary classrooms, especially in the early grades, citizenship and patriotism are synonymous. Many state standards require learning about the importance of patriotism in addition to U.S. symbols and songs of national pride. From their first days in school, students learn that a good citizen loves their country. But what love of one's country *means* and *looks like* is rarely discussed. Thus, young children are left with popular messages that being patriotic and loving your country means following the rules and not questioning authority. A *critical* version of patriotism is rarely introduced to young learners. Critical patriotism is what Black writer and civil rights activist James Baldwin (1955) described when he stated, "I love America more than any other country in the world and, exactly for this reason, I insist on the right to criticize her perpetually" (p. 5).

Teaching citizenship differently might feel intimidating. But that's the only way to help students understand how *complex* citizenship is. It isn't just about good or bad behavior. It's about a set of rights that people are entitled to and about understanding that many people have historically been denied those rights on the basis of their identities. Moreover, some people *continue* to struggle with fully accessing and exercising their rights as citizens. Still others are caught in limbo, legally unable to become citizens despite their roots in our society. So, given how important citizenship is because of its direct connection to the rights that one *is* or *is not* afforded, you have to know some of the technical details. In particular, an understanding of documented national identity (what is commonly known as "legal" citizenship) and its history explains why so many social groups have struggled to achieve citizenship in order to access all the rights and privileges that come with it.

WHY SHOULD WE HISTORICIZE CITIZENSHIP?

The United States has long been called a nation of immigrants and a melting pot. More recently, recognizing that "melting" requires assimilation, the metaphor of a salad bowl has become popular, but using any of these metaphors leaves out several important considerations. First, we must acknowledge that Asian Americans, like all other non-Indigenous communities, are settlers in the United States. Indigenous communities lived and continue to live on the land we now call the United States. They are not immigrants, so to describe the U.S. as a nation of immigrants erases their presence since time immemorial. Central to this erasure are the many treaties broken by the U.S. government that fail to acknowledge the lands, rights, and governments of tribes. In addition, for Indigenous communities, membership in the United States via legal citizenship was not even an option until 1924. Before this, birthright citizenship (automatic citizenship granted when born in the United States), which is guaranteed by the 14th Amendment, was denied to Indigenous Peoples by the U.S. Supreme Court.

A second consideration is the citizenship of Black Americans. Enslaved Africans were not immigrants as they were brought to the United States *against their will*. Some curricula term this "involuntary migration," but we find this euphemism unnecessary and inappropriate. Describing their experience as being kidnapped and threatened with violence is far more accurate and less misleading. As enslaved peoples were considered *property* rather than *people*, they, their descendants, and any other free Black individuals were not guaranteed citizenship until 1868 when the 14th Amendment was passed, granting them equal protections from racial (and other) discrimination. Although this right was inscribed into law, the accompanying rights and privileges were never guaranteed and remain tenuous to this day. Many systems were put in place to keep the rights of citizenship away from Black communities, such as Jim Crow laws, unequal school funding, poll taxes and tests, and government benefits that were only granted to white workers.

JIM CROW LAWS

After the Civil War, the U.S. government passed several amendments that were meant to ensure the rights of Black communities. These are known as the Reconstruction Amendments. Reconstruction (1865–1877) was the time period following the Civil War when the Confederate states were reincorporated into the United States. A priority of Reconstruction was to address the many inequities accrued from decades of enslavement. Federal troops and officials stayed in southern states to ensure that free and newly freed Black Americans would be able to vote (men only!), run for office, go to schools, buy land, and work for themselves.

Historian W. E. B. DuBois (1935/1992) called those few years "a brief moment in the sun" (p. 30), as federal protections proved effective and Black Americans in the South made political and economic gains. Reconstruction ended when a contested presidential election resulted in a compromise between mostly Northern Republicans and Southern white Democrats, in which the Republican candidate, Rutherford B. Hayes, became president. Federal troops and influence were removed from southern states, and Jim Crow laws designed to take away the civil rights of Black Americans were quickly passed. These laws, named after a Black minstrel character, enforced racial segregation, including separate facilities for restrooms, restaurants, and seating on buses.

Finally, the Asian struggle for access to U.S. citizenship reveals how civic membership into this so-called nation of immigrants or salad bowl is and always has been based on white supremacy (see the Forever Foreigner section in Chapter 2). That is, a racial hierarchy exists in our society where white people are at the top and enjoy all rights and privileges while other racial groups, including Asian Americans, are denied full access to the rights of citizens. The rest of this chapter will focus on this third consideration.

WHO CAN BE A CITIZEN?

Asians in America often used the court system in their fight for citizenship. Whether successful or not, these cases reveal a lot about who the United States wanted as citizens and who they did not. Even when the government finally began to shift the laws away from Asian exclusion, political interests rather than social progress were often the dominant motivation.

Birthright Citizenship

In 1898, the Supreme Court affirmed the right to citizenship to anyone born on U.S. soil through the 14th Amendment. This is known as *birthright* citizenship. The 14th Amendment is best known for the equal protection clause, which was intended to ensure the equal treatment of Black Americans. The catalyst for this amendment was a Chinese American man named Wong Kim Ark. He was born in the U.S. and often traveled to China, where his family members lived. On one return trip in 1895, Wong was refused entry by immigration and customs officials who stated that, because he was of Chinese descent, he could not be a U.S. citizen. Wong challenged the Bureau of Immigration in the court case *United States vs. Wong Kim Ark*, and the Supreme Court ruled in his favor, upholding the 14th Amendment right that any individual born on U.S. soil would be granted citizenship no matter their race or the citizenship status of their parents.

I AM AN AMERICAN: THE WONG KIM ARK STORY BY MARTHA BROCKENBROUGH WITH GRACE LIN, ILLUSTRATED BY JULIA KUO

This picturebook describes Wong Kim Ark's life and his legacy of birthright citizenship for all, detailing the challenges many Chinese immigrants and their U.S.-born children faced. Some challenges are clearly stated, while others are implied in the illustrations. For example, when the author describes how Chinese people were blamed during difficult financial times, the illustration shows a broken window. Teachers should help students make these connections more explicit (i.e., people threw stones at the windows and broke them).

The peritext includes primary sources as well as brief explanations about the 14th Amendment, citizenship laws, and the arguments used for and against keeping Wong's U.S. citizenship. While the authors describe the lawyers who argued against Wong as untrustworthy, they stop short of identifying racism as the root of the lawyers' reasoning. When *you* discuss these arguments in the classroom, make sure you don't tiptoe around racism.

Naturalized Citizenship

In 1790, the founders of the United States designated free white persons as the only group of people who could *naturalize* to become a citizen; that is, white people could become citizens of the U.S. even if they were born outside of the country. Asians, however, were lawfully barred from citizenship because they were not white. This law is an important part of understanding several key events in Asian American history. Birthright citizenship and the 14th Amendment meant that Wong Kim Ark's U.S. citizenship was established, but his own parents and all Asian immigrants were still legally barred from naturalized citizenship since they were not white.

***Ozawa v. U.S.* and *U.S. v. Thind*.** In 1922 and 1923, two Asian immigrant men separately challenged the denial of citizenship and took their cases all the way to the Supreme Court. In 1922, Takao Ozawa argued for citizenship based on his assimilation to white U.S. culture. The following year, Bhagat Singh Thind used the Supreme Court's own words to make the scientific case that he should be classified as Caucasian and, thus, would be eligible for citizenship. In both cases, the Court made clear that Asian meant "not white" and, therefore, Asians were unable to become U.S. citizens. The table below outlines their stories.

TABLE 4.1 The Stories of Takao Ozawa and Bhagat Singh Thind

NATIONALITY ACT OF 1790 "any alien being a free white person . . . may be admitted to become a citizen . . ."	
***Ozawa v. U.S.* (1922)**	***U.S. v. Thind* (1923)**
Takao Ozawa was born in Japan in 1875. He immigrated to the United States in 1894. He attended high school and college in California and then moved to Hawai'i. Ozawa was fluent in English, practiced Christianity, and worked for an American company. He was married to a Japanese woman who was educated in America, and the couple had two children. In 1914, Ozawa applied for naturalization. During that time, only white persons and persons of African descent were allowed to become naturalized citizens. Ozawa argued that, because his skin was as white as other white people, he should be allowed to become a U.S. citizen. The Supreme Court denied his request, saying that being white meant that one had to belong to the Caucasian race, and as part of the Mongolian race, Ozawa could not be considered white.	Bhagat Singh Thind was born in 1892 in India. He came to the United States in 1913. He studied at a university and served in the U.S. Army during World War I. After the war, he applied for and was granted citizenship in 1920. However, the Bureau of Naturalization appealed the case, which went to the U.S. Supreme Court. Thind thought he would win because a few months earlier in the Ozawa ruling, the Court said that being white meant being Caucasian. Thind, like most North Indians, was Caucasian. However, during this case, the Supreme Court changed the definition of being white from being Caucasian to what most people believed it to mean. The Court said that, although Thind was Caucasian, most people wouldn't see him as white because of his cultural background, and therefore denied Thind's request.

Created by Sohyun An & Esther Kim.

Ozawa v. U.S. and *U.S. v. Thind* clearly show how citizenship was not about what a good citizen should do, but rather about who was the "right" race. The different definitions of "white" offered by the same Supreme Court within one year also reveal how race and whiteness are constructs that shift depending on which definition will best uphold white supremacy.

From Exclusion to Inclusion In Chapter 3, we described how the earliest Chinese immigrants had to pay the Foreign Miner's Tax because they were ineligible to become citizens. The Chinese Exclusion Act of 1882 legally prohibited them from naturalizing—going through the citizenship process as adults who were born outside of the United States. This prohibition on naturalization was then applied to all the Asian groups who immigrated after the Chinese in the late 1800s and early 1900s: Koreans, Japanese, Filipinx, South Asians, and more. We also

FIGURE 4.1 Bhagat Singh Thind with his battalion at Camp Lewis, Washington on November 18, 1918. DONATED BY DAVID THIND. SOUTH ASIAN AMERICAN DIGITAL ARCHIVE (HTTPS://WWW.SAADA.ORG/ITEM/20110802-264).

noted that exclusion and the subsequent ban on naturalization ended during World War II. We will revisit this part of history briefly below. If you'd like to see a detailed list of the various pieces of legislation related to U.S. citizenship over time, visit the Citizenship section of the Immigration History website (https://immigrationhistory.org/lesson-plan/citizenship).

In Chapter 3, we discussed how the Cold War led to gradual changes in U.S. immigration policies. The Immigration and Nationality Act of 1952 (also known as the McCarran–Walter Act) dropped all racial restrictions on naturalization. Then the Immigration and Nationality Act of 1965 (also known as the Hart–Celler Act) eliminated racist quotas. Many education standards and texts tell proud narratives of U.S. progress and exceptionalism, but it is important to keep in mind that these pieces of legislation were all strategic. They weren't the result of a sincere desire to abolish racist policies. Instead, these changes were politically motivated. Simply put, they made the U.S. look good! Being honest about these histories makes clear that the U.S. has yet to achieve the democratic ideals that it promises.

DISCUSSION QUESTIONS ABOUT CITIZENSHIP

Introduce and explain the Luce–Celler Act (the 1946 law that ended Filipinx and Indian exclusion from the U.S., see Chapter 3) and the McCarran–Walter Act. Then lead a class discussion around the following questions:

- Why did the U.S. government pass the Luce–Celler and McCarran–Walter Acts?
- Who was affected by these changes in immigration policy?
- What do these reasons suggest about what elected U.S. government officials believed to be important?
- Do you agree with their reasoning? If not, which reasons, in your opinion, should govern U.S. immigration policy?
- What do you think is a good reason to change laws that discriminate against people?

Inquiry Lesson: Who Can Be A Citizen?

In Chapter 1, we described inquiry as a way for young learners to wrestle with authentic questions about problems in our world. Using an excerpt from the Naturalization Act of 1790 and primary sources related to the *Ozawa* and *Thind* Supreme Court Cases, guide students through the inquiry question "Who can be a citizen?" This lesson has two parts: first, understanding available pathways to citizenship and second, introducing the history of obstacles present in these pathways.

Pathways to Citizenship. Begin with a twist on the traditional KWL chart ("What I know," "What I want to know," and "What I learned"). Lead a whole-class discussion using the headings of the chart below, and list students' answers in each column.

TABLE 4.2 Citizenship Chart

CITIZENSHIP		
What we *think* it takes to become a citizen	What it *actually* takes to become a citizen	What we think it *should* take to become a citizen

After students have the opportunity to speculate about pathways to citizenship, read *I Am an American: The Wong Kim Ark Story* (see the description earlier in this chapter). Then ask students what they have learned about who can be a U.S. citizen from Wong's story. The class should be able to define and add the term "birthright" to the second column.

Support students as they define "naturalization" (a process where someone can become a citizen). Using the United States Citizenship and Immigration Services website (https://www.uscis.gov), add information about naturalization to the second column. Students may have questions about what each qualification may mean (e.g., what does it mean to "demonstrate a good moral character?"). Draw attention to the fact that *anyone* who wants to naturalize has to pass a test showing they know facts about U.S. history and government. Upper elementary students can take a shortened version of the citizenship test available on the Citizenship and Immigration Services website and assess their performance. For an at-home extension, students can have family members take the quiz and compare results. We've found that most of the birthright citizens we know often struggle with the questions, whereas folks who are pursuing naturalization or have recently gained it usually get every question right!

To wrap up this part of the lesson, review the second column about available pathways to citizenship and ask students what they think about the qualifications. In the third column, add any ideas they have about what they think should be qualifications for citizenship for *everyone*. If they had the chance to revise citizenship laws, what requirements would they add or eliminate? Give students a chance to weigh the pros and cons of any suggestions.

A History of Obstacles. The second part of the inquiry lesson focuses on the history of obstacles faced by those who attempted to gain citizenship. With your students, analyze an army photograph of Bhagat Singh Thind from World War I (Figure 4.1). Review the qualifications for naturalization on the chart. Remind students that naturalization is also offered to people who have served in the U.S. military and ask why the government would create this specific benefit. Then, have students apply the naturalization qualifications to Thind to determine if he was eligible for citizenship based on his story.

Thind was clearly eligible for naturalization based on his qualifications, but the Naturalization Act of 1790 presented an obstacle. Share this excerpt from the Act with students: "any alien being a free white person . . . may be admitted to become a citizen." Follow up with questions such as: Who wrote and approved this law? What did this mean for Thind and other people like him from Asia?

In primary grades, students can illustrate what this law means to them and depict who is included and excluded because of it. They can also describe or illustrate how Thind might have felt after he was denied citizenship. For upper grades, create a class timeline that begins with this Act. This will show students how long U.S. society and Asian American experiences have been shaped by this particular law. As you move through the lesson and throughout the school year, continue to add events relevant or similar to *Thind v. U.S.* in 1923.

The Immigration and Nationality Act of 1952 was passed during the Cold War, in large part to convince the world that the U.S. was not racist. On the timeline, mark 1952 as the year when the U.S. government got rid of all racial restrictions on naturalization. Remind students that these restrictions were removed *162 years* after passing the Naturalization Act of 1790. This meant that in 1952, Asians could naturalize as U.S. citizens for the first time in U.S. history. However, they were still restricted from immigrating to the U.S. Returning to the chart, ask students if there are any other qualifications they want to add to the third column and explain why they think these additions would be important.

Proving Citizenship Through Documentation

Just as the 14th Amendment did not guarantee equal treatment of and protection to Black Americans, Wong Kim Ark's citizenship did not guarantee that he, as a Chinese American, would be treated like a citizen. For Black Americans, the Supreme Court ruling of "separate but equal" in *Plessy v. Ferguson* (1896) essentially negated the 14th Amendment. Transportation, schools, water fountains, swimming pools, and many other public facilities were legally separated between Black and white people but were far from equal in quality. For example, schools for Black children had far less funding than schools for white children, an inequity that continues today (Givens, 2021; Love, 2019).

Chinese Americans were required to register with local authorities in order to receive a Certificate of Residence. If they were ever caught without this document, they could be detained and deported (Lee, 2016). In 1901, after he was declared a U.S. citizen by the Supreme Court, Wong Kim Ark was arrested in El Paso, Texas. Until

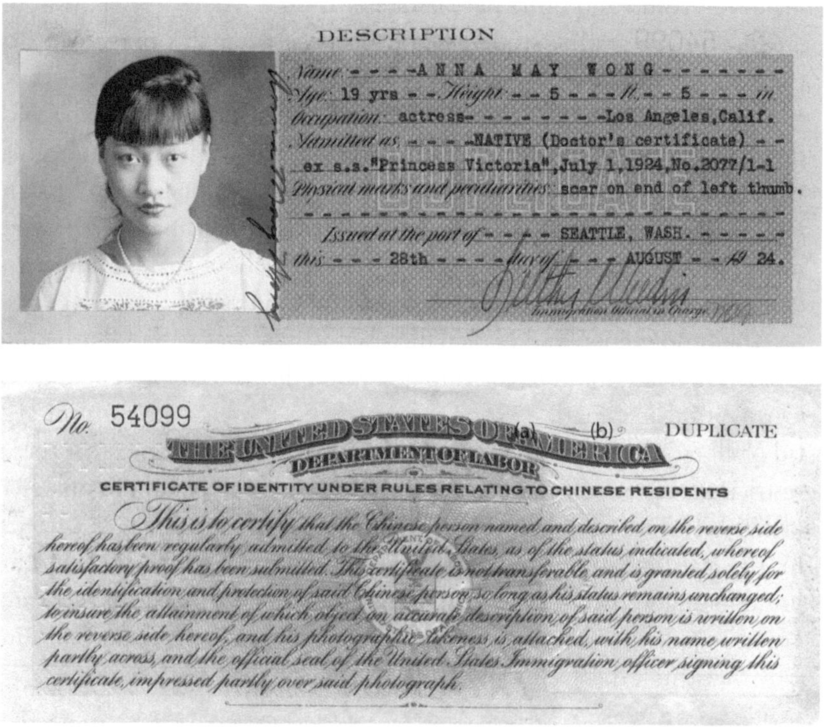

DESCRIPTION

Name - - - -ANNA MAY WONG - - - - - - -
Age 19 yrs - - Height - - 5 - - - ft. - - 5 - - - in.
Occupation actress- - - - - - - - -Los Angeles,Calif.
Admitted as - - - -NATIVE (Doctor's certificate) - -
ex s.s."Princess Victoria",July 1,1924,No.2077/1-1
Physical marks and peculiarities scar on end of left thumb.
Issued at the port of - - - - SEATTLE, WASH. - - - - -
this - - - 28th - - - - day of - - - AUGUST - - 19 24.
Immigration Official in Charge.

No. 54099 (a) (b) DUPLICATE
THE UNITED STATES OF AMERICA
DEPARTMENT OF LABOR
CERTIFICATE OF IDENTITY UNDER RULES RELATING TO CHINESE RESIDENTS

This is to certify that the Chinese person named and described on the reverse side hereof has been regularly admitted to the United States, as of the status indicated, whereof satisfactory proof has been submitted. This certificate is not transferable and is granted solely for the identification and protection of said Chinese person so long as his status remains unchanged; to insure the attainment of which object an accurate description of said person is written on the reverse side hereof, and his photographic likeness is attached, with his name written partly across, and the official seal of the United States Immigration officer signing this certificate, impressed partly over said photograph.

FIGURE 4.2 Duplicate certificate of identity of Anna May Wong, 1924.
NATIONAL ARCHIVES CATALOG (HTTPS://CATALOG.ARCHIVES.GOV/ID/5720287).

a U.S. Commissioner declared him a U.S. citizen *again* several months later, Wong was under suspicion of violating Chinese Exclusion and illegally residing in the U.S. (Frost, 2021). Even a Hollywood star like Anna May Wong, whose family had been in the United States since the 1850s, was viewed as a foreigner and had to prove her right to be in the U.S. (see Figure 4.2). White and Black Americans did not have to carry any such certificates or other documentation proving their citizenship.

Documentation and Citizenship Today. The selective requirement of carrying documentation of legal status is still used today and to the same effect. Members of Latine communities, especially in areas of the Southwest, have experienced racial profiling by law enforcement who require them to prove legal citizenship. Although politicians and the media often associate undocumented immigrants with the Latine community, Asian Americans are estimated to be approximately 13% of all undocumented immigrants in the United States (Wong, 2015).

Jose Antonio Vargas, a human rights activist, was born in the Philippines and immigrated to the U.S. as a child. When he was in high school, Vargas discovered that his immigration papers were forgeries and that he was undocumented. Since then, he has dedicated his award-winning career as a journalist, filmmaker, and producer to uplifting marginalized voices. Vargas founded the organization Define America, which seeks to humanize immigrant narratives so that *all* people in the United States are considered American, regardless of their immigration status. Part of his work includes raising awareness about how dehumanizing it is to call undocumented people "illegal" and how who and what is considered legal is a result of who holds legislative power (Vargas, 2018). He is considered one of the most famous undocumented Americans in the country, and an elementary school in Mountain View, California was named after him in 2019.

RACE IN U.S. CITIZENSHIP

By barring Asians from U.S. citizenship, discrimination was built into laws. Both the laws and discrimination were reinforced by ordinary folks doing their everyday jobs, such as the customs officials who detained Wong Kim Ark in San Francisco and later in El Paso. In both places, a U.S. government official with greater power intervened to ensure Wong's rights as a U.S. citizen. But sometimes discrimination comes from the highest powers and, unfortunately, even the courts can fail to protect civil rights.

Japanese American Incarceration

Japanese American incarceration during World War II is known more commonly in schools and standards as "internment." When teaching this history, one of the first issues educators must address is terminology. As historian Roger Daniels (2005) explains, the intentional and continued use of the term "internment" conceals the great harm done to Japanese Americans by the U.S. government. Internment is a legal process where U.S. residents who are citizens of another country at war with the U.S. can be legally removed from their homes, and their movement can be confined to wherever the government decides. For example, during World War II, some German and Italian citizens living in the U.S. were *interned*. In contrast, two-thirds of the 120,000 people of Japanese ancestry forcibly removed and relocated during World War II by the U.S. government were U.S. citizens. The rest were legally barred from naturalizing as citizens. Because most of the Japanese Americans who were imprisoned were U.S. citizens, the term "internment" by definition *cannot* apply to them. Therefore, a more accurate term is Japanese American *incarceration*. Densho (densho.org) offers more information and a sample activity on euphemistic terms like "evacuation" (instead of "forced removal") and "relocation centers" (instead of "concentration or prison camps").

We begin with this clarification because too many teacher resources and state standards continue to use the euphemistic term "internment," despite the fact that historians and scholars of Asian American studies have long argued for more historically and legally accurate language (An, 2022a). When educators refuse to change euphemistic language like this, they continue to perpetuate the image of Asian Americans as forever foreigners (see Chapter 2) whose experiences and histories are less valued in curriculum.

So what might you do when you and your students encounter internment in a book or film? Remind students of commonly used euphemisms in everyday life. For example, what are some "nice" ways to say that you're going to the bathroom? Why would people choose to use euphemisms rather than blunter language? Then discuss what it means when euphemisms are used in historical narratives. Why might a particular group choose to use a euphemism rather than a more honest description of what happened? How might they benefit from a "nicer" narrative? And how might these "nicer" narratives disguise the harms inflicted by those in power? Students could create a T-chart listing euphemisms that are not harmful and euphemisms that can mislead in harmful ways to consider the power of language.

When teaching Japanese American incarceration to young learners, emphasize that the majority of those incarcerated were U.S. citizens, and that the rest were *not allowed* to become citizens because of their race. Remember, no Asian immigrants were allowed to become naturalized citizens until 1952. Clearly, incarceration during World War II was about race. Even the U.S. government acknowledges this! The U.S. was at war with many countries, including Japan, Germany, and Italy. But, unlike Japanese Americans, U.S. citizens of German and Italian ancestry were not incarcerated. Newspapers as well as government and military officials made it clear that people of German and Italian descent were no longer German or Italian, but *American*. But in U.S. society in the 1940s, people of Japanese descent were only viewed as Japanese, never as Americans. For instance, the *Los Angeles Times* published an editorial in February of 1942 that claimed: "A viper is nonetheless a viper wherever the egg is hatched—so a Japanese-American, born of Japanese parents—grows up to be Japanese, not an American" (Anderson, 1942, para. 2-3). The perception of Japanese Americans as forever foreigners, regardless of their place of birth or loyalties, was widespread.

On the rare occasions when Japanese American incarceration is taught in elementary classrooms, it is often presented as a necessary act of national security. Japan's attack on Pearl Harbor is presented as the reason for President Franklin Roosevelt's Executive Order 9066. This Order gave power to the military to forcibly remove Japanese and Japanese Americans on the West Coast to incarceration camps.

FIGURE 4.3 Children Wearing "Evacuation Tags": Two children from the Mochida family wait for a bus that will forcibly remove their family from their home. One of the children is already tagged with her family number and eating a sandwich given to her by a local church group. Hayward, California on May 8, 1942.
PHOTOGRAPH BY DOROTHEA LANGE. DENSHO DIGITAL REPOSITORY (HTTPS://DDR.DENSHO.ORG/DDR-DENSHO-151-54).

However, the U.S. government found no evidence of espionage by Japanese Americans before *or* after Pearl Harbor, and actively hid or destroyed these findings. Moreover, high ranking U.S. military officials and media reported that, no matter how many generations a Japanese American family had lived in the United States—even if they were U.S. citizens—they would still be Japanese, and therefore, the enemy. These linked forms of racism and patriotism/nationalism are partly why teaching about the bombing of Pearl Harbor is so closely tied to the teaching of Japanese American incarceration. Focusing on Pearl Harbor offers a rationale to educators who seek to minimize U.S. wrongdoing and racism.

PHOTOGRAPHS BY TOYO MIYATAKE AND DOROTHEA LANGE

Toyo Miyatake was a photographer who opened his own studio in Los Angeles in 1923. When Japanese American families were forcibly removed from their homes in 1942, they were not allowed to take cameras with them. Miyatake managed to smuggle camera equipment into the camp at Manzanar, California and secretly documented life in the prison camp. His son recalled Miyatake explaining, "This kind of thing should never happen again. I have to record everything" (Nakamura, 2002). Miyatake's photos depicting life in Manzanar can be found at Toyo Miyatake Studio (toyomiyatake.com), which is still run by his family today.

Famous photographer Dorothea Lange took pictures of Japanese Americans as they first reported to War Relocation Authorty (WRA) assembly centers and later when they lived in isolated prison camps. Her photographs show families with babies and young children crowded into lines, each person tagged with their family's number (Figure 4.3). She documented the harsh living conditions of the horse stables converted into temporary family residences, the barbed wire, and the soldiers with guns who ensured that no one left the prison camps.

Like Miyatake, Lange's work shows how incarcerated Japanese and Japanese Americans found joy and purpose in the camps through the gardens they created and the everyday life of children playing and learning. Lange's photographs of incarceration were originally censored by the U.S. Army for revealing the harsh conditions of camps, particularly in contrast to the more sanitized photos by her contemporary Ansel Adams. Many of Lange's images are available on Densho.org and through the Library of Congress (www.loc.gov). Miyatake's and Lange's photographs are primary sources that can be paired with children's literature to show the reality of Japanese American incarceration while centering the humanity of those who were imprisoned.

FIGURE 4.4 Concentration Camp Scene: Children walking back to their family's barracks after school in Manzanar, California, on June 29, 1942.
PHOTOGRAPH BY DOROTHEA LANGE. DENSHO DIGITAL REPOSITORY (HTTPS://DDR.DENSHO.ORG/DDR-DENSHO-151-69).

Surviving and Seeking Justice. Executive Order 9066 led to the creation of the WRA, which was the organization responsible for relocating Japanese Americans living on the West Coast. Ten long-term sites were identified, and camps were hastily constructed. They were intentionally located in desolate and remote areas surrounded by barbed wire and guard towers. First, Japanese Americans reported to assembly centers, which were quickly set up at racetracks and fairgrounds. Then they were assigned and transported to prison camps. The 10 WRA camps were: Amache, Colorado; Gila River, Arizona; Heart Mountain, Wyoming; Jerome, Arkansas; Manzanar, California; Minidoka, Idaho; Poston, Arizona; Rohwer, Arkansas; Topaz, Utah; and Tule Lake, California. Each camp provided inmates with basic food, housing, medical care, and some clothing. Eventually, school buildings, libraries, and other facilities like barbershops and newspapers were established at the camps.

BASEBALL IN PRISON CAMPS

Baseball has been a popular sport in Japan since the late 1800s. When Japanese people began to immigrate to the U.S., they created Japanese American baseball leagues. Kenichi Zenimura built several all-star teams that toured nationally and internationally. He even played an exhibition game with baseball Hall of Famers Lou Gehrig and Babe Ruth! When the U.S. government incarcerated him and his family, Zenimura organized a baseball league at the Gila River prison camp. Baseball in the prison camps is an example of the joy and agency of Japanese and Japanese Americans while incarcerated.

There are several children's books about prison camp baseball, including *Barbed Wire Baseball* (Moss, 2013) which tells the story of Zenimura. While books like *Baseball Saved Us* (Mochizuki, 1993) are quite popular with educators, we caution you from using them in ways that highlight resilience without complicating the stories' focus on happy endings. Please ensure that the joy of baseball does not erase the unjust and dehumanizing reality of incarceration.

Prison camp conditions were challenging. Families had little or no privacy as they were forced to share small wooden barracks with tar-paper walls that were poorly constructed and let in cold air and dust. Many restroom facilities were communal and lacked individual stalls. In the Manzanar camp, the city of Los Angeles drained land that once belonged to the Paiute people, leaving a dry and dusty landscape. Those who were incarcerated had to find creative ways to make these camps habitable. And through community support they did, but without any help from the government. For example, college students became teachers for young children, while people like Kenichi Zenimura built baseball diamonds and set up teams and leagues.

On January 2, 1945, the U.S. Army lifted West Coast exclusion and Japanese Americans began to be released from the camps. The WRA closed all camps in 1945 with the exception of Tule Lake, which was the last camp to close in March 1946. On June 26, 1946, President Harry Truman signed Executive Order 9742 that officially terminated

FIGURE 4.5 Japanese American Working in Garden: William Katsuki working in a desert garden he created next to his barrack in Manzanar, California on June 30, 1942. PHOTOGRAPH BY DOROTHEA LANGE. DENSHO DIGITAL REPOSITORY (HTTPS://DDR.DENSHO.ORG/DDR-DENSHO-151-425).

the WRA. However, despite regaining their freedom, most West Coast Japanese Americans had little to return to. Many of their homes and businesses had been sold or taken over by others, and their ethnic communities were destroyed. Some went back to the places they called home before their imprisonment while others relocated or stayed in the states where the WRA camps had been previously located.

JAPANESE AMERICANS AND INDIGENOUS SOLIDARITY

Each year, Japanese American camp survivors, their families, and other community members (including elders from local Indigenous tribes) make a pilgrimage to Manzanar. When the Los Angeles Department of Water planned to use the land for solar panels, the two groups came together to preserve the landscape of Manzanar as a monument to the injustices that occurred against both groups. Examples of similar solidarity between different communities is rarely found in curriculum and should be highlighted whenever possible.

In the decades that followed, Japanese American activists sought compensation for the extraordinary financial losses they experienced during World War II. As illustrated in Uchida's *The Bracelet* (1996), families sold their belongings far below market rate as they often only had a number of days to figure out what to do with their property and possessions before leaving for the assembly centers. The Japanese Americans Citizens League lobbied heavily for the McCarran–Walter Act so that first-generation Japanese Americans could become naturalized and own land (alien land laws from earlier generations had prevented them from doing so). The League also worked with Japanese American activists (see Yuri Kochiyama in Chapter 6) and politicians to demand redress, or financial reparations, from the U.S. government.

In 1980, President Jimmy Carter and Congress approved the creation of the Commission on Wartime Relocation and Internment of Civilians. The Commission gathered information from government documents, academic research, and the personal papers of officials who shaped the decision to incarcerate and conducted interviews with 750 witnesses, including more than 500 former detainees. In 1983, the Commission published their findings in a report entitled *Personal Justice Denied*. The report clearly stated that there was *no* justification for the detention of Japanese Americans and blamed their incarceration on "race prejudice, war hysteria, and a failure of political leadership" (p. 459). The condemnation of the U.S. government's actions was unpopular among many groups and individuals, including then-President Reagan.

In 1988, over 40 years after Japanese Americans were released from WRA prison camps, the U.S. government passed the Civil Liberties Act. This act issued a formal presidential apology and paid reparations in the amount of $20,000 to each formerly incarcerated survivor. When teaching about Japanese American incarceration, make sure to include excerpts from the Civil Liberties Act of 1988, such as the following:

> Congress recognizes that . . . a grave injustice was done to both citizens and permanent resident aliens of Japanese ancestry by the evacuation, relocation and internment of civilians during World War II . . . These actions were carried out without adequate security reasons and without any acts of espionage or sabotage, and were motivated largely by racial prejudice, wartime hysteria, and a failure of political leadership . . . For these fundamental violations of the basic civil liberties and constitutional rights of these individuals of Japanese ancestry, the Congress apologizes on behalf of the Nation . . . (Pub. L. 100–383, title I, August 10, 1988, 102 Stat. 903-904, 50a U.S.C. § 1989b et seq.)

The Civil Liberties Act is one of the few instances where the U.S. government admitted to doing something wrong (even if begrudgingly). This is an opportunity to show students how the efforts of a community led to change and a measure of justice!

RECOMMENDED CHILDREN'S LITERATURE ABOUT JAPANESE AMERICAN INCARCERATION

- *The Bracelet* by Yoshiko Uchida, illustrated by Joanna Yardley
- *Desert Diary: Japanese American Kids Behind Barbed Wire* by Michael O. Tunnell
- *Enemy Child: The Story of Norman Mineta, a Boy Imprisoned in a Japanese American Internment Camp During World War II* by Andrea Warren
- *It Began with a Page: How Gyo Fujikawa Drew the Way* by Kyo Maclear, illustrated by Julie Morstad
- *Journey to Topaz* by Yoshiko Uchida
- *Love in the Library* by Maggie Tokuda-Hall, illustrated by Yas Imamura
- *Fred Korematsu Speaks Up* by Laura Atkins and Stan Yogi, illustrated by Yutaka Houlette
- *Paper Wishes* by Lois Sepahban
- *Stealing Home* by J. Torres, illustrated by David Namisato

- *Sylvia and Aki* by Winifred Conkling
- *They Called Us Enemy* by George Takei, Justin Eisinger, and Steven Scott, illustrated by Harmony Becker
- *We Hereby Refuse* by Frank Abe and Tamiko Nimura, illustrated by Ross Ishikawa and Matt Sasaki
- *Write to Me: Letters from Japanese American Children to the Librarian They Left Behind* by Cynthia Grady, illustrated by Amiko Hirao

DISCUSSION QUESTIONS ABOUT JAPANESE AMERICAN INCARCERATION

- Why do you think the U.S. government incarcerated Japanese American children?
- How do you think Japanese American children felt while they were waiting to be taken away from their homes?
- Using primary sources included in this chapter, describe the locations of the WRA camps. What do you notice about the geographical features in these locations? Why do you think the U.S. government built them in those locations?
- Explore a map of WRA Camps. Who do you think lived in those locations before the camps were built?
- What are some ways that Japanese Americans made living in the prison camps more bearable?

RELIGION IN U.S. CITIZENSHIP

To be seen as a citizen, as someone who belongs in the United States, your religion matters. Throughout most of U.S. history, Protestant Christianity was the only "acceptable" religion one could follow in order to be viewed as fully American. Even some variations of Protestantism, like the Society of Friends (whose followers are known as Quakers), faced persecution. Although religious freedom in the U.S. is guaranteed by the First Amendment, there are many ways that Protestant Christianity determines what is normal and acceptable. The national calendar revolves around Christian holidays. Most office and professional jobs do not involve work on weekends, which are so designated to honor the sabbath, and school vacation days are planned around Christmas. Hallmark's beloved holiday movies didn't even feature a Hanukkah-focused film until 2021! We can't only recognize the First Amendment in theory; we need to uplift it in practice, with and for all of our students.

When we discussed Asian American identity in Chapter 2, diversity was a key characteristic. In this section, we highlight the religious diversity of Asian America. Keep in mind that by religious diversity, we also mean diversity *within* religions (all faiths are interpreted and practiced in innumerable ways) as well as atheism and agnosticism. A recent survey found that 34% of Asian American and Pacific Islander Americans are unaffiliated with any religion (Public Religion Research Institute, 2021). Christianity, with its many sects and denominations, is practiced by many Asians and Asian Americans. However, because Christianity is dominant in U.S. culture, we provide a general overview of Islamophobia and major religions followed by Asian Americans aside from Christianity. We urge teachers to explore these religions further on their own and with their students.

Islamophobia In and Out of the Classroom

Throughout his presidential campaign and presidency, Donald Trump attacked many marginalized communities. From labeling Latin American immigrants as criminals to his thoughts on the "Muslim problem" and his claim that "Islam is at war with us" (Trump, 2016), the former president drew from a long history of xenophobia in the United States. In 2017, President Trump channeled these prejudices into immigration policies. He issued an executive order that barred travel and immigration from several countries, most of which were predominantly Muslim, and referred to this order as a "Muslim ban." The Supreme Court decided that a variation of this ban was legal because, even though it was discriminatory, it upheld national security. Four of the Supreme Court justices strongly dissented, describing the policy and claims of supposed national security as a way to disguise a ban based on religion. Remember when we talked about Dusky Peril, Orientalism, and Islamophobia in Chapter 2? They're still around, and were fiercely reignited during the Trump administration.

MOHAMMAD SALMAN HAMDANI

Prejudice in the U.S. against Muslims and Arabs existed long before 9/11 and shaped how 9/11 was investigated. Mohammad Salman Hamdani, a Pakistani American police cadet, lived in New York City and went to the Twin Towers on 9/11 to provide rescue aid, ultimately sacrificing his life. Initially, law enforcement suspected Hamdani of helping the terrorists due to his name, Muslim faith, and birthplace of Pakistan. Even after his sacrifice came to light, his Muslim name was not listed with other first responders on the 9/11 memorial. In 2014, Hamdani was finally honored by his community in Queens when they renamed the corner of 204th Street at 35th Avenue "Salman Hamdani Way."

Muslims and those perceived as Muslim continue to face various forms of discrimination and violence. This includes governmental bans on entering the country as well as surveillance in their homes, places of work, and religious spaces. They are profiled at airports and by fellow U.S. citizens who consider them a threat to national security and culture. In classrooms, this violence continues through the lack of curricular representation and the ways that schools prioritize Christian holidays and culture.

Many educators unknowingly reinforce this violence. Esther will never forget (and shouldn't!) when one of her students had to remind her that Ramadan had started. The student had to explain why she was so tired during the day and why she would not partake in the provided snacks. This may seem trivial, but this lack of awareness on Esther's part meant that the student could not participate the same way as her classmates and therefore felt isolated. Noreen met a Pakistani American teacher who, as a child, was suspended from school because she had mehndhi (traditional henna patterns drawn on the skin for Muslim holidays like Eid) on her hands. Simply including non-Christian religious holidays in our teaching calendars and recognizing how students may be celebrating them can make a big difference for students whose faiths are currently ignored at school.

But there is so much more we need to do. Politicians and media pundits continue to portray Islam as a foreign religion steeped in violence. You can disrupt these narratives by teaching about Islam and Muslims in the United States. Islam is not any more foreign to the U.S. than Christianity. Indeed, both religions originated in the same part of the world! Muslims are not foreigners. In fact, the first Muslims in the U.S. were enslaved Africans who arrived in the earliest years of the nation.

Visit local mosques with your students. Invite imams (the leaders of mosques, similar to a minister, priest, or rabbi) and other Muslim community leaders into your classroom. Teach histories and stories that center Muslim American voices, like the incredible career of U.S. Olympic fencer Ibithaj Muhammad. Bring in Asian American Muslim characters like *Ms. Marvel*, a Pakistani American superhero, and share Saadia Faruqi's *Yasmin* and *Marya Khan* series with students in early grades. Incorporate picturebooks such as *Muslim Girls Rise* by Saira Mir (2019), which features short biographies of Muslim American women activists including Amani Al-Khatahtbeh, founder of MuslimGirl.com, and Dalia Mogahed, the first hijabi to advise a U.S. president.

Hinduism as a Lived Faith

Hinduism began in South Asia. It was inspired by oral traditions from approximately the 1500s Before the Common Era (BCE) and written down in the early centuries of the Common Era (CE). These texts, the Vedas and the Upanishads, were held as sacred, especially by the Brahmin or priestly class of South Asia. In the caste system that developed out of this early Vedic society, in which people were born into a specific position in the social hierarchy, higher-status castes like the priestly class typically had fewer members than lower-status castes. As a result, a popular form of Hinduism emerged to address the needs of the masses, focused on how anyone, not just priests, could faithfully follow the religion.

Within the great Indian epic poem the Mahabharata, the Bhagavad Gita is a foundational text that describes faithful adherence to Hinduism. In the Bhagavad Gita, the princely warrior Arjuna confides in his charioteer Krishna—the earthly avatar of the God Vishnu—his doubts about the morality of going to war against friends and family. Through their dialog, the Bhagavad Gita conveys the idea of reincarnation: the death of the body does not mean the death of the soul. The soul continues in a cycle of perpetual rebirth. An individual obtains release from this cycle and attains true liberation with devotion to the deity and upholding their caste duties.

There are many ways that Hinduism is practiced around the world. Diverse traditions exist even within the United States. Diwali, also known as the Festival of Lights, is a common holiday celebrated not only by Hindus, but also by Sikhs and some Buddhists. For this holiday, clay lamps decorate homes as a symbol of protection against evil. People celebrate Diwali for different reasons, including commemoration of the significant historical event in Hinduism where a good god or king triumphed over evil. Family and friends gather at different times over five days, including a time for puja (prayer) to the Goddess Lakshmi who will bring prosperity.

On a cautionary note, polytheistic religions are often taught only as bygone myths, like those of the Greeks and the Romans, rather than as beliefs that people have today. The stories and images of Hindu deities, who have different skin colors or animal heads, are often presented as exotic mythology. Avoid doing this in your classrooms! When teaching about Hinduism, center the stories and voices of currently practicing Hindus.

Buddhism in Asia and the United States

Buddhism began in the 500s BCE in South Asia with Siddhartha Gautama, a sheltered regional prince distressed by the suffering he encountered when he first ventured beyond the palace walls. In his determination to overcome his personal suffering, he followed the practices of holy ascetics of the time. Ultimately disenchanted with the result, after 40 days of continuous meditation he finally attained enlightenment: overcoming suffering and gaining release from the cycle of reincarnation. Thereafter known as the Buddha, or "the awakened one", he described the path by which anyone can attain enlightenment. These early Buddhist teachings center on the Four Noble Truths: all life is suffering; desire causes suffering; suffering can be overcome;

and the path to overcoming suffering lies in the Noble Eightfold Path (encapsulated in the tenets of right-view, right-intention, right-speech, right-action, right-livelihood, right-effort, right-mindfulness, and right-concentration).

The Buddha's teachings spread along the Silk Road throughout Asia and branched into different traditions, many still followed today. In some traditions, the Buddha maintains a unique role; others focus on the role of Bodhisattvas, individuals who have attained enlightenment, but forgo a release from reincarnation out of a wish to help others who are still suffering. In the Tibetan tradition, the Dalai Lama is considered the reincarnation of a past Bodhisattva whose work continues in this world.

As with Hinduism, some Buddhist traditions include beliefs in beings who may be regarded as mystical and exotic. Ensure that your lessons on Buddhism build respect for the traditions, no matter how unfamiliar they may seem. Many Buddhist traditions also celebrate the Buddha's birth. Though the historical date is unknown, different traditions choose a conventional date that is set using the lunar calendar and subsequently changes each year in the Western calendar. In many Asian countries, the Buddha's birthday is a holiday and is celebrated with lantern festivals to symbolize the Buddha's gift of wisdom to the world.

As Asians migrated to the United States, they brought many Buddhist traditions (including the well-known Mahayana and Theravada branches) that they and their descendants continue to practice in local temples. Buddhist beliefs have been taken up by many white Americans that dominate depictions of Buddhism in the U.S. It is, therefore, important to keep in mind that Buddhism originated in Asia, continues to be practiced there, and that most Buddhists in the U.S. are Asian and Asian American. Consider learning from local Buddhist temples and monasteries with an understanding and respect for the history and experiences of Asian and Asian American Buddhists.

Sikhism, a Commitment to Equality and Service

Guru Nanak ("Guru" means "religious leader"), born in 1469 CE, founded Sikhism when he began to teach in the northern region of South Asia and gathered followers. After Guru Nanak died, 10 more

Gurus led the Sikh community. Sikhs follow a sacred text known as the Guru Granth Sahib, which was put together by the Gurus as messages revealed by God. They also have five articles of faith: kesh (unshorn hair), kanga (a comb), kara (a steel bracelet), kirpan (a sword), and kachera (knee-length shorts). The articles of faith have deep symbolic meaning that reminds them of Sikh teachings and are viewed as gifts from one of the Gurus. Sikhs believe in one God who created all people to be equal. One way that Sikhs express this belief is through their names. Sikh men often take the surname Singh and women take the surname Kaur, as one way to show that all are equal no matter their social or economic levels.

Sikhism is the fifth-largest religion in the world. A dedication to justice and service for humanity is a central part of Sikhism. Turbans, mostly worn by Sikh men and some women, are a way that Sikhs show their commitment to living their faith. Faith is also demonstrated through Sikh houses of worship, called gurdwaras, where they serve the community through gatherings and communal meals. As human rights are a central concern in Sikhism, learning and teaching about the religion as people practice it now is one way to show the agency and activism of Sikhs. Chapter 2 detailed the importance of teaching about this faith as a step in disrupting the misconceptions about Sikhism.

Teaching for Religious Diversity

Here are some ways to teach about religious diversity in your own classroom as a part of antiracist and antioppressive education:

- Share a survey with your students and their families to see which religions they follow and which holidays they celebrate. In your survey, allow family members to note if they would be willing to teach your students about any of the holidays they celebrate. Emphasize that this information will be used to better support *all* students in the classroom.
- Once you're aware of the holidays celebrated by your students, note when they occur and integrate them into your classroom calendar. Do some research as to how these holiday celebrations might impact students in terms of eating, prayer practices, etc.

(e.g., fasting during school hours, missing class to attend prayers) so you can plan accordingly.

- Seek out nonfiction and realistic fiction books that are written by members of the faiths that are depicted in the texts. Not sure about the author's identity? Use search engines to learn about them and check out book reviews that might reveal what members of that religion think about the book's accuracy. And while you are looking up information, search for audio pronunciations of names and other important words!
- Emphasize common symbols and celebrations across religions, like the significance of light and acts of service. Avoid focusing solely on religious differences, which can alienate students who are not in the religious majority.
- Don't ask students to teach *for* you—while you can certainly invite them to share what they know, don't tokenize them by having them serve as a cultural expert. Moreover, the way they as an individual celebrate something is just *one* story out of many. Remind students that people celebrate in many different ways all around the nation and world!
- When reading books or discussing current events, guide students to identify and then challenge how one's religion affects whether the person is regarded and treated as "American."

RECOMMENDED RESOURCES FOR TEACHING ABOUT RELIGIOUS DIVERSITY

- Harvard University's The Pluralism Project (https://pluralism.org/home)
- The Council on American–Islamic Relations (https://www.cair.com)
- The Sikh Coalition (https://www.sikhcoalition.org)
- Tanenbaum Center for Interreligious Understanding (https://tanenbaum.org)

CITIZENSHIP MATTERS

Citizenship as patriotism is woven throughout standards and curriculum in elementary classrooms, promoting unquestioned obedience to laws and the status quo. As we have described in this chapter, many laws and the status quo have been and continue to be harmful to many communities on the basis of race, religion, and other aspects of one's identity. By teaching about the histories and identities of these communities, alongside what is already set in curriculum, you can guide students towards James Baldwin's definition of patriotism: knowledge of both U.S. civic ideals and of the ways the country falls short, alongside a commitment to the work that must be done to achieve those ideals for *everyone.*

5

War and Displacement

Asian Americans have entered America as refugees, adoptees, brides, laborers, students, and immigrants largely because of U.S. wars and military involvement in Asia. In this chapter, we describe why and how to make clear the connections between U.S. wars in Asia and Asian migration to the United States. We also include two lessons that use children's literature and primary sources to engage upper elementary students in inquiries about these connections.

WHY TEACH WAR CRITICALLY?

War has been ever-present in American lives throughout the nation's history. Born out of war against the British empire, the United States has been at war in all but 11 years of its existence (Vine, 2020). The United States launched numerous wars against Indigenous nations in the conquest of their lands, then invaded and conquered islands in the Pacific and Caribbean, and later used its military power to back pro-U.S. dictators and regimes in Asia, Africa, and Latin America, inciting coups and waging wars abroad (Vine, 2020). The many wars and military actions conducted by the U.S. have generated more violence than peace. Moreover, they have served the economic and political interests of elites, while leaving tens of millions—including children—dead or displaced, with trauma and pain (Vine, 2020).

DOI: 10.4324/9781032662695-5

These not-so-glorious facts about U.S. wars are generally avoided in elementary classrooms. When lessons on U.S. wars or related historical figures are taught—the American Revolution, the Civil War, "Westward Expansion," World Wars, George Washington, Abraham Lincoln, Theodore Roosevelt, Franklin D. Roosevelt, etc.—educators tend to avoid violent realities and focus instead on patriotism and national pride. Elementary students are rarely asked to consider human suffering and the other costs of U.S. wars. On even rarer occasions are they encouraged to evaluate whether or not those costs are justified or to consider the perspectives of invaded nations and their peoples. Such lessons communicate a clear message: U.S. wars are *always* noble, necessary, and inevitable. They are fought in the best interests of our nation *and* the world.

We believe that it is irresponsible to teach about war and conflict without attention to those who are harmed in myriad ways. We know that children often reenact violence in their play, shooting pretend or toy guns and playing with soldier figurines. So, while some educators may wish to avoid negative and potentially scary realities, they often allow such reenactment in play to occur with little intervention. Social justice teaching demands harm reduction *and* discussion of injustice. We do not suggest that you share gory images and detail the brutal effects of napalm with young learners, but you can certainly engage children in trauma-informed conversations around displacement and related emotions (Venet, 2021). To only focus on the U.S. perspective of war is inaccurate and harmful, as it promotes and justifies endless U.S. military interventions around the world (Zinn, 2010). Instead, we need to teach American wars honestly and critically, so that children can develop a more accurate understanding of how the U.S. military has influenced global society. With this knowledge, they can take informed action to create a less violent, more peaceful world.

The United States waged several wars in Asia, including the Philippine-American War, the Korean War, and the Vietnam War. These wars caused countless deaths, destruction, and displacements, generating conditions for many Asians to enter the United States as refugees, asylum seekers, adoptees, spouses, laborers, students, and other types of migrants (Lee, 2015). Indeed, Asians are in the United States because the U.S. went to Asia.

However, lessons on U.S. wars in Asia, if they are ever taught substantively in elementary classrooms, typically present the wars as rescue-and-liberation missions. They neglect the complex causes of war and the United States' role as a violent aggressor. Instead, the United States is positioned as a savior: a caring big brother simply trying to spread the gospel of democracy. Relatedly, lessons on Asian migration (which also rarely occur!) tend to explain how Asians fled poverty and oppression in their home countries to find freedom and prosperity in the United States. Ignoring the United States' role in *generating* the refugee crisis through war in the first place, such lessons depict the United States as a generous host welcoming desperate Asians.

Taken together, these ideas contribute to an inaccurate understanding of Asian migration, which contributes to persistent and prevalent racism against Asian Americans. Common verbal attacks such as, "Go back to your country!," discriminatory deportation policies, and hate crimes against Asian Americans all emerge from the misconception that the U.S. has been nothing but welcoming to ungrateful and undeserving Asians.

Therefore, we call for the *critical* teaching of U.S. wars in Asia that empowers children to understand the connection between war and migration in Asian American history. We suggest lessons for grades 4–6 that focus on the Philippine-American War and Korean War as well as children's literature recommendations for teaching the Vietnam War. Some states, such as Alabama, Georgia, and South Carolina, include these wars in their elementary social studies curriculum standards, whereas others do not. When not directly mentioned in state standards, these wars and lesson ideas can be part of an instructional unit on war, immigration, and/or refugees.

CRITICAL TEACHING OF THE PHILIPPINE-AMERICAN WAR

The Filipinx American community is the third-largest Asian American group with a population of over 4.2 million (U.S. Census Bureau, 2021). Although Filipinxs in North America were first documented in the 16th century, mass migration did not begin until the United States seized control of the Philippines after the Spanish-American War of 1898.

FIGURE 5.1 Illustration shows Uncle Sam offering on one hand a soldier and on the other a "School Teacher" to a group of reluctant Filipinos, telling them that the choice is theirs. LIBRARY OF CONGRESS (HTTP://WWW.LOC.GOV/PICTURES/ITEM/2010651486).

Prior to becoming a U.S. colony, the Philippines had been a Spanish colony for more than 300 years. When the United States came to the Philippines during the Spanish-American War in 1898, Filipinxs had already begun an anticolonial revolution against Spain for their liberation. Filipinx revolutionaries believed that the United States was their ally and helped the U.S. win the Spanish-American War. However, when the war ended, the United States ignored the Filipinx people's desire for independence and colonized the Philippines. According to then-president William McKinley, U.S. colonization of the Philippines was necessary to "educate the Filipinos, and uplift and civilize and Christianize them" (Rusling, 1903, pp. 137–138), preparing them for eventual self-rule.

As you can imagine, Filipinxs resisted, and the War of Philippine Independence (1899–1902) began. Although commonly called "the Philippine-American War" in the U.S., this was, for Filipinxs, a war of independence that continued their fight for sovereignty against foreign empires—first Spain, then the United States. This three-year war was brutal, involving mass killing, torture, and the burning of villages, because many U.S. military leaders dehumanized Filipinxs and viewed them as barbaric savages (Immerwahr, 2020). After winning this war, the United States ruled the Philippines until 1946, when it finally granted independence to its people. The four decades of U.S. colonial rule Americanized the Philippines, transforming its language, education, political system, and economy according to U.S. customs (Baldoz, 2011; David, 2011).

This historical context is central to Filipinx migration to the United States. Between 1903 and 1939, many young Filipinxs went to the U.S. to pursue education. As poverty increased under colonial rule, more Filipinxs came to the U.S. for work (Lee, 2015). Unlike other Asian groups who were banned by a series of anti-Asian immigrant laws in the early 1900s (see Chapter 3), Filipinxs could still travel to and work in the U.S. because, as subjects of a U.S. colony, they held special status as U.S. nationals who pledged allegiance to America and lived under U.S. rule. Most early Filipinx migrants worked in canneries and fields along the West Coast. They suffered from racism and discrimination similar to what other Asian migrant groups faced. And, like other Asian migrant groups, Filipinxs were not powerless. They fought against workplace exploitation and demanded justice in solidarity with Mexican migrant workers (see Chapter 6).

We suggest engaging students in the study of early Filipinx migration in relation with the U.S. war and colonization of the Philippines through primary sources and the picturebooks *Tucky Jo and Little Heart* by Patricia Polacco (2015) and *Journey for Justice: The Life of Larry Itliong* by Dawn B. Mabalon and Gayle Romasanta (2018).

TUCKY JO AND LITTLE HEART BY PATRICIA POLACCO

Johnnie was a young boy from Kentucky. When he heard the news about the Japanese attack on Pearl Harbor, Johnnie decided to fight for his country and was sent to the Pacific theater. After many battles, Johnnie's unit landed in the Philippines, which was invaded and occupied by Japan. One day in a forest, Johnnie met a little girl. She did not speak at all, and Johnnie began to call her Little Heart. Their friendship grew, and Johnnie helped Little Heart and the people in her village by sharing his food. One day Johnnie heard the news that the United States would bomb the forest to fight the Japanese army nearby. He and his fellow American soldiers raced to the village and evacuated Little Heart and other villagers to avoid the bombing. After World War II ended, Johnnie returned home. Years later, as an old man in poor health, Johnnie regularly visited a hospital. One day a new nurse came in and took good care of him, and she turned out to be Little Heart! Finally, she reunited with Johnnie and thanked him for helping her village.

Through Johnnie's eyes and voice in *Tucky Jo and Little Heart* (Polacco, 2015), students can vividly see the wartime suffering of U.S. soldiers and Filipinx civilians. Students can also note human resilience during war. The friendship, kindness, and caring that Johnnie and Little Heart built during wartime suggests the possibility for a better future. A limitation, however, is the absence of the larger historical context. For example, it is unclear whether Johnnie knew that the Philippines was a U.S. colony and that Little Heart and the Filipinx villagers were once U.S. nationals. When Johnnie met Little Heart's grandfather in the village, he was surprised that the grandfather could speak English, but the book does not explain why. The grandfather learned English at school because English was the official language of education in the U.S.-occupied Philippines. Finally, a significant limitation is the lack of Filipinx perspective. Like most textbooks and curricular materials, this story is told from the point of view of a white American savior.

With these strengths and limitations in mind, you can use this book as a springboard for an inquiry into the U.S. war and colonization of the Philippines as well as into the impact of these events on Filipinx migration. Begin the inquiry by reading *Tucky Jo and Little Heart* as a class. After reading, encourage students to share their feelings, thoughts, and questions about the story. Then, pose the question: What was the relationship between the Philippines and the United

States in the early 1900s? To explain the inquiry further and to spark students' curiosity, ask, "How did Little Heart's grandfather learn to speak English? Were Little Heart's grandfather and the Filipinx villagers considered foreigners or Americans?"

After hearing students' initial thoughts, engage them in analysis of primary sources. First, present a map of the United States from the early 1900s, which includes the Philippines as well as Alaska, Hawai'i, Guam, Wake Island, American Samoa, Puerto Rico, and the Panama Canal Zone in boxes as part of the United States territories. Such a map can be found on the Stanford Library website (https://exhibits.stanford.edu/nhdmaps/catalog/xr731vr4463). Support students to make inferences about what this map reveals about the status of the Philippines in relation to the United States during the early 1900s.

Second, analyze the interview of President McKinley explaining his decision to colonize the Philippines. Guide students in identifying how McKinley justified taking over the Philippines and how his racist beliefs about Filipinxs shaped his decision to colonize the Philippines. Encourage students to imagine how Filipinxs would have felt about this rationalization of U.S. colonization.

INTERVIEW WITH PRESIDENT WILLIAM MCKINLEY IN 1899

When I next realized that the Philippines had dropped into our laps, I confess I did not know what to do with them . . . And one night late it came to me this way . . . (1) That we could not give them back to Spain—that would be cowardly and dishonorable; (2) that we could not turn them over to France and Germany—our commercial rivals in the Orient—that would be bad business and discreditable; (3) that we could not leave them to themselves—they were unfit for self-government—and they would soon have anarchy and misrule over there worse than Spain's was; and (4) that there was nothing left for us to do but to take them all, and to educate the Filipinos, and uplift and civilize and Christianize them, and by God's grace do the very best we could by them, as our fellow-men for whom Christ also died.

After analyzing these primary sources, read aloud *Journey for Justice: The Life of Larry Itliong* (Mabalon & Romasanta, 2018). This picturebook tells the story of Itliong, who was a Filipino migrant worker and labor activist (see Chapter 6). Like many people in the Philippines, Itliong left his home and family in search of the American dream, only to be met with discriminatory and unjust working conditions in the California fields. While the book focuses on Itliong's journey as a leader of the farmworkers movement, the first part vividly describes the larger structural forces behind Filipinx migration to the United States. After reading, ensure that students understand why Itliong wanted to leave home to go to the U.S. and how the U.S. colonization of the Philippines spurred this migration.

"ASIANS, IT MUST BE REMEMBERED, DID NOT COME TO AMERICA, AMERICANS WENT TO ASIA."

Historian Gary Okihiro wrote these words in 1994 (pp. 28–29). They apply to nearly all of the Asian continent, and particularly to the history of the Philippines. Many understand imperialism to be solely about taking natural resources, including land. But imperialism also means the recruitment of cheap labor, draining the colony of its educated, professional class (also known as the "brain drain"), and forcing the adoption of imperialist culture. In the Philippines, this meant setting up an education system in English that promoted U.S. interests and ideals as superior. Culturally, it meant that the light skin, pointed noses, and straight hair of Anglo colonizers were the standard for what was considered beautiful. In order to understand why people like Larry Itliong left their families and homeland in search of the "American dream," U.S. imperialism (physical and cultural) must be a part of the conversation.

CRITICAL TEACHING OF THE KOREAN WAR

The Korean American community is the fifth-largest Asian American subgroup with a population of 1.9 million today (U.S. Census Bureau, 2021). The first significant wave of Korean immigration started in

1903, when a shipload of Koreans, most of whom were Christians converted by U.S. missionaries, arrived in Hawaiʻi to work on pineapple and sugar plantations. The number of Korean immigrants remained small during the first half of the 20th century because of anti-Asian immigration laws (see Chapter 3) and Japan's colonization of Korea from 1910 to 1945. The notable change in Korean migration to the United States was due to the Korean War.

Often called the "Forgotten War," the Korean War gets little curricular attention. When taught in elementary classrooms, it is generally explained as America's benevolent mission to rescue South Koreans from communist North Korea and to stop the spread of communism. However, the Korean War is much more complex and controversial than the feel-good narrative of the U.S. rescue and liberation of desperate Asians (Cumings, 2010).

For example, the United States was not a purely liberating force. Prior to the Korean War, Koreans were under Japanese colonial rule and had been fighting for independence since 1910. When World War II ended and Japan withdrew from Korea in 1945, the winners of the war—namely the Soviet Union and the United States—denied Koreans the independence they were ready for and had long desired. Instead, the two world powers divided Korea into two, each occupying half of the country. This initial division sowed discord, which resulted in the Korean War in 1950. The two divided Koreas created their own states under U.S. and Soviet influences respectively, each one aiming to reunite Korea under its own ideological system. This led to a full-scale war between communist North Korea and capitalist South Korea (Cumings, 2010).

When the Korean War began, the United States intervened to support South Korea, while China joined the war to help North Korea. After three years of bloody fighting, the United States, Soviet Union, China, North Korea, and South Korea signed an armistice. Although the fighting ceased, a formal peace treaty was never signed, meaning the Korean War has not officially ended. The two Koreas remain divided. Furthermore, three years of active fighting resulted in countless deaths, destruction, and displacement. The United States was not exempt from committing war atrocities. For example, in the No Gun

Ri massacre, U.S. troops killed hundreds of South Korean civilians. U.S. warplanes also dropped 635,000 tons of bombs along with 32,557 tons of napalm, which wiped out cities and towns in Korea and caused innumerable civilian deaths (Cumings, 2010).

In the aftermath of this tragic war, 15,000 Koreans came to the United States. These migrants were the wives of American soldiers and war orphans adopted by American families, as well as students, businessmen, and intellectuals who fled their war-torn country. Due to the 1965 Immigration Act (see Chapter 3), along with the continued presence of the U.S. military bases in South Korea (remember, the Korean War is still not over!), Korean migration to the United States has continued to increase.

We recommend two picturebooks and two primary sources to engage students in an inquiry into the Korean War to establish historical context for Korean migration to the United States.

These two picturebooks complement each other's strengths and weaknesses. *When Spring Comes to the DMZ* (Lee, 2019) highlights the unfinished nature of the Korean War and the continued human suffering. However, this book does not describe the war itself. In contrast, *Peacebound Trains* (Balgassi, 1996) focuses on what happened *during* the Korean War. It vividly describes human suffering caused by the war. However, it does not detail the complex causes of the war, instead simply mentioning that North Korea invaded South Korea. Also, the book only presents the United States in a positive light, illustrating the U.S. as a big brother who helped South Koreans during the war and allowed them to resettle in the U.S. Unfortunately, most children's books published in the United States tend to avoid the U.S.'s complex role in the Korean War (An, 2021). Therefore, a critical unpacking of the storyline is key.

Begin the lesson by reading *When Spring Comes to the DMZ* as a class. Ask students to share their feelings, thoughts, and questions about the unfinished Korean War and to consider how its legacy affects Korean people today. Based on students' previous knowledge, possible discussion topics may include borders, walls, family separation, and/or environmental protections. Next, read *Peacebound Trains* and identify what happened during the active fighting of the Korean War. Guide

***WHEN SPRING COMES TO THE DMZ* BY UK-BAE LEE**

The DMZ (Korea's demilitarized zone) is a strip of land 160 miles long and about 2.5 miles wide between the border fences of South Korea and North Korea. Along the DMZ, the North and South Korean militaries are positioned against each other, and people cannot cross the border freely. Meanwhile, an untouched haven for wildlife has flourished inside the DMZ, where animals and plants cross the border freely. A young boy in South Korea accompanies his grandfather on his visits to the DMZ every season. He describes beautiful wildlife thriving inside in juxtaposition to the soldiers conducting seasonal military practice on both sides of the DMZ. He also describes his grandfather's sorrows and desire for a united Korea so that he can finally meet his long-lost family and friends in North Korea.

***PEACEBOUND TRAINS* BY HAEMI BALGASSI**

Sumi, a Korean American girl, listens to her grandmother's stories about the Korean War. Grandmother and her family lived in South Korea, and one day North Korea invaded her town. Grandmother and her two children (including Sumi's mother) had to leave home and flee further south. Sumi's grandfather, however, decided to remain and fight against communist soldiers. He died during the war. When the fighting ended, Grandmother and her children immigrated to the U.S. and built a new life.

students in assessing how the United States is depicted in the text and illustrations.

Then ask students if there may be different perspectives on the United States' role in the Korean War. To provide different views on U.S. roles in the war, students can analyze two primary sources. The first source (Figure 5.2) is a propaganda poster produced in China during the Korean War. The man in uniform is a caricature of Douglas MacArthur, the commander of the U.S. troops in South Korea. While he was committing war crimes in Korea, a U.S. airplane bombed a factory in China. The poster depicts the United States as a violent war aggressor. The second source (Figure 5.3) is a photo of MacArthur being greeted by South Korea President Syngman Rhee during the war. This photo was taken by the U.S. military. One interpretation of this photo is that General MacArthur, as a representative of the United States, is a benevolent rescuer of South Korea from the communist attack.

Students can juxtapose the two sources and identify how and why General MacArthur and the United States are depicted in such starkly different ways. Then, ask students to compare and contrast the representation of the United States in the two primary sources with the depictions from *Peacebound Trains.* Challenge students to evaluate each image to draw their own conclusion about the United States' role in the Korean War and to explain their rationales.

Next, explore how the Korean War spurred Korean migration to the United States. Ask students to analyze Table 5.1 and make inferences about the increase in Korean migration to the United States. Remind them that the active battles of the Korean War were fought from 1950 to 1953, and that the U.S. military forces have stayed in South Korea ever since because the war remains unfinished. Students should consider the cause-and-effect relationship between the Korean War and Korean migration and explain how the war caused forced displacement. Then, encourage students to think about Sumi's grandmother in *Peacebound Trains* and how the grandmother's story of the Korean War and her journey to the United States might be reflected in the table.

TABLE 5.1 Number of Annual Korean Immigrants to the U.S., 1946–1964

Year	Number of Korean Migrants to the U.S.
1946–1950	107
1951–1955	581
1956–1960	6182
1961–1964	8014

Created by Sohyun An based on *Koreans' immigration to the United States: History and contemporary trends*. Research Report No 3. Research Center for Korean Community at Queens College, City University of New York.

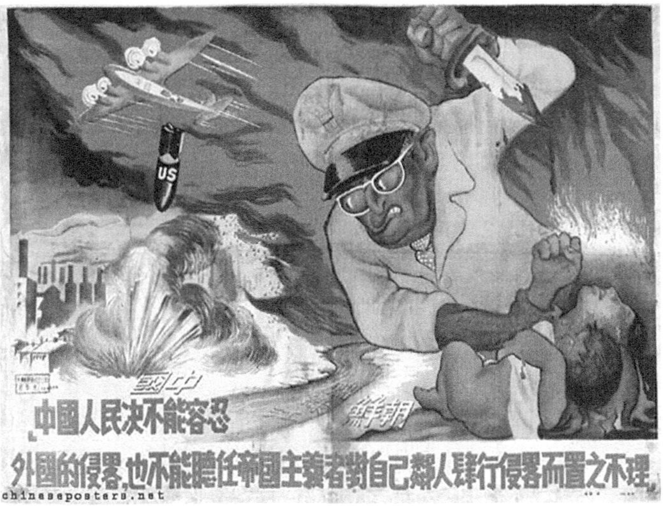

FIGURE 5.2 A propaganda poster produced by the Chinese government during the Korean War. THE INTERNATIONAL INSTITUTE OF SOCIAL HISTORY COLLECTION (HTTPS://CHINESEPOSTERS.NET/GALLERY/E27-169)

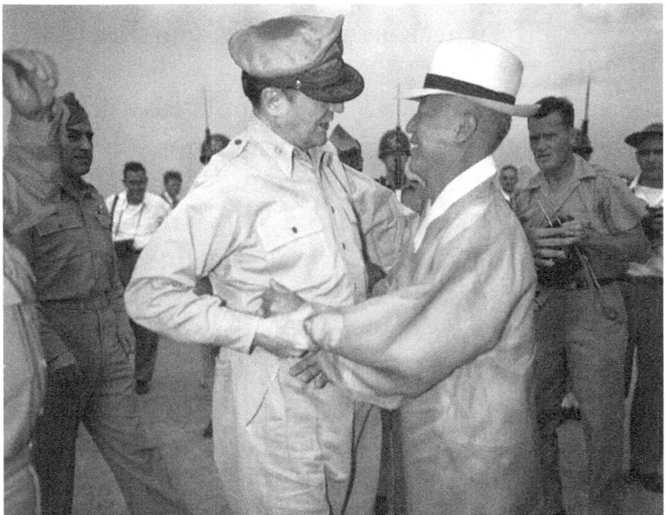

FIGURE 5.3 Douglas MacArthur and Syngman Rhee. U.S. ARMY (HTTPS://COMMONS.WIKIMEDIA.ORG/WIKI/FILE:SYNGMAN_RHEE_2.JPG).

To conclude the lesson, invite students to share the thoughts, feelings, and questions that emerged. Make sure that students are able to situate Korean migration within the historical context of the Korean War and to discuss the complex roles of the United States both in the war and in Korean people's lives.

CRITICAL TEACHING OF THE VIETNAM WAR

Southeast Asian Americans represent the largest refugee community ever to be resettled in the United States after being forcefully displaced by U.S. wars in Vietnam, Laos, and Cambodia. The roots of the Vietnam War go back to the late 1800s, when Vietnam, Laos, and Cambodia were under French colonial rule. During World War II, Japan drove out France and occupied the region. When the war ended with Japan's defeat, France sought to recolonize its former Southeast Asian subjects, resulting in the First Indochina War (1946–1954). In this war, the United States sided with France because it preferred French imperial rule to independent communist governments in Southeast Asia. After eight years of fighting, the First Indochina War ended with a French defeat. Laos and Cambodia gained independence from France, whereas Vietnam was temporarily divided into North and South (Nguyen, 2012).

In this context, the United States began to more deeply intervene in the region to prevent the spread of communism. By the 1960s, the United States entered a full-blown war against communist North Vietnamese forces and their allies in South Vietnam, which ended with a U.S. defeat. More than 58,000 Americans and three million Vietnamese lost their lives in the war, and 12 million Vietnamese became refugees. Furthermore, most of Vietnam's infrastructure was destroyed, and its land and water were poisoned with defoliating chemicals (Nguyen, 2012).

Even worse, the Vietnam War spread to neighboring Laos and Cambodia as Vietnamese communist forces moved into those regions. U.S. bombings killed tens of thousands of Cambodians, fueling Cambodian civilian support of the Khmer Rouge, a communist group that initiated a brutal genocide upon taking power in 1975. In Laos, two million tons of U.S. bombs were dropped, which was equal to a planeload of bombs every eight minutes, 24 hours a day, for nine years. To hide these military actions from public eyes and ears and to minimize American casualties, the United States recruited the Hmong, an ethnic minority in Laos, to fight the United States' secret war in Laos (Kurlantzick, 2017).

When the United States withdrew from the region in 1975, communist governments had come to power in all three countries. People who sided with the United States during the war or suffered under the new communist regimes began to flee. Some were airlifted and taken to U.S. military bases in the Pacific for resettlement processing. Others fled on foot or by boat. Many died from drowning, shipwrecks, starvation, thirst, and violent pirate attacks. Those who survived the dangerous journey still had to endure poor conditions in refugee camps in neighboring countries, waiting with uncertainty, sometimes indefinitely, to be resettled in the United States or elsewhere. The stories of 1.2 million Vietnamese, Lao, Hmong, and Cambodian people who entered the United States as refugees reveal the complex legacies of U.S. war and military interventions in Southeast Asia (Espiritu, 2014).

We recommend Southeast Asian refugee children's literature as an instructional tool to engage students in understanding the relationship between U.S. wars in Southeast Asia and Southeast Asian migration to the United States. These books tell stories of the Vietnam War through Southeast Asian refugees' experiences, naturally linking war and displacement. However, research shows that many Southeast Asian refugee children's books published in the United States omit the U.S.'s role as a violent war aggressor that spurred the deaths and displacements of Southeast Asians. Instead, many texts present the United States as a benevolent rescuer or a safe haven for desperate refugees (An, 2022b). Therefore, critical reading of this body of children's literature is key.

Recommended books and discussion questions are provided on page 131. In order for students to critically read and discuss these texts, they should understand how the Vietnam War directly led to Southeast Asian migration to the U.S.; identify complex roles that the

FIGURE 5.4 Vietnamese Boat People: Vietnamese refugees wait to be taken aboard the amphibious command ship USS Blue Ridge. They are being rescued from a 35 foot fishing boat 350 miles Northeast of Cam Ranh Bay, Vietnam, after spending eight days. U.S. NAVY AND PUBLIC DOMAIN.

United States played in the war and refugee crisis; center Southeast Asian voices and experiences in understanding of the war and forced displacement; and recognize the struggles and resilience of Southeast Asian migrant communities.

RECOMMENDED CHILDREN'S LITERATURE ABOUT THE VIETNAM WAR AND SOUTHEAST ASIAN MIGRATION

- *A Different Pond* by Bao Phi, illustrated by Thi Bui
- *A Path of Stars* by Anne Sibley O'Brien
- *Dia's Story Cloth* by Dia Cha
- *Grandfather's Story Cloth* by Linda Gerdner and Sarah Langford, illustrated by Stuart Loughridge
- *Half Spoon of Rice* by Icy Smith, illustrated by Sopaul Nhem
- *Inside Out and Back Again* by Thanhha Lai
- *The Most Beautiful Thing* by Kao Kalia Yang, illustrated by Khoa Le
- *Yang Warriors* by Kao Kalia Yang, illustrated by Billy Thao
- *Mali Under the Night Sky* by Youme Landowne
- *When Everything Was Everything* by Saymoukda Duangphouxay Vongsay, illustrated by Cory Nakamura

DISCUSSION QUESTIONS ABOUT THE VIETNAM WAR AND SOUTHEAST ASIAN MIGRATION

- Who are the main characters? What happened to the main characters during the war, escape, and/or resettlement? What challenges did the main characters face and how did they navigate these challenges?
- What role did the United States play in the Vietnam War and the Southeast Asian refugee crisis?
- What did the main characters feel and think about the war, displacement, and the resettlement?
- What did you learn about the Vietnam War, Southeast Asian migration, the United States, and Southeast Asian Americans?

ASIAN MIGRATION AS ADOPTEES

Some Asians migrated to the U.S. as adoptees because of U.S. wars and military presence in Asia. About 200,000 adoptees came from South Korea as a result of the Korean War (Kim, 2010). Many early adoptees were the multiracial children of U.S. military men and Korean women. During the last days of the Vietnam War in 1975, the U.S. government airlifted approximately 3,000 Vietnamese orphans to the U.S. Many of these babies were fathered by U.S. military men and adopted by white families.

Aside from U.S. wars, the domestic contexts of U.S. and Asian countries also generated the migration of Asian children as adoptees. Beginning in the 1960s, there was a shortage of white babies available for adoption in the U.S., partly because contraception became more widely available and single mothers gained more social acceptance. Prospective parents then looked overseas to adopt newborn babies. Meanwhile, the Chinese government implemented family planning with the one-child policy in the late-1970s. Chinese parents who preferred sons left their daughters at orphanages, leading to the adoptions of more than 85,000 Chinese children by people in the U.S. The stereotype of Asian Americans as model minorities has promoted the idea of Asian children as model adoptees.

Knowing the history of transnational and transracial Asian adoptees is important because you may have Asian American students who have not been raised in households where Asian culture—in any of its forms—is present. Scholars and transnational adoptees Melanie McCormick and Alycia West (2022) have a powerful open-access article that draws from their own schooling experiences to offer educators advice on how to better support adopted students. Their article also recommends children's literature about adoption, including the books on the next page. We would be remiss if we didn't note that most books about transnational adoption are narrated by white adoptive mothers who frequently erase Asian voices; consequently, popular trade books about adoption rarely attend to transracial complexities of the adoption process (Yi, 2021).

RECOMMENDED CHILDREN'S LITERATURE ABOUT ADOPTION

- *Over the Moon: An Adoption Tale* by Karen Katz
- *And That's Why She's My Mama* by Tiarra Nazario
- *I Don't Have Your Eyes* by Carrie A. Kitze, illustrated by Rob Williams
- *Star of the Week: A Story of Love, Adoption, and Brownies with Sprinkles* by Darlene Friedman, illustrated by Roger Roth
- *We Belong Together: A Book about Adoption and Families* by Todd Parr

WAR AND DISPLACEMENT MATTER

We recognize that teaching about U.S. wars through a critical lens is not easy. A feel-good narrative of these wars as honorable, inevitable, just, and necessary is deeply entrenched in our society, including in books, movies, video games, national holidays, and textbooks. Discussions of these wars—if they occur at all—often go no deeper than to proclaim that "we support the troops." In this context, a critical take on U.S. wars may quickly be labeled as unpatriotic or anti-American. Despite the risks, however, the stakes are too high to avoid this lens. Avoidance would only reinforce existing perceptions that U.S. military interventions occur around the world to spread freedom and democracy. As educators, we have an obligation to empower children to follow Dr. Martin Luther King Jr.'s call, "War is not the answer!" and begin to explore peaceful alternatives.

The three lessons outlined in this chapter are examples of such anti-war, pro-peace education. By guiding students to understand the relationship between U.S. wars in Asia and Asian migration to the United States, and by centering the experiences and perspectives of Asian migrants in the study of war and displacement, these lessons can help students challenge the myth that U.S. wars are well-intentioned rescue-and-liberation missions. Despite the educational benefit of such approaches, however, U.S. wars in Asia and Asian migration to the U.S. are rarely included in most states' elementary curriculum standards. Therefore, educators must think creatively to address this complex content in meaningful ways.

Above all, war and displacement in Asian American history can be part of a unit on other wars or migration that is typically taught in elementary education, whether it is the Revolutionary War, "Indian Wars," Trail of Tears, the Civil War, "Westward Expansion," the World Wars, or the Great Migration. With essential questions such as, "What causes people to migrate?", "How does war affect human lives?", and "How does war often result in forced migration?", students can learn about topics included in the curriculum standards along with Asian migration spurred by U.S. wars in Asia.

6

Activism and Resistance

When you think about activism and resistance in U.S. history, who comes to mind? For many of us, only a few names might surface, and most will probably be from the same time period, the Civil Rights era of the 1950s and 1960s. We want to make sure that young learners can answer this question with more depth and breadth. History shows us that, whenever and wherever there has been oppression, there has also been activism and resistance by many people and in many different ways. *All* children should be able to see their identities represented in these histories. As teachers, we have the opportunity and obligation to bring diverse narratives of civic action into the classroom.

The stories in this chapter highlight a term that has become mainstream but is often misconstrued: *intersectionality*. Patricia Hill Collins and Sirma Bilge (2016) define intersectionality as "a way of understanding and analyzing the complexity in the world, in people, and in human experiences . . . shaped by many factors in diverse and mutually influencing ways" (p. 2). Specifically, intersectionality allows us to consider how particular identities are subjected to complex and multiple types of discrimination. The most common misuse of the term is the layering of multiple identities without the consideration of oppression.

In this chapter, we consider how racial discrimination intersects with other forms of oppression. We begin with Asian and Asian American

DOI: 10.4324/9781032662695-6

activism in women's rights in the 20th century. Next, we discuss Asian American women who were active in the Civil Rights Movement of the 1960s across several communities. Then we address labor rights, focusing on the work of Larry Itliong and his role in the Delano Grape Strike, and LGBTQ+ rights. We conclude with resources for teachers to stay current on issues affecting Asian American communities today.

WOMEN'S RIGHTS

In social studies curriculum, women historical figures are rarely present. Women with political influence often enter the curriculum with the introduction of Susan B. Anthony and Elizabeth Cady Stanton. Ida B. Wells, a Black suffragist, writer, former teacher, and civil rights leader, may be mentioned to address racism in suffragist movements, because many white suffragists actively fought *against* the vote for Black women. But there are so many more individuals and organizations that should be a part of this story in classrooms. In this section, we will describe two incredible Asian Americans who fought for women's rights: Mabel Ping-Hua Lee and Patsy Mink.

Defying Stereotypes: Mabel Ping-Hua Lee, a Chinese Suffragist in New York

Mabel Ping-Hua Lee's life shows how feminism and women's rights in Asian American history were not simply achieved with the passage of the 19th Amendment, as citizenship and racism were always in tension (see Chapter 4). Unraveling her experiences can help students understand the hope and progress of the suffrage movement, while also recognizing that the movement fell far short of encompassing the humanity and the dignity of *all* women.

Lee was born in China in the late 1890s (the exact year is unknown). Her father was a Chinese missionary who moved his family to New York to lead a Baptist church for Chinese immigrants in 1905. Although Lee would spend much of her life in the United States, one of her primary concerns was the growing call for women's rights in China. Her ideas around feminism and women's rights were shaped by both Chinese and U.S. thinkers and movements. As women and their allies in more and more states began to fight for the right to vote, Lee did the same,

MABEL LEE.
The young Chinese woman who wants a vote.
CHINESE GIRL WANTS VOTE
Miss Lee Ready to Enter Barnard, to Ride in Suffrage Parade.

FIGURE 6.1 Mabel Ping-Hua Lee featured in the *New-York Tribune.* *NEW-YORK TRIBUNE,* 1912, APRIL 13. CHRONICLING AMERICA, NATIONAL ENDOWMENT FOR THE HUMANITIES AND THE LIBRARY OF CONGRESS (HTTPS://CHRONICLINGAMERICA.LOC.GOV/LCCN/SN83030214/1912-04-13/ED-1/SEQ-3).

encouraging Chinese and Chinese Americans in New York to fight for women's suffrage. As a teenager, Lee's leadership in the Chinese community came to the attention of white suffragists who asked her to lead the 1912 suffrage parade.

In college, Lee was heavily involved in the Chinese Students' Alliance and came into contact with other students interested in women's rights, including some Chinese Americans. Together, these young activists debated and sharpened their thoughts on women's rights and why they are necessary in any civilization, but especially in a post-dynasty, rapidly changing China. Lee began to view women's rights as greater than the single issue of suffrage; she defined feminism broadly as "equality of opportunity" and "the application of democracy to women" (Cahill, 2020, p. 152).

A SUFFRAGIST AND A SCHOLAR

As a Chinese woman in the U.S. suffrage movement, Mabel Lee worked to break down stereotypes that U.S. citizens held about China. She would write and give talks in New York about Chinese culture and history, including elements that would be seen as progressive. She continued to defy stereotypes by choosing to study economics for her doctorate when the field was dominated by men. Her 600-plus page dissertation about China's economic history with an emphasis on agriculture culminated in her being the first Chinese woman in the U.S. to earn a Ph.D. in 1921. Some of her research is still used by scholars today!

While Lee's engagements with white suffragists illustrate the broad hopes of the movement early on, her identity as a Chinese-born woman exposes how many women were actually left behind after the passage of the 19th amendment. Despite her support of women's right to vote, Lee would never be able to exercise the right herself, as the Naturalization Act of 1790 and the Chinese Exclusion Act of 1882 prevented *all* Asian immigrants from becoming U.S. citizens. This legislation was not fully reversed until 1952 (see Chapters 3 and 4). Similarly, Indigenous women could not become citizens and vote until 1924, although several states still found ways to deny suffrage to Indigenous communities for decades afterward. The passage of the 1965 Voting Rights Act finally secured the vote for most communities of color. An extension of the Act in 1975 ensured that people who did not speak English would also have access to voting.

Fighting Inequity Through the Law: Patsy Mink, U.S. Representative of Hawai'i

Women's suffrage and civil rights are often taught as separate issues. Congresswoman Patsy Mink's work brings the two together, as her story shows how civil rights struggles for people of color and women did not end in 1964 with the Civil Rights Act. Mink was born in 1927 in Hawai'i before it became a state. While her Japanese American family was not incarcerated during World War II, her father, a

FIGURE 6.2 U.S. Representative Patsy Mink speaking at a press conference on the introduction of legislation on gender equity in education, Washington D.C. PHOTOGRAPH BY MICHAEL R. JENKINS, 1993. LIBRARY OF CONGRESS (HTTPS://WWW.LOC.GOV/RESOURCE/PPMSCA.72551).

second-generation civil engineer, was questioned by authorities after the bombing of Pearl Harbor. When he returned from the interrogation, Mink recalled him burning all their Japanese mementos. Any tie to Japan and Japanese culture was viewed with suspicion by the U.S. Consequently, many Japanese American families felt the need to distance themselves from the land of their ancestors and to hide any connections they had to it.

In spite of the discrimination that Japanese Americans faced during World War II, Mink ran for student government in high school and successfully won the position of student president. She later graduated from the University of Hawaiʻi with degrees in zoology and chemistry, and then applied to medical schools. Mink was denied admission because, as some schools outright explained, she was a woman. She shifted her ambitions and graduated from law school, but had difficulty getting a job at top law firms because she was a mother. Mink decided to run for Congress after Hawaiʻi became a state, and in 1964, she became the first Asian American woman elected to the U.S. House of Representatives (Wu & Mink, 2022).

While a member of Congress, Mink was one of the main authors and sponsors of Title IX. Title IX states that "no person in the United States shall, on the basis of sex, be excluded from participation in, be denied the benefits of, or be subjected to discrimination under any education program or activity receiving Federal financial assistance" (Title IX, Education Amendments of 1972, 20 U.S.C. §§ 1681-1688). While Title IX is perhaps best known for opening up school sports programs so women could participate, the reforms were also applied to education, including to law and STEM programs that traditionally denied access to most women. In sponsoring the reform, Mink drew from her personal experiences of discrimination. After Mink's death in 2002, Title IX was officially renamed the "Patsy T. Mink Equal Opportunity Education Act."

In addition to Title IX, much of Mink's political work addressed the multiple forms of discrimination she faced as a Japanese American citizen and woman. She and Representative Norman Mineta (California) created the Congressional Asian Pacific American Caucus in 1994 to highlight Asian and Pacific American issues in Congress. Mink spoke out against Supreme Court nominees who supported whites-only policies and who were accused of assaulting women. As a politician, she advocated for ending the Vietnam War and diverting its financial resources into social programs, even though this went against the opinions of many voters in her region. Mink also supported bilingual education and, as a working mother, affordable childcare. Throughout her career, she prioritized what she believed to be right for as many people as possible, rather than make political decisions that would get her re-elected.

Any classroom-based discussion of women's suffrage should distinguish between those who fought for women's right to vote and those who actually benefited from the 19th Amendment. Rather than solely focusing on white figures like Susan B. Anthony and Elizabeth Cady Stanton, include the stories of Ida B. Wells—we love Walter Dean Myers' picturebook *Let the Truth be Told* (2015) about her life! —and Mabel Ping-Hua Lee, exploring her broad definition of feminism in both her words and actions. Make sure to extend women's rights to Patsy Mink in the 1960s and 1970s. Her life reveals the continued discrimination against women and the work she and others have done to address these injustices.

RECOMMENDED CHILDREN'S LITERATURE ABOUT WOMEN'S RIGHTS

- *Equality's Call: The Story of Voting Rights in America* by Deborah Diesen, illustrated by Magdalena Mora
- *Finish the Fight!: The Brave and Revolutionary Women Who Fought For the Right to Vote* by Veronica Chambers and the staff of *The New York Times*
- *Fall Down Seven Times, Stand Up Eight: Patsy Takemoto Mink and the Fight for Title IX* by Jen Bryant, illustrated by Tashiki Nakamura
- *Loujain Dreams of Sunflowers* by Lina AlHathloul and Uma Mishra-Newbery, illustrated by Rebecca Green
- *She Persisted: Patsy Mink* by Tae Keller
- *An Equal Shot: How the Law Title IX Changed America* by Helaine Becker, illustrated by Dow Phumiruk

DISCUSSION QUESTIONS FOR TEACHING ABOUT WOMEN'S RIGHTS

- The 19th Amendment states that, "The right of citizens of the United States to vote shall not be denied or abridged by the United States or by any State on account of sex." In addition to voting, what are other rights that women have had to fight for? See the National Women's History Museum (womenshistory.org) for more resources, and the American Civil Liberties Union for major Supreme Court cases on women's rights (https://www.aclu.org/other/timeline-major-supreme-court-decisions-womens-rights).
- What are some of the ways women have fought for their rights throughout U.S. history? (see *Finish the Fight!* listed above).
- What are women's rights issues that Mabel Ping-Hua Lee and Patsy Mink fought for?

- What are some changes that happened thanks to Lee's and Mink's work?
- Why do you think Lee and Mink tried to make changes that they themselves would not directly benefit from?
- What are some challenges that today's women face in the U.S.? In the world?

"YELLOW POWER" IN THE CIVIL RIGHTS MOVEMENT

In 1969, five college students decided to start a newspaper named *Gidra* that featured essays, poems, and illustrations about the Asian American experience. One of the first essays published in *Gidra* was "Yellow Power!" by Larry Kubota. Kubota wrote,

> Yellow power is a call for all Asian Americans to end the silence that has condemned us to suffer in this racist society and to unite with our black, brown and red brothers of the Third World for survival, self-determination and the creation of a more humanistic society. (p. 2)

Remember Emma Gee and Yuji Ichioka from the Introduction? The Asian American Political Alliance they formed sought to unify Asian Americans against racism and imperialism. The Alliance also committed to solidarity with other communities of color or, as Kubota described them, the "Third World."[1]

One example of Third World unity began on college campuses when multiple organizations came together to form the Third World Liberation Front. It was made up of the Black Student Union, Latin American Student Organization, Mexican American Student Coalition, Pilipino American Collegiate Endeavor, Chinese for Social Action, and the Asian American Political Alliance (Maeda, 2009). Together, they led a student strike demanding, among other issues, the creation of ethnic studies at their university. After several months of student protests that resulted in police violence, the Third World Liberation Front succeeded in establishing ethnic studies departments at San Francisco State University and University of California Berkeley.

Examples of this Third World unity are often left out of curricula. Instead, we mostly learn and teach about civil rights activism separately by race or gender. This completely leaves out several communities, including Asian Americans (An, 2022a). You can address these challenges by crossing—as the Third World Liberation Front did—the boundaries typically drawn around and between communities. People hold many identities and belong to multiple communities. It's the same for activists, many of whom—past and present—have worked in solidarity with others. It's time to highlight some of these histories.

Yuri Kochiyama: Solidarity Beyond Borders

Yuri Kochiyama was born Mary Yuriko Nakahara in San Pedro, California in 1921 to Japanese immigrants. The local hospital did not allow Japanese to deliver their babies there, so Kochiyama and her siblings were all delivered by a family friend. They had a comfortable middle-class childhood as a result of Kochiyama's parents' successful fish business (Fujino, 2005).

In the early hours of Sunday, December 7, 1941, Japan bombed Pearl Harbor. Within 24 hours of the bombing, more than 700 Japanese Americans were arrested without charges. Those were mostly immigrant men and community leaders, including Kochiyama's father Seiichi Nakahara—but some second-generation U.S. citizens like Patsy Mink's father were also arrested. Nakahara, who had surgery a week before his arrest, was detained for six weeks, which aggravated his health issues. On January 21, 1942, the day after his release, he died at home. Two months later, as a result of Executive Order 9066 (see Chapter 4), the family was forced to leave their home in San Pedro, California and relocate to a horse stable at the Santa Anita racetrack. Shortly afterward, they were moved to the WRA camp in Jerome, Arkansas. While incarcerated, Kochiyama became increasingly aware of the discrimination that she and other Japanese Americans were facing. For the first time, working with others like her, Kochiyama started to proudly see herself as a Japanese American. She and other activists wrote letters to Japanese American soldiers to show them support. This is how she met her future husband Bill Kochiyama, a private in the U.S. army.

In 1945, the war ended, and Japanese Americans were released from the WRA camps. In 1946, Kochiyama moved to New York City to marry Bill, who had just returned to the U.S. after being discharged from the military. Bill went to school while she worked as a waitress. Moving to Harlem allowed Kochiyama to meet people directly involved in the struggle for civil rights, and she became involved in various political activities.

In the summer of 1963, Kochiyama worked with the Brooklyn chapter of the Congress of Racial Equality, a civil rights organization that led campaigns including the Freedom Rides, the March on Washington, and Freedom Summer. She attended protests against racially discriminatory hiring practices, often bringing her children with her. During one protest, Kochiyama and her son Billy were among over 600 protesters arrested.

The Kochiyamas joined the Harlem Parents Committee, which called for a boycott of every Harlem school with the goal of upgrading the quality of education in the Harlem community. Despite the desegregation ruling of *Brown v. Board* a decade earlier, Harlem schools were still segregated and had inferior facilities, textbooks, and learning opportunities. The boycott was successful, and the Harlem Parents Committee, along with other civil rights groups, continued several other campaigns in the schools and community. The Harlem Parents Committee opened Freedom School, which the Kochiyama family attended each Saturday. The school exposed Kochiyama to the work of Black activists and intellectuals like James Baldwin, Fannie Lou Hamer, and W. E. B. DuBois, who helped Kochiyama develop historical and political understandings of structural racism.

Kochiyama's friendship with Malcolm X truly changed her political vision. She met Malcolm X in October of 1963 at the hearing for her arrest during a protest by the Congress of Racial Equality. Months later, she organized a meeting between Japanese atomic bomb survivors and Malcolm X in her home; this event highlights how Kochiyama and Malcolm X envisioned justice beyond U.S. borders. Malcolm X began corresponding with the Kochiyamas during his travels. His postcards show a significant evolution of his political ideas about race and class. When he founded the Organization of AfroAmerican Unity, Malcolm invited Kochiyama to join its Liberation School to take classes. She was the only Asian American in attendance and learned more about the role of racism in American society.

On February 21, 1965, Kochiyama was present in the Audubon Ballroom when Malcolm was shot and killed. She was one of the few attendees who ran onstage to help him rather than hide for safety. A *Life* magazine cover photograph shows Kochiyama cradling Malcolm X's head in his final moments. Although only 16 months passed between their meeting and his death, Malcolm X greatly influenced Kochiyama's politics, and she dedicated herself to his vision (Fujino, 2005).

INCLUDING MALCOLM X IN THE MOVEMENT

Although Malcolm X is rarely included in elementary curriculum, his part in the Civil Rights Movement of the 1950s and 1960s can and should be introduced to students in upper elementary grades. Malcolm X and the Organization of AfroAmerican Unity did not focus on racial integration and viewed nonviolence as a tactic to be used depending on the circumstances. At the same time, they were firm about the need for self-defense. Malcolm X shifted the responsibility for violence from the oppressed to the perpetrators, which made sense to Kochiyama. She was also attracted to the sense of pride that Malcolm X elicited in Black communities and to his emphasis on encouraging people to learn their own history. While she did not agree with all of Malcolm X's ideas, she was not afraid to associate with him and wanted to learn more from him.

Instead of presenting Malcolm X as oppositional to the nonviolent Martin Luther King Jr., teachers can show how both leaders adapted ideas to their contexts and experiences throughout their lives. King and Malcolm X had very different childhood experiences with racial violence. Both fought for rights for Black communities but they had different ideas for how to achieve this goal, and these ideas changed as they gained more experiences. Both were religious, and their faiths ultimately guided their visions of justice. To learn more about these revolutionary leaders, we recommend the adult-level text *The Sword and the Shield: The Revolutionary Lives of Malcolm X and Martin Luther King, Jr.* by Peniel Joseph.

Kochiyama's wide-reaching advocacy is premised on the broadest possible definition of humanity; this definition is easily tied to the work of Malcolm X and King. All of them were concerned about the injustices faced by many communities in the U.S., but they also saw the need to actively challenge injustice abroad, including injustices against the Vietnamese or other communities affected by imperialism. In 1967, King spoke about common problems in the U.S. and the world: racism, poverty, and war. Kochiyama, King, and Malcolm X's global definition of humanity and their work caring about global humanity would thematically fit within any civil rights lesson. Moreover, this information can expand traditional ideas about the Civil Rights era in the United States.

Kochiyama saw parallels between the experiences of Black Americans and of Japanese Americans in the WRA camps. The Kochiyama home in Harlem became a hub for activists, bringing her into contact with many communities and individuals, including nine-year-old Tupac Shakur, whose family were political prisoners in the U.S. In the 1970s and beyond, Kochiyama became involved in demonstrations for Puerto Rican independence. She also promoted awareness about injustices in other countries that often were a result of U.S. foreign policies (e.g., the Peruvian government's war with Peru's Indigenous and economically marginalized communities) (Kochiyama, 2004). Kochiyama and her husband were integral to the redress movement, which demanded that the U.S. government apologize and pay for the countless damages and losses experienced by formerly incarcerated Japanese Americans during World War II. Kochiyama continued actively working towards justice for a range of communities throughout her life until her passing in 2014.

In 2011, the hip hop group Blue Scholars wrote an ode to Kochiyama detailing the long arc of her life as an advocate and inspiration for challenging injustices: "Never got to talk to anybody who done lived

FIGURE 6.3 Yuri Kochiyama (1980, printed 2016) takes a stand in the streets of New York City's Chinatown neighborhood to defend the rights of Silver Palace restaurant workers. PHOTOGRAPH BY CORKY LEE, COURTESY OF THE CORKY LEE ESTATE

this . . . and still exist. Or better yet . . . she still resist" (Blue Scholars, 2011). Kochiyama was active in the civil rights struggles of the 1950s and 1960s that students commonly learn about, but her activism did not stop there. Her life is evidence that the common approach to teaching the Civil Rights Movement is too confined and superficial. The song's chorus describes a desire to be like Yuri Kochiyama, an activist who cared deeply about self-determination and liberation for all. This ode is a testament to her legacy among young activists.

Grace Lee Boggs: A Community Activist for Human Rights

Grace Lee Boggs was born above her father's restaurant in Providence, Rhode Island in 1915. Her parents were Chinese immigrants who opened a chain of Chinese restaurants in the Northeast called Chin Lee's. Boggs attended Barnard College, then continued her education at Bryn Mawr College in Pennsylvania, where she earned a Master's and a doctorate in philosophy.

Despite her education, Boggs was unable to find work with a livable wage after earning her doctorate in the 1940s. Philosophy departments in schools of higher education were dominated by white men who actively resisted the hiring of women colleagues; an *Asian American* woman colleague would have been simply unacceptable. Unable to find a position that would allow her to teach philosophy after graduation, Boggs moved to Chicago in 1940 and began working with a tenants organization. It was her first time interacting with Black communities and working with real people outside of the academic world, and it inspired her to become a movement activist in Black communities. Boggs eventually ended up in Detroit, where she became well known for her work on labor, civil, and women's rights in partnership with her husband James Boggs, a Black auto worker and political thinker. They published radical newsletters and worked to elect more Black Americans to political positions. While their efforts drew the attention and respect of Detroit community members, the Boggs also attracted the attention of the FBI, which erroneously speculated that Grace was "Afro Chinese."

SOLIDARITY

Very rarely is solidarity between communities highlighted in any curriculum. Instead, curriculum and media tend to address ethnoracial groups individually and/or emphasize conflict between communities of color. For example, during the COVID-19 pandemic, more than 75% of violence towards people of Asian descent was committed by white people (Borja & Gibson, 2020). However, the news focused on images and stories about Black individuals as the offenders. Teachers can change this narrative! In addition to teaching about people like Yuri Kochiyama and Grace Lee Boggs, thread the theme of solidarity throughout the curriculum. Ask students to look for instances of solidarity both in and out of the classroom. For example, the children's book *Today is Different* by Doua Moua (2022) tells the story of a Hmong American girl and her Black best friend as they join Black Lives Matter protests.

Due to the Boggs' deep involvement in the Black Power movement, their fight for economic justice in Detroit, and their close connections to Black Marxist scholar C. L. R. James, the FBI labeled the couple as radicals and began to surveil them (along with other prominent activists, including Martin Luther King Jr. and Rosa Parks). Undeterred, the Boggs continued writing for various causes. They worked towards racial and economic justice and equity in their city by organizing local projects. These projects included creating gardens in vacant lots, painting murals, supporting the elderly and people with disabilities in demanding services and rights, and gathering young people in Detroit to conduct activist work.

In 1992, the Boggs founded Detroit Summer, a community movement that brought together people of all ages, races, and cultures to rebuild Detroit. Detroit Summer is still active today! In 2013, a charter school in Detroit was opened in Jimmy and Grace's name with Grace Boggs' support. The Boggs School was created to "nurture creative, critical thinkers who contribute to the well-being of their communities" (The James and Grace Lee Boggs School, 2022). The Boggs School is a testament to the many ways the Boggs inspired change through their writing, conversations, and local community efforts.

MAKING MEANING OF POWERFUL QUOTES

Here we offer a few of our favorite quotes by several of the individuals spotlighted in this chapter.

> "We have to build things that we want to see accomplished, in life and in our country, based on our own personal experiences to make sure that others do not have to suffer the same discrimination." —Patsy Mink, *Honolulu Star-Bulletin* (1975)

> "You were bombed and have physical scars. We too have been bombed and you saw some of the scars in our neighborhood. We are constantly hit by the bombs of racism—which are just as devastating." —Malcolm X, addressing Hiroshima atomic bomb survivors at Yuri Kochiyama's home (1964)

"Injustice anywhere is a threat to justice everywhere."
—Martin Luther King Jr.,
"Letter from a Birmingham Jail" (1963)

These quotes offer young learners an opportunity to reflect on the activists' stances and goals, as well as on students' own lives and communities. Students can interpret and paraphrase each quote, add their own illustrations, or consider them in combination.

WORKERS' RIGHTS

Teaching about labor rights in elementary school may seem like a challenge. But some of the earliest labor laws were about children, which is one of the reasons why your students are required to be in school! Therefore, this history truly belongs in elementary grades. In Asian American communities, there is a long history of labor activism and resistance. Like most of the content included in this book, those histories tend to be missing in schools. However, popular narratives of Cesar Chavez and Mexican American farm workers in California are the perfect opportunity to include the story of the Filipino American farm workers who worked alongside them. Here, we highlight Larry Itliong, a Filipino migrant worker who initiated the Delano Grape Strike and later co-founded the United Farm Workers with Chavez. We also briefly explore other examples of Asian American involvement in worker's rights across time and place.

Larry Itliong and the Delano Grape Strike

Larry Itliong was born in the Philippines in 1913, when the country was colonized by the U.S. (see Chapter 5). The textbooks that Itliong read in school promoted the idea that the U.S. was a place where anyone who worked hard would be rewarded. Without easy access to education in his hometown, Itliong moved to the U.S. as a teenager, determined to go to college and become a lawyer. However, he quickly realized that as a non-white person, life and work in the United States would be more challenging than he was led to believe.

FIGURE 6.4 Larry Itliong, assistant director of the United Farm Workers Organizing Committee, surveys an unidentified picket line, c. 1960s.

WALTER P. REUTHER LIBRARY, ARCHIVES OF LABOR AND URBAN AFFAIRS, WAYNE STATE UNIVERSITY

He struggled financially as a migrant worker in Montana, moving up and down the West Coast from California farms to Alaska canneries, and eventually gave up his dreams of pursuing higher education (Mabalon, 2013).

Itliong experienced firsthand the exploitation of Filipino workers, who received less pay for harder jobs, were exposed to dangerous pesticides, were given little or no time off during the work day or week, lived in substandard housing, and received less food compared to white workers. Even when Itliong and fellow Filipino workers joined their white counterparts in a strike to receive better pay, the strike ended with only white workers receiving a wage increase while Filipino workers were left without jobs (see Chapter 3 for a similar story of Chinese workers who were not allowed to join unions).

This experience did not discourage Itliong from continuing his fight for justice. He joined the Agricultural Workers Organizing Committee and recruited members throughout California in 1959. When Filipino and other workers in the Committee went on strike for better working conditions, owners brought in Mexican workers. Itliong knew that the two groups would keep fighting each other while white owners continued to grow rich by exploiting both communities. Therefore, he approached Cesar Chavez and Dolores Huerta of the largely Mexican American National Farm Workers Association. Together they agreed that, if the two largest ethnic groups in agricultural work united, their chances for success would increase.

The two groups went on strike in vineyards around Delano, California from 1965 until 1970. Many workers lost their homes since they lived in company housing. When growers brought in workers from other states, the strike progressed to calling for boycotts with the support of other workers' unions. This brought a lot of attention to and general support for the farm workers. During the strike, the Agricultural Workers Organizing Committee and National Farm Workers Association merged to become the United Farm Workers. The United Farm Workers finally won concessions from the growers, such as higher pay and medical insurance. The legacy of the Delano Grape Strike and the many people who sacrificed for those efforts should be taught in all their fullness.

AGBAYANI VILLAGE

When the Delano Grape Strike ended, many Filipino workers were elderly with little to no retirement savings. As farmworkers, they could not rely on retirement funds or pension plans from their employers or the government. California laws at that time did not allow mixed race marriages and actually passed antimiscegenation laws that made such marriages illegal. As a result, many Filipino laborers remained single and had no families to care for them. Under the leadership of Larry Itliong and Philip Vera Cruz, the United Farm Workers built a retirement village for many of these men in Delano, CA. They named it Paolo Agbayani Village, after a Filipino worker who died while picketing. Agbayani Village served as a model for other such residences and continues to provide a dignified retirement for elderly workers today.

FIGURE 6.5 Filipino farmworkers gather to plan construction of Agbayani Village, Delano, California, October 1972. The Paolo Agbayani Village was created to house retired Filipino farm workers who had no family in the United States. WALTER P. REUTHER LIBRARY, ARCHIVES OF LABOR AND URBAN AFFAIRS, WAYNE STATE UNIVERSITY.

Young children have a strong sense of what is fair and unfair, but they often underestimate the type of labor that is required in order for them to enjoy everyday foods. A discussion about what students know about how food gets from farms to their tables is a natural starting point that combines concepts from science and geography. For a striking journey backwards from table to farm, watch the music video for La Santa Cecilia's cover of the Beatles song "Strawberry Fields Forever," which begins with a strawberry cake then explores how the strawberries were harvested. Ask students which parts of the process are unfamiliar to them, then discuss the various skills required of workers at each stage of the harvest and the challenges such work may present.

Math skills can be utilized to compare workers' hourly wages and the prices that consumers may pay for items. *Journey for Justice: The Life of Larry Itliong* (Mabalon & Romasanta, 2018) notes the amount of money that Itliong made doing different types of manual labor. Revisit the Mathematics section in Chapter 1 for details on using *Journey for Justice* to teach place value through a lesson created by educators Gloria Gallardo and Cathery Yeh (2022).

If time allows, look online for a short clip from the CNN show *Inside Man* featuring filmmaker Morgan Spurlock picking oranges as a day laborer. Spurlock explains how the work impacts his body; graphics featured in the video illustrate how much workers are expected to pick each day and how their pay is dependent on that amount. To make clear how farm workers continue to be exploited today, students can research contemporary produce boycotts to learn about current injustices in the fields. They can also learn about organizations that advocate for more just working conditions, such as the Coalition for Immokalee Workers, and read about agricultural cooperatives.

RECOMMENDED RESOURCES ABOUT THE DELANO GRAPE STRIKE

- *Delano Manongs* (documentary) directed by Melissa Aroy
- *Journey for Justice: The Life of Larry Itliong* by Dawn B. Mabalon and Gayle Romasanta
- *Viva la Causa* (documentary) available online, teaching guide available at http://www.learningforjustice.org
- Labor Archives at the Walter P. Reuther Library at Wayne State University
- Welga Archive at the University of California Davis

DISCUSSION QUESTIONS ABOUT LABOR RIGHTS

- What were some of the labor conditions that workers wanted to change?
- What are some ways that workers have fought for change?
- What did solidarity look like during the Delano Grape Strike?
- According to activists like Larry Itliong, why might solidarity be important in the struggle for labor rights?

Other Asian American Labor Histories

Many of the earliest Asian communities in the United States were recruited to work as laborers (see Chapter 3). From the beginning, resistance and activism were a part of Asian American life. For example, after years of being underpaid and subjected to racial prejudice, Chinese railroad workers in the Sierra Nevada mountains engaged in mass collective action in June 1867. Days after an accidental tunnel explosion claimed the lives of five Chinese and a white man, 3,000 Chinese workers spread across nearly 30 miles laid down their tools and refused to work for a week. Although the Chinese workers were not successful in negotiating wages equal to white workers, Central Pacific Railroad slowly increased wages for skilled and experienced workers after the strike (Chang, 2019).

Elementary students are often introduced to labor activism through stories about garment workers' rights, whether through the picturebook *Brave Girl: Clara and the Shirtwaist Makers' Strike of 1909* (Markel, 2013) or through nonfiction texts about the Triangle Shirtwaist Factory. While these famous examples took place in New York City in the early 1900s, by the 1930s the garment industry was the largest employer in San Francisco's Chinatown. Like garment workers in New York City, Chinatown workers labored in sweatshop conditions for meager wages. In 1938, the Chinese Ladies Garment Workers Union Local 361 successfully went on strike to improve working conditions and to demand increased wages from their employer, National Dollar Stores. However, the owner of National Dollar Stores sold his facility to Golden Gate Manufacturing, a "new" company led by the National Dollar Stores factory manager. This change of ownership allowed Golden Gate to ignore the union contract. Workers went on strike again for 15 weeks until the owner agreed to provide a 5% raise, 40-hour workweek, and to enforce better health and safety conditions (Yung, 1999).

Moving to the contemporary period, the New York Taxi Workers Alliance has a majority membership of South Asian drivers. In 1998, under the leadership of Indian American Bhairavi Desai, they organized a successful strike against the Taxi and Limousine Commission that was increasing insurance costs and charging unfair fines to drivers. About 98% of all taxi drivers in New York participated in this strike, with many of the planning meetings taking place in ethnic restaurants. The diversity of their membership was also reflected in their memos, which were written in multiple South Asian languages. Historian Rohma Khan (2018) notes this moment as significant in showing how South Asian communities that have historically been in conflict were able to come together over mutual labor interests as immigrants in the United States.

More recently, Taiwanese American labor organizer Ai Jen Poo co-founded the National Domestic Workers Alliance in 2007. The Alliance fought to pass state legislation establishing and protecting the rights of domestic workers, such as minimum wage, overtime pay, safe working conditions, and protections from sexual harassment. During the COVID-19 pandemic, they raised over $20 million dollars to provide emergency assistance to domestic workers who lost jobs or needed protective equipment to continue their work caring for vulnerable populations.

This is just a small sampling of regional and national efforts to support workers' rights. While these specific examples involve Asian American workers and leaders, it is important to emphasize labor solidarity, both in terms of diverse ethnoracial workers *and* consumers who buy products and pay for services. The classic picturebook *Click, Clack, Moo* (Cronin, 2000) is an excellent primer on boycotts and protests for young learners that can launch questions for further exploration about labor rights in the past and present.

LGBTQ+ RIGHTS

At the time of writing, at least 45 anti-LGBTQ bills have been signed into state law. Some of these laws threaten parents who support their transgender children. Others claim to protect parental rights and allow parents, *not* teachers, to determine what is appropriate curriculum for children in the classroom with regard to anything related to sexuality or "morality," with specific language targeting conversations about LGBTQ+ identities. Countless school districts have similarly constrained teachers from representing LGBTQ+ figures in curricula through book bans and in classroom spaces by discouraging the display of photographs of families with same-sex partners. Often, these constraints are amplified at the elementary level by politicians and conservative groups. Their purpose is to erase LGBTQ+ representation, but they code this desire with language such as "age appropriate content" or protecting the "innocence" of children. The reality is that teachers are responsible for *all* the children who cross through their classroom doors, who represent a range of races, ethnicities, religions, socioeconomic classes, gender expressions and identities, sexual orientations, and abilities.

While we recognize that having conversations that forefront LGBTQ+ communities may be considered controversial in some contexts, we want to be clear these identities are not actually controversial. LGBTQ+ people have always been a part of communities throughout history, all around the world. In this section, we highlight three Asian American activists who have worked in distinctly different ways to support Asian American communities as well as LGBTQ+ rights.

Kiyoshi Kuromiya, Activist Across Communities

Like many of the Asian American activists detailed in this chapter, Kiyoshi Kuromiya fought for many issues, both on a personal level and for broader humanity. He was born in the Heart Mountain, Wyoming WRA camp in 1943. After Japanese Americans were released, Kuromiya grew up in California where he had limited LGBTQ+ mentors and resources. He recalls his experience of coming out as a young boy of 11, when he was accused by police of "consorting in a public park" (Gossett & Lincoln, n. d.) with another boy.

Kuromiya became active in the Civil Rights Movement in the 1960s. He led a voter registration march in Alabama, where he was beaten by police and hospitalized. He spoke of this experience as revealing what it was like to be "black in Mississippi or a peasant in Vietnam" (Vaughan, 1968, p. 92). Kuromiya's activism was clearly both local and global. He drew attention to the use of napalm by the U.S. government on Vietnamese civilians by announcing a fake demonstration of napalm use on a dog in Philadelphia. When protesters arrived, the largest protest group to have gathered in that city during the Vietnam War, they were congratulated for saving one dog and urged to focus on the lives of countless human beings, including children, being targeted in Vietnam.

Kuromiya represented the LGBTQ+ community as a delegate to the Blank Panther Party and was integral in using the internet to disseminate information about AIDS when many healthcare institutions avoided informing the public about the disease. He also brought attention to and fought for people of color who were largely not being represented in AIDS research. While most of these topics are more likely to be addressed in secondary curriculum, Kuromiya can inspire a justice-oriented lesson around access and medicine for younger learners. Students can be inspired by Kuromiya's activism, and can research contemporary issues related to health care inequities and access. For example, young learners can investigate why certain essential medicines and treatments are harder for some individuals to access than others; insulin is one example that has received substantial news coverage. Students can also calculate the costs of medicines, learn how those costs are decided, and how health insurance impacts their affordability. Kuromiya is an example of an Asian American who worked to change health care inequity through technology and protest.

Helen Zia, Activist Writer

Helen Zia, a Chinese American journalist, was born in New Jersey to parents who met in New York City's Chinatown. Zia was born in 1952, before the Hart–Celler Act allowed significantly more Asian immigration, when the Asian American population was still very low. Her father made sure she knew enough of China's history to disrupt negative perceptions of China in the U.S., but much of her childhood

FIGURE 6.6 Vincent Chin's mother, Lily Chin being comforted. PHOTOGRAPH BY CORKY LEE, COURTESY OF THE CORKY LEE ESTATE

understanding of race was within the Black–white binary (Zia, 2000). After Zia graduated from Princeton University, she moved to Detroit, where she worked in the auto industry and began her journalism career.

As a journalist, Zia brought attention to the 1982 racially-motivated killing of Vincent Chin in Detroit. Chin and his friends were celebrating his bachelor party at a strip club when they had a racist altercation with two disgruntled auto workers. The auto workers assaulted Chin so severely that he went into a coma and died days later. His assailants were fined $3,000 and placed on 3 years of probation. They served *no* jail time for their horrific actions. When Zia read about this case, not only did she write her own news story, but she helped organize a multiethnic, multiracial and multireligious group to work towards finding justice for Chin and his surviving family. The Chin case was only the beginning of her long career as an investigative journalist, editor, and author.

Zia and her partner were also one of the first same-sex couples to marry in California when the state finally instituted marriage equality in 2008. In fact, a photograph of the two saying their vows was published in a *New York Times* article about the California law. Shortly after her marriage took place, voters in California tried to limit marriage to a man and woman only. Zia testified as an expert witness during the Supreme Court case *Hollingsworth v. Perry* (2013) which ensured marriage equality in California. Zia continues to be a voice for human and women's rights in the United States and around the world. She exemplifies the important role of journalists in spreading awareness about civil rights and injustice.

Sameer Jha, Youth Activist

Activism does not have to wait until adulthood; youth advocate Sameer Jha is an excellent example of how young people can initiate change in their communities. After dealing with bullying at their California school in 2016 due to their gender expression, Jha founded The Empathy Alliance at age 14 to support LGBTQ+ youth programming. Jha convinced leaders at their predominantly Asian American former middle school to create the school's first Gay-Straight Alliance, to provide queer literature in the library, and to offer professional development to teachers. By 2018, The Empathy Alliance shared LGBTQ+ curriculum and resources with all 42 schools and 35,000 students in Jha's hometown school district. That same year, at age 16, Jha published *Read This,*

Save Lives: A Teacher's Guide to Creating Safer Classrooms for LGBTQ+ Students (2018) in an effort to make schools safer spaces for all students.

While Jha's advocacy is deeply focused on changing homophobic and cis-heteronormative school environments, they also want to encourage conversations about gender and sexuality in South Asian American communities, particularly given the lack of representation of LGBTQ+ Asian Americans in popular culture. Fortunately, this is starting to change, albeit slowly: in 2019, transgender Indian American actress Aneesh Seth starred as a transgender character in the Marvel series *Jessica Jones*; Indian American actor Kal Penn came out in 2021; and Pakistani Canadian Bilal Baig became the first queer South Asian Muslim character to lead a primetime Canadian television series in 2021 with their show *Sort Of.* Additionally, organizations have been created to support LGBTQ+ members of South Asian American communities, like Desi Rainbow and the Muslim Alliance for Sexual and Gender Diversity. Together, these shifts in pop culture representation, curricular resources, and community organization can offer today's LGBTQ+ youth the supports that Jha was missing in their early years of school.

CURRENT EVENTS AND SOLIDARITY NOW

Contemporary narratives of activism and resistance are important in all classrooms. Learning about activism in the past and the present allows students to understand why things are the way they are and what must be changed today. For instance, immigration exclusion by race meant that only educated or wealthy people from Asia could come to the United States. Knowing this helps explain the number of Asian and Asian Americans in the STEM field as well as the model minority myth. Immigration laws that barred Asians, Africans, and Latin Americans from entering the U.S. for several decades make clear the numeric dominance of whites in our country today. Past efforts for change show us what *was* possible and effective, while efforts for change now show us what *is* possible, and provide space for students to dream of what *can be* possible.

In recent years, there have been many accusations of educators training students to become activists. As social studies scholars, we consider informed action to be a crucial final component of any inquiry (see Chapter 1 for the role of informed action in the C3 Framework). As almost anyone in public education (and many people in private education as well) can attest, the world is *not* a fair and just place. We want our students to be passionate and informed members of their communities in and out of the classroom no matter the political climate, and that involves being active citizens in our democratic society.

RECOMMENDED CHILDREN'S LITERATURE ABOUT TAKING INFORMED ACTION

- *Art of Protest: Creating, Discovering, and Activating Art for Your Revolution* by De Nichols, illustrated by Diana Dagadita, Molly Mendoza, Olivia Twist, Saddo, and Diego Becas
- *Enough!: 20 Protesters Who Changed America* by Emily Easton, illustrated by Ziyue Chen
- *I Walk with Vanessa* by Kerascoët
- *Just Help!: How to Build a Better World* by Sonia Sotomayor, illustrated by Angela Dominguez
- *Librarian on the Roof!* by M. G. King, illustrated by Stephen Gilpin
- *No Voice Too Small: Fourteen Young Americans Making History* by Lindsay H. Metcalf, Keilva V. Dawson, and Jeanette Bradley, illustrated by Jeanette Bradley
- *Peaceful Fights for Equal Rights* by Rob Sanders, illustrated by Jared Andrew Schorr
- *Rise Up!: The Art of Protest* by Jo Rippon
- *Say Something!* by Peter H. Reynolds
- *Sometimes People March* by Tessa Allen
- *Speak Up* by Miranda Paul, illustrated by Ebony Glenn
- *Speak Up!: Speeches by Young People to Empower and Inspire* by Adora Svitak, illustrated by Camila Pinheiro
- *Together We March: 15 Protest Movements that Marched into History* by Leah Henderson, illustrated by Tyler Feder
- *What Can a Citizen Do?* by Dave Eggers, illustrated by Shawn Harris

DISCUSSION QUESTIONS FOR TAKING INFORMED ACTION

- What are parts of your community that you love?
- What are parts of your community that you want to change?
- What are steps you can take to make the change happen? Who can you ask for help?

- Who is already doing work to make changes in your community? How can you be an ally to them?
- How can you let people in your community know that you are interested in helping them?

ASIAN AMERICAN CIVIL RIGHTS ORGANIZATIONS

- 18 Million Rising (https://18millionrising.org)
- Asian Americans Advancing Justice (https://www.advancingjustice-aajc.org)
- Asian Pacific American Labor Alliance, AFL-CIO (https://www.apalanet.org)
- Asian Pride Project (http://asianprideproject.org)
- Asian Solidarity Collective (https://www.asiansolidaritycollective.org)
- Desis Rising Up and Moving (https://www.drumnyc.org)
- MPower Change (https://www.mpowerchange.org)
- National Asian Pacific American Women's Forum (https://www.napawf.org)
- National Queer Asian Pacific Islander Alliance (https://www.nqapia.org)
- Sikh Coalition (https://www.sikhcoalition.org)
- South Asian Americans Leading Together (https://saalt.org)
- The Visibility Project (http://www.visibilityproject.org)

One starting point for teaching about Asian American activism and resistance is to expand the teaching of the Civil Rights Movement (usually confined to Black Americans in the 1950s and 1960s) to what scholar Jacqueline Dowd Hall (2005) refers to as the "long Civil Rights Movement." The denial of certain rights on the basis of various identities has affected every ethnoracial group. Throughout the academic year, support your students in asking, "Who is missing in this history?" This question can spark student investigation into what these groups did to make themselves seen and heard, even if those narratives are missing in the curriculum. As you support this work, be careful to avoid assertions that you or anyone else can be a "voice for the voiceless." Instead, consider Arundhati Roy's (2004) powerful dismissal of this notion: "There is really no such thing as the 'voiceless.' There are only the deliberately silenced, or the preferably unheard" (p. 1). As much as possible, center the stories and experiences of the group in question rather than other people's interpretations of those stories and experiences.

Specific to Asian American activism and resistance, teaching the long Civil Rights Movement means extending discussions about civil rights to before *and* after the 1950s and 1960s. For example, teaching about the rights of women should begin with Black abolitionist women such as Sojourner Truth and should extend far beyond the 19th Amendment to Patsy Mink and the passage of Title IX through today. School desegregation, which we detail in Chapter 7, offers another opportunity to include Asian American struggles in the fight for public schooling. And the court case *Lau v. Nichols* was brought by Chinese students who did not speak English and made clear that students who did not speak the language of instruction were being deprived of their right to an education. The Supreme Court's decision in favor of the Chinese American plaintiffs led to the significant development of bilingual education and linguistic support for *all* English language learners across the United States.

ACTIVISM AND RESISTANCE MATTER

The reality of teaching in a politicized time and place means that we may not be able to teach everything we want in the ways we want to. But that's one reason why teaching is an intellectual, creative, *and* courageous act. We know that the Asian American activism and resistance we outlined in this chapter parallels the many ways that teachers do what is best for their students. We hope some of the stories, individuals, organizations, and texts we spotlighted here inspire your students to take informed action in your communities in whatever ways they can. Indeed, democracy is not a spectator sport!

Endnote

1. While "Third World" was a term popularized by student activists in the late 1960s who fought for campus reforms and ethnic studies, it is

generally considered derogatory, as it was developed by French demographer Alfred Sauvy to describe nations with little global political influence. Various terms have been used since then to classify countries based on their socioeconomic status and stability; the current terms that we suggest using are "Global North" and "Global South."

7

Contention and Complexity

Asian American experiences are diverse, and like any ethnoracial group, contentions exist among and within Asian American communities. In this chapter, we provide instructional approaches and resources to teach a complete history that recognizes the contention and complexity present in Asian American experiences. But why should we teach about contention and complexity in the first place?

WHY TEACH ABOUT CONTENTION AND COMPLEXITY?

There is no single Asian American experience. Asian American experiences have always been as diverse as the people who make up Asian America. Regarding anti-Black racism, for example, Asian Americans have stood in solidarity with Black communities to demand justice. During the 1968 Third World Liberation Front strike (see Chapter 6), Asian American college students joined Black and other marginalized student groups to fight against Eurocentric curriculum. In the case of the #Asians4BlackLives, Asian American communities joined the Black Lives Matter movement and protested police violence against Black communities.

There are, however, moments when Asian Americans have been and continue to be complicit in sustaining anti-Black racism. Examples include the *U.S. v. Thind* (1923) and *Lum v. Rice* (1927) cases, when Asian immigrants relied on white supremacy in their fight for naturalized citizenship or integrated schools, as well as the recent case of

DOI: 10.4324/9781032662695-7

Chinese right-wing organizing against affirmative action at Harvard University. In 2014, a group called Students for Fair Admissions sued Harvard University, arguing that Harvard used a "racial quota" that discriminated against Asian American applicants. Although about 70% of Asian Americans support affirmative action, some conservative Asian Americans oppose race-conscious college admissions (Lee et al., 2021).

Asian Americans have also responded to settler colonialism in different ways. Many Asian residents in Hawai'i, for example, voted for Hawai'i statehood in the 1950s. Asian economic and political elites have also pushed for U.S. defense industry and tourism-driven land development in Hawai'i. These actions by Asian Americans are at the expense of the Native Hawaiian decolonization movement (Fujikane & Okamura, 2008). In contrast, there were and are cases when Asian Americans stood in solidarity with Indigenous Peoples. Local Japanese Women for Justice, a collective of Japanese American women in Hawai'i, publicly spoke out against Japanese American political elites like Senator Daniel Inouye and their actions against Native Hawaiian sovereignty (Yoshinaga & Kossa, 2000).

Contentions and divisions exist among various Asian ethnic groups as well. In the early 1900s, Chinese and Korean immigrants organized boycotts of Japanese goods when Japan invaded and occupied their homeland. Later, when Japanese Americans were forcibly removed to WRA prison camps during World War II (see Chapter 4), some Asian Americans criticized this unjust action and supported Japanese Americans in whatever ways they could. For instance, they helped by looking after the homes, stores, or farms of their Japanese American neighbors who were jailed in remote camps. However, some Chinese and Korean immigrants, particularly those who identified with their ancestral countries that had been conquered by Japan, transferred their hatred of Japan to Japanese Americans, endorsing the unjust government action against Japanese American communities (Niiya, 2017).

As these examples illustrate, Asian American experiences are diverse and complex. Teaching only positive stories or telling a single story of any group of Asian Americans does not help students develop an accurate understanding of Asian American histories. According to Black history education scholar LaGarrett King (2020), "To represent Black humanity . . . we should not merely teach and present positive Black histories and images. We need to introduce a complete history that addresses humanity that includes Black people's deficiencies and vulnerabilities" (p. 340). We agree wholeheartedly. Anti-Black racism in Asian American communities and Asian American complicity in settler colonialism are particularly important to discuss if we want students to learn about the challenges and possibilities of creating interracial coalitions for justice. In this chapter, we suggest three lessons to teach a more complete and complex history of Asian Americans.

COMPLEXITY IN THE ASIAN AMERICAN STRUGGLE FOR CITIZENSHIP

In Chapter 4, we noted that only "free white persons" were allowed to become naturalized citizens after the founding of the United States. Then, the right of naturalization was extended to "aliens of African nativity and persons of African descent" after the Civil War. We also described *Ozawa v. U.S.* (1922) and *U.S. v. Thind* (1923)—two Supreme Court cases brought by Asian immigrants in their quest for citizenship in the face of discriminatory naturalization laws. Building on this knowledge, let's turn to complexity and contention in the Asian American struggles for citizenship.

The *Ozawa* and *Thind* cases clearly reveal Asian American agency and resistance against discrimination. However, it is important to note that Ozawa's and Thind's pursuit of citizenship rights did not challenge the racist laws that restricted naturalization to "free white persons" and "aliens of African nativity and persons of African descent." Instead, both Ozawa and Thind argued that *they* should be considered *white,* due to their pale skin color in the case of Ozawa or by belonging to the Caucasian race as Thind argued. Of course, it is not hard to recognize that, if Ozawa and Thind tried to gain citizenship by challenging the racist law itself, their cases likely would not have reached the Supreme Court at all. However, by complying with the racist law and contesting the denial of their whiteness, both men were complicit in supporting the oppressive structure of white supremacy.

To explore this complexity with students, ask them to consider the difficult choice Asian immigrants had to make in their quests for equal rights to become U.S. citizens. Begin with students reading a brief biographical summary about Ozawa and Thind (see Chapter 4). Then, have students analyze the two court cases using a graphic organizer (see Table 7.1). After conducting a short court case analysis, use the suggested questions in the box to facilitate a whole-class discussion. Make sure that students consider the challenges Asian immigrants faced in a white-dominant world as well as their complicity in sustaining white supremacy when choosing to comply with the legal status quo in their fight for equal rights.

TABLE 7.1 Court Case Analysis of Ozawa and Thind

NATURALIZATION ACT OF 1906: Only "free white persons" and "aliens of African nativity and persons of African descent" have the right to naturalized citizenship.	
Ozawa v. U.S. (1922)	***U.S. v. Thind*** (1923)
Ozawa's argument Ozawa argued his skin was as white or whiter than many other white people and thus, he was eligible for naturalization.	**Thind's argument** Thind argued that he should be eligible for naturalization because he was of the Caucasian race.
Supreme Court's argument "The federal and state courts, in an almost unbroken line, have held that the words 'white person' were meant to indicate only a person of what is popularly known as the Caucasian race." "The appellant, in the case now under consideration, however, is clearly of a race which is not Caucasian . . ."	**Supreme Court's argument** "It may be true that the blond Scandinavian and the brown Hindu have a common ancestor in the dim reaches of antiquity, but the average man knows perfectly well that there are unmistakable and profound differences between them today . . ." "What we now hold is that the words 'free white persons' are words of common speech, to be interpreted in accordance with the understanding of the common man, synonymous with the word 'Caucasian' only as that word is popularly understood".
• What was Ozawa's argument for his right to naturalized citizenship? • What was the Supreme Court's argument to deny Ozawa naturalized citizenship? • What was Thind's argument for his right to naturalized citizenship? • What was the Supreme Court's argument to deny Thind naturalized citizenship? • How did the Supreme Court's definition of "white" change from the *Ozawa* case to the *Thind* case?	

Created by Sohyun An & Esther Kim

DISCUSSION QUESTIONS ABOUT THE OZAWA AND THIND CASES

- Why do you think the court used different definitions of "white" in the *Ozawa* and *Thind* cases? Do you think it was fair or right?
- Why do you think both Ozawa and Thind argued that they were white instead of challenging the racist laws that excluded Asian immigrants in the first place?
- If you were Ozawa or Thind, how would you have responded to the racist laws and why?

COMPLEXITY IN THE ASIAN AMERICAN STRUGGLE FOR SCHOOL DESEGREGATION

Now let's move on to school segregation. You may have taught a lesson that involves reading a text about Ruby Bridges, Thurgood Marshall, or the *Brown v. Board of Education* decision. What is often missing from these lessons is the long and multiracial history of school segregation. First, the fight against school segregation in the courts goes back to 1849, when 5-year-old Sarah Roberts and her family sued the city of Boston, Massachusetts for segregating Black children in *Roberts v. Boston*. After 1849, there were more than 90 court cases in which Black families and communities across the country challenged separate and unequal schooling prior to the landmark *Brown v. Board of Education* decision (Martinez-Cola, 2022).

Second, the struggle against school segregation goes beyond the Black–white racial binary (Martinez-Cola, 2022). Alice Piper, a 15-year-old Paiute girl, and her community challenged the Big Pine school district in California for denying Indigenous students entrance into public schools in the 1924 *Piper v. Big Pine School District* case. Most Mexican American children in California were forced to attend "Mexican only" schools in the early 1900s. Sylvia Mendez and her family, along with several other Mexican American families, challenged segregated and unequal schooling in the 1946 *Mendez v. Westminster* case. Asian Americans were also no strangers to the history of school (de)segregation. Here are two pivotal Asian American court cases related to this fight.

Tape v. Hurley (1885)

Joseph and Mary Tape immigrated from China and had a successful business in California. In 1884, they tried to enroll Mamie, their 8-year-old U.S.-born daughter, in Spring Valley Primary School, the white school in their neighborhood. The school principal refused to admit Mamie because she was Chinese. Although state law guaranteed all children admission to public schools, the city of San Francisco had excluded Chinese American children from public schools for more than a decade. The Tapes found the exclusion unfair and sued the San Francisco Board of Education. The Superior Court ruled in favor of the Tape family, declaring that she should be able to attend her local public school. On appeal, the state Supreme Court upheld the 1885 lower court decision in *Tape v. Hurley.*

Dissatisfied with the ruling, the superintendent of San Francisco Andrew Moulder lobbied the state legislature to amend the state's school law by adding the line: "trustees shall have the power . . . to establish separate schools for children of Mongolian or Chinese descent. When such separate schools are established Chinese or Mongolian children must not be admitted into any other schools" (CA Assembly Bill, 1885, p. 100). Mary Tape (1885) protested by writing an open letter to a local newspaper:

> Mamie Tape will never attend any of the Chinese schools of your making! Never!!! I will let the world see sir what justice there is when it is governed by the race of prejudiced men! Just because she is of Chinese descent, not because she doesn't dress like you because she does. Just because she is descended from Chinese parents. I guess she is more of an American than a good many of you that is going to prevent her being educated. (para. 2)

Regardless, the school board quickly opened a segregated school for Chinese American students in San Francisco and ordered the Tapes and other Chinese American children to attend that school. Mamie and her younger brother Frank were among the first students who had to attend the Chinese primary school when it opened in Chinatown on April 13, 1885.

Lum v. Rice (1927)

California was not the only place where Chinese American children faced educational discrimination. After the Civil War, dominant whites in the South tried to maintain their power over freed Black Americans by encouraging Chinese and other people of color to work for them (Lee, 2015). In this context, some Chinese migrants began to move to the Jim Crow South, and soon a question arose: Where should Chinese American children go to school there? In Mississippi, the state constitution stated that separate schools were to be provided for the "white" and "colored" races. Conventionally, the term "colored" meant Black in the South. Excluded from this racial binary, Chinese immigrants taught their children at home or sent them to China for education. Some were able to send their children to the local white school if there were only one or two Chinese families living in the district and white residents did not consider them a threat.

Martha Lum's story unfolded against this backdrop. Her parents, Katherine and Jeu Gong Lum, migrated from China and settled in Rosedale, Mississippi, where they ran a grocery store. During the 1923–1924 academic year, 8-year-old Martha and her sister Berda attended the all-white Rosedale public school in their neighborhood. On the first day of the next school year, they were told that they were no longer welcome at the school.

Martha's parents filed suit in local court, arguing that their daughters were not "colored" and, as U.S.-born citizens, they had the right to attend a public school. The county ruled in favor of the Lum family, but the school district's board of trustees appealed to the state Supreme Court, which reversed the previous decision in *Rice v. Lum* (1925), stating:

> We think that the constitutional convention used the word "colored" in the broad sense rather than the restricted sense; its purpose being to provide schools for the white or Caucasian race, to which schools no other race could be admitted, carrying out the broad dominant purpose of preserving the *purity and integrity of the white race* [emphasis added] and its social policy. (p. 786)

The Lum family appealed, and the case went to the federal Supreme Court. Gong Lum argued that Martha should not have to attend the school for colored children in Mississippi because " 'colored' describes only one race, and that is the negro" (Lum v. Rice, 1927, p. 79 . . .). Because his daughter was "pure Chinese," Gong Lum argued that she ought to have been classified with white people rather than with Black people (Lum v. Rice, 1927). The Court rejected this reasoning. Citing *Plessy v. Ferguson,* the federal court said that the states had the authority to establish "separate but equal" schools without violating the 14th Amendment. Frustrated with the decision, the Lum family moved to a town in Arkansas where Martha and her siblings could attend a white school.

It is important to note that, although the Lums tried very hard to provide their daughters with access to a quality education, their lawsuit did not challenge the *constitutionality* of segregated schools. Instead, the Lums challenged their daughter's classification as colored and argued that *they* should be eligible to attend a white school. The Tape family also did not challenge the educational policies of segregated schools; instead, they, too, sought to gain admission to a white school. In doing so, the Tape and Lum cases show the complexity of Asian American struggles in schooling. Caught between the Black–white racial binary, Asian Americans had to choose whether to challenge white supremacy by seeking school desegregation for *all* races or to align with white supremacy by seeking admission to a segregated white school by distinguishing themselves as non-Black.

Students can explore this complexity through an inquiry-based court case analysis. First, summarize the stories of Mamie Tape and Martha Lum drawing from the historical content provided above. You can find photos of Tape, Lum, and their respective families at the Smithsonian National Museum of American History (https://americanhistory.si.edu/brown/history/2-battleground/detail/tape-family.html) and Stanford University Libraries (https://exhibits.stanford.edu/riseup/feature/martha-and-berda-lum). Next, guide students in analyzing the two court cases via a graphic organizer (Table 7.2), then facilitate a class discussion with the questions suggested in the box that follows. Make sure that students identify and discuss the challenges Asian Americans faced in a white-dominant world and the difficult choices they had to make: Join the collective struggle to fight white supremacy or sustain white supremacy by resorting to the status quo in their fight for equal rights?

TABLE 7.2 Court Case Analysis of Tape and Lum

Tape v. Hurley (1885)	*Lum v. Rice* (1927)
California School Law of 1880 "Every school, unless otherwise provided by law, must be open for the admission of all children between six and 21 years of age residing in the district."	**Mississippi State Constitution in Early 1900S** Separate schools were to be provided for the "White" and "colored" races.
San Francisco School District 1884 Provided segregated public schools for whites, African Americans, and Native Americans, but not for Asian American students.	**Rosedale Public School** Allowed Martha and her sister to attend the all-white school in 1924. But next year, the school did not allow Martha and her sister because they were not white.
Tape Family's Argument As a U.S.-born citizen, Mamie Tape had the right to attend a public school.	**Lum Family's Argument** Martha was not "colored" and, as a U.S.-born citizen, she had the right to attend a public school.
California State Supreme Court Decision "To deny a child, born of Chinese parents in this State, entrance to the public schools would be a violation of the law of the State and the Constitution of the United States."	**Mississippi State Supreme Court Decision** "We think that the constitutional convention used the word 'colored' in the broad sense rather than the restricted sense; its purpose being to provide schools for the white or Caucasian race, to which schools no other race could be admitted, carrying out the broad dominant purpose of preserving the purity and integrity of the white race and its social policy."
California State Assembly In response to the court ruling, the state assembly passed a bill to establish separate schools for children of "Mongolian or Chinese" descent and, once such schools were established, those children would not be admitted into any other schools.	**U.S. Supreme Court Decision** "A child of Chinese blood, born in, and a citizen of the United States, is not denied the equal protection of the laws by being classed by the State among the colored races who are assigned to public school separate from those provided for the whites, when equal facilities for education are afforded to both classes."

continues

Tape v. Hurley (1885)	*Lum v. Rice* (1927)
Result The San Francisco school district quickly opened a Chinese primary school and ordered Mamie and other Chinese American children to attend the school.	**Result** Frustrated with the court decision, Martha's family moved to Arkansas and settled in a town where Martha and her siblings could attend a white school.
• What was the Tape family's argument for Mamie's right to attend a white school? • What was the court's argument to rule in favor of the Tape family? • How did the San Francisco school district respond to the court decision? • What was Lum family's argument for Martha's right to attend a white school? • What was the court's argument to rule against the Lum family?	

Created by Sohyun An

DISCUSSION QUESTIONS ABOUT THE TAPE AND LUM CASES

- What challenges did the Tapes and the Lums face and why?
- What do you think about the court decisions as well as about the school districts' actions related to these families?
- Why do you think Mamie's and Martha's parents fought for their children to attend a white school? Why do you think they chose to do that instead of challenging racist laws that segregated schools based on race?
- If you were Mamie, Martha, or their parents, what would you do when the school laws segregated or excluded Asian American students from public schools?

AOKI V. DEANE (1907)

Keikichi Aoki, a Japanese American student, had a slightly different experience from Mamie Tape and Martha Lum. Unlike the Chinese, the number of Japanese immigrants was very low until the early 1900s. Japanese American children could attend white schools as long as white residents did not object. By 1910, however, the number of Japanese immigrants reached about 72,000, since they became a new source of cheap Asian labor after the passage of the Chinese Exclusion Act. As the Japanese American population grew, so did the anti-Japanese movement. Consequently, the San Francisco Board of Education ordered Japanese American students to attend the segregated school for Chinese American students instead of white schools. The Japanese immigrant community protested, keeping their children at home and appealing to the Japanese government about their mistreatment.

President Theodore Roosevelt intervened. On the morning of January 17, 1907, Aoki, accompanied by representatives of the U.S. Attorney's office, went to San Francisco's Redding School, where Principal Deane refused his entry. After this prearranged confrontation, the Attorney General filed his brief in both a Federal District Court and the State Supreme Court in *Aoki v. Deane* (1907). In the meantime, Roosevelt met with San Francisco school officials and California legislative leaders to negotiate. Ultimately the U.S. and Japanese governments settled on the Gentlemen's Agreement, which included Japan ending laborer migration to the United States in exchange for several compromises, including the San Francisco Board of Education rescinding its segregation order. By the 1920s, most of the 30,000 Japanese American students in California attended white public schools.

Unlike the Tape and Lum cases, *Aoki v. Deane* was settled out of court via political means, partly due to international politics. China held little political clout on the world stage at the turn of the 20th century, whereas Japan was a rising international power. To maintain a good relationship with Japan, the U.S. federal government intervened on behalf of Japanese Americans. This demonstrates how domestic *and* international contexts shape Asian American lives and anti-Asian racism.

COMPLEXITY IN THE ASIAN AMERICAN STRUGGLE FOR CIVIC RECOGNITION

Now, let's examine Asian American stories related to settler colonialism. One question we all need to consider is, "Are Asian Americans settlers who are responsible for U.S. settler colonialism?" It is important to note that not every Asian migrant voluntarily immigrated to the United

States for a better job and economic opportunity. Not every Asian immigrant or refugee has the privilege of choosing or being allowed to settle in the United States. Regardless of their intent or direct participation in settler colonialism, however, Asian migrants and their descendants are implicated in the building and development of the United States—a settler nation that is responsible for the ongoing displacement and dispossession of Indigenous Peoples (Fujikane & Okamura, 2008; Saranillio, 2013). We argue that this complex positionality of Asian Americans needs to be considered when teaching about Asian American histories.

Let's consider the construction of the Transcontinental Railroad. As we explained in Chapter 3, Chinese migrants played a significant role in building the railroad. They cleared trees, blasted rocks, and laid tracks. Many died during the winter when snowstorms covered construction workers and trapped them under snowdrifts. Others lost their lives while laying dynamite to create tunnels through the mountains. Once the railroad was completed, however, the Chinese workers were nowhere to be found in official photographs commemorating the occasion. They were erased from history. Teaching about the struggles and contributions of Chinese workers to the construction of the Transcontinental Railroad is therefore an act of justice to reclaim these erased and forgotten histories.

Yet, when teaching this content, we must remember the Indigenous Peoples whose displacement and dispossession were central to the railroad construction in the first place. As the Chinese were imported to the United States by capitalists in search of cheap labor, Indigenous Peoples were displaced and uprooted through wars and treaty violations to make way for railroads and white settlement (Karuka, 2019). As such, the histories of Indigenous dispossession parallel and intersect with the history of Chinese migration in the creation of the settler colonial state. Possibly without knowing and intending to do so, Chinese railroad workers contributed to the United States' violence against Indigenous Nations and Peoples.

Therefore, more accurate, responsible, and ethical lessons about the Transcontinental Railroad must bring together the Chinese migrant experiences *and* Indigenous Peoples' experiences in order to unpack their interconnected histories. Such lessons can promote solidarity against settler colonialism. We underscore that demanding national recognition of Chinese belonging in the United States and their contribution to nation-building without acknowledging Indigenous dispossession stands against Indigenous struggles for decolonization. To engage students in an inquiry into the complex Transcontinental Railroad story, we recommend using the picturebook *Coolies* alongside primary sources.

COOLIES BY YIN

A young boy learns the story of his great-great-great-grandfather Shek and Shek's little brother Wong. In the mid-1800s, Shek and Wong made the difficult sea voyage to the United States to work and support their family in China. The two brothers joined other Chinese workers, toiling under dangerous conditions as they built the Transcontinental Railroad. Later, the brothers joined fellow Chinese laborers in a strike after they found out white workers were paid more. However, the strike failed when the bosses withheld food and water. The brothers and other Chinese laborers endured dangerous tasks until the railroad was completed. However, on the day celebrating the railroad's completion, everyone but the Chinese were invited. The two brothers eventually settled in the United States and their families in China later joined them.

After reading *Coolies* (Yin, 2001) as a class, have students share their feelings, thoughts, and questions about the story. Then, go deeper into the storyline by exploring primary sources. First, regarding the page on Chinese struggles with unfair treatment, challenge students to think about possible reasons behind the mistreatment. Use Figure 7.1 to help students identify how racist beliefs about the Chinese led to the unequal treatment they experienced.

Second, reference the page about the railroad completion ceremony at Promontory Point and compare the illustration of the ceremony in *Coolies* with the 2014 photo taken by Corky Lee, who invited

FIGURE 7.1 A picture for employers. LIBRARY OF CONGRESS (HTTPS://WWW.LOC.GOV/PICTURES/ITEM/2002720432).

FIGURE 7.2 Descendants of Chinese laborers reclaim Railroad's history. PHOTOGRAPH BY CORKY LEE, COURTESY OF THE CORKY LEE ESTATE

FIGURE 7.3 Across the Continent: "Westward the Course of Empire Takes Its Way." NATIONAL GALLERY OF ART.

descendants of Chinese railroad workers to recreate the original photograph (Figure 7.2). Ask students to reflect on why Chinese railroad workers were excluded from the original ceremony in 1869 and to consider the purpose of the 2014 photo and the ceremony reenactment.

To transition to the interwoven stories of Chinese workers and Indigenous Peoples in railroad construction, ask students, "Whose land was the railroad built on?" and "Who were the original caretakers of the land before the railroad was built?" After gathering students' initial thoughts, encourage them to analyze Figure 7.3 and identify the dispossession and displacement of the Indigenous Peoples by railroad construction.

After this second round of analysis, encourage students to share their new understandings about how Chinese experiences were connected to Indigenous experiences. Then, prompt students to brainstorm an ethical and responsible way to commemorate the construction of the Transcontinental Railroad. After students share their thoughts, encourage them to generate ideas on how to take informed action to promote a more responsible remembrance of railroad history. Some possible actions are listed in the box.

RESPONSIBLE REMEMBERING OF THE TRANSCONTINENTAL RAILROAD

Option 1. Drawing inspiration from Corky Lee's historical reenactment photo, students will sketch a photo scene commemorating the construction of the Transcontinental Railroad. In designing their image, students should consider the following questions:

- What should the title of the image be?
- Who should be included in the image?
- What will these people be doing?
- What message will this image send to the viewers?

Option 2. The picturebook *Coolies* does not explicitly talk about what happened to Indigenous Peoples who lived in the areas affected by railroad construction. Students will create a page that can be inserted into *Coolies* so that the storyline will include the interconnected stories of Chinese and Indigenous Peoples. In creating the text and illustration for the page, students will need to consider what message they want to send to the readers and should conduct research on the Indigenous tribes that live/lived in the lands that the railroad passed through.

CONTENTION AND COMPLEXITY MATTER

The three topics and lessons we described in this chapter do not constitute an exhaustive approach to teaching a complete and complex history of Asian Americans. Yet, like many of the suggestions in this book, we hope they can serve as a starting point. We encourage you to continue learning about more topics while recognizing the contention and complexity in Asian American experiences.

Of course, we understand the reality of limited resources for these narratives. The court cases of Takao Ozawa, Bhagat Singh Thind,

Mamie Tape, and Martha Lum, as well as the stories of Chinese railroad workers, are not included in most states' curriculum standards or popular elementary curriculum materials. However, through primary sources and picturebooks like those recommended in this chapter, they can be easily woven into popular elementary lessons on citizenship, civil rights, school segregation, and "Westward Expansion," deepening student inquiry and sparking rich discussions about racism and settler colonialism. Teaching diverse, complex, and contentious histories of Asian America is important *and* possible.

• Epilogue •

We need to raise our voices a little more, even as they say to us "This is so uncharacteristic of you." To finally recognize our own invisibility is to finally be on the path toward visibility. Invisibility is not a natural state for anyone.

—Mitsuye Yamada, *Invisibility is an Unnatural Disaster: Reflections of an Asian American Woman*

Asian American invisibility is not a natural state. It has always been a choice—a set of decisions and omissions by many stakeholders who were intent on limiting U.S. history to the heritage of white America. We hope this book demonstrates that, as teachers, you also have a choice. You can choose to make visible the histories of Asian America in your classrooms. When we choose visibility and diverse representations, we recognize the humanity of communities whose voices have always been present, but were ignored and suppressed for too long. We make clear our commitment to teach about our pluralist democracy in all its fullness and complexity, not just the mythical stories of the powerful few.

We write this book at a time when culture wars unfortunately position this more democratic vision of teaching and learning as somehow *less* American. Nonetheless, we must fight for marginalized histories—including those of Asian Americans—to be brought to the fore. As educators Wayne Au and Moé Yonamine (2021) remind us, this "is a fight that requires solidarity—not just solidarity among Asian Americans, but with all communities battling for racial justice. It is a fight that requires us to teach and learn about each other, together, in struggle" (para. 11). We hope that the many people whose histories and work turned this book from our dream into our reality will also inspire you to teach in solidarity with Asian Americans and other communities recognizing their humanity in all elementary classrooms.

• Appendix •

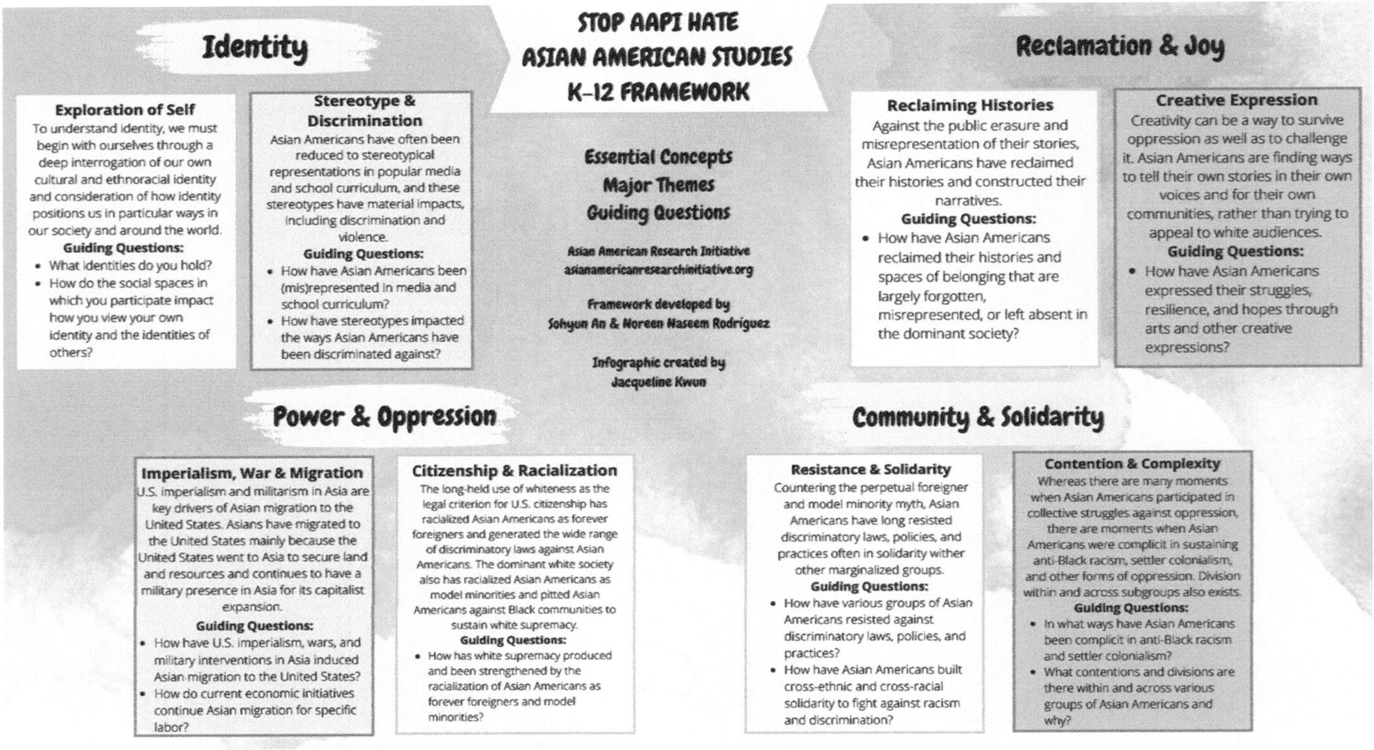

STOP AAPI HATE
ASIAN AMERICAN STUDIES
K-12 FRAMEWORK
Essential Concepts
Major Themes
Guiding Questions
Asian American Research Initiative
asianamericanresearchinitiative.org
Framework developed by
Sohyun An & Noreen Naseem Rodríguez
Infographic created by
Jacqueline Kwon
Identity
Exploration of Self
To understand identity, we must begin with ourselves through a deep interrogation of our own cultural and ethnoracial identity and consideration of how identity positions us in particular ways in our society and around the world.
Guiding Questions:
• What identities do you hold?
• How do the social spaces in which you participate impact how you view your own identity and the identities of others?
Stereotype & Discrimination
Asian Americans have often been reduced to stereotypical representations in popular media and school curriculum, and these stereotypes have material impacts, including discrimination and violence.
Guiding Questions:
• How have Asian Americans been (mis)represented in media and school curriculum?
• How have stereotypes impacted the ways Asian Americans have been discriminated against?
Reclamation & Joy
Reclaiming Histories
Against the public erasure and misrepresentation of their stories, Asian Americans have reclaimed their histories and constructed their narratives.
Guiding Questions:
• How have Asian Americans reclaimed their histories and spaces of belonging that are largely forgotten, misrepresented, or left absent in the dominant society?
Creative Expression
Creativity can be a way to survive oppression as well as to challenge it. Asian Americans are finding ways to tell their own stories in their own voices and for their own communities, rather than trying to appeal to white audiences.
Guiding Questions:
• How have Asian Americans expressed their struggles, resilience, and hopes through arts and other creative expressions?
Power & Oppression
Imperialism, War & Migration
U.S. imperialism and militarism in Asia are key drivers of Asian migration to the United States. Asians have migrated to the United States mainly because the United States went to Asia to secure land and resources and continues to have a military presence in Asia for its capitalist expansion.
Guiding Questions:
• How have U.S. imperialism, wars, and military interventions in Asia induced Asian migration to the United States?
• How do current economic initiatives continue Asian migration for specific labor?
Citizenship & Racialization
The long-held use of whiteness as the legal criterion for U.S. citizenship has racialized Asian Americans as forever foreigners and generated the wide range of discriminatory laws against Asian Americans. The dominant white society also has racialized Asian Americans as model minorities and pitted Asian Americans against Black communities to sustain white supremacy.
Guiding Questions:
• How has white supremacy produced and been strengthened by the racialization of Asian Americans as forever foreigners and model minorities?
Community & Solidarity
Resistance & Solidarity
Countering the perpetual foreigner and model minority myth, Asian Americans have long resisted discriminatory laws, policies, and practices often in solidarity wither other marginalized groups.
Guiding Questions:
• How have various groups of Asian Americans resisted against discriminatory laws, policies, and practices?
• How have Asian Americans built cross-ethnic and cross-racial solidarity to fight against racism and discrimination?
Contention & Complexity
Whereas there are many moments when Asian Americans participated in collective struggles against oppression, there are moments when Asian Americans were complicit in sustaining anti-Black racism, settler colonialism, and other forms of oppression. Division within and across subgroups also exists.
Guiding Questions:
• In what ways have Asian Americans been complicit in anti-Black racism and settler colonialism?
• What contentions and divisions are there within and across various groups of Asian Americans and why?

FIGURE A.1 (An, S. & Rodríguez, N. N. (2022, June 2). Stop AAPI Hate Asian American Studies K–12 Framework. Asian American Research Initiative. https://asianamericanresearchinitiative.org/asian-american-studies-curriculum-framework/)

STOP AAPI HATE ASIAN AMERICAN STUDIES K–12 FRAMEWORK

The figure opposite introduces the Asian American Studies Framework to K–12 educators. The framework avoids common multicultural approaches that only include communities of color and marginalized groups through disjointed, superficial lessons focused on food, fun, and festivals. It also recognizes that Asian American studies as a field is interdisciplinary and offers a thematic approach to teach Asian American studies across curriculum and throughout the year.

The framework has four components: (a) definition of the term "Asian American" and Asian American studies; (b) essential concepts and major themes within each concept; (c) teaching considerations; and (d) a glossary of terms mentioned in the essential concepts and themes. A compendium of resources is available on the website (https://asianamericanresearchinitiative.org/asian-american-studies-curriculum-framework) to support teachers in developing lessons based on the framework.

ARCHIVES

Chinese Railroad Workers in North America Project at Stanford University http://web.stanford.edu/group/chineserailroad/cgi-bin/website

Dr. Seuss Political Cartoons at UC San Diego https://library.ucsd.edu/speccoll/dswenttowar/#intro

Japanese American National Museum https://www.janm.org

Go For Broke National Education Center https://goforbroke.org/history/archives

Museum of Chinese in America https://www.mocanyc.org

Roz Payne Sixties Archive https://rozsixties.unl.edu

Pioneering Punjabis Digital Archive https://pioneeringpunjabis.ucdavis.edu

Southeast Asian Digital Archive at UMass Lowell https://www.uml.edu/research/sea-digital-archive

Southeast Asian Archive Digital Collections at UC Irvine https://seaa.lib.uci.edu/digital

Third World Liberation Front at the Berkeley Revolution Archive https://revolution.berkeley.edu/projects/twlf
United Farm Workers Image Gallery at the Walter P. Reuther Library, Wayne State University https://reuther.wayne.edu/image/tid/21
Welga Archive at the Bulosan Center for Filipino Studies at UC Davis https://welgadigitalarchive.omeka.net
Wing Luke Museum https://www.wingluke.org

ASIAN AMERICAN BIOGRAPHICAL COLLECTIONS

Amara, P., & Chi, O. (2020). *Awesome Asian Americans: 20 stars who made America amazing*. Immedium.
Cho, T. (2022). *Asian American women in science: An Asian American history book for kids*. Rockridge.
Hirahara, N. (2022). *We are here: 30 inspiring Asian Americans and Pacific Islanders who have shaped the United States*. Running Press Kids.
Wolf, A. Q. (2019). *Asian-Americans who inspire us*. *Self-published.
Yang, K. (2022). *Yes we will: Asian Americans who shaped this country*. Dial Books.

TABLE A.1 Matrix of Asian Americans Listed in This Book and Biographical Collections That Include Them

	Asian-Americans Who Inspire Us (Wolf, 2019)	*Awesome Asian Americans: 20 Stars Who Made America Amazing* (Amara & Chi, 2020)	*We Are Here: 30 Inspiring Asian Americans and Pacific Islanders Who Have Shaped the United States* (Hirahara, 2022)	*Yes We Will: Asian Americans Who Shaped This Country* (Yang, 2022)
Grace Lee Boggs			*	
H.E.R.				*
Larry Itliong	*			
Yuri Kochiyama		*		
Sunisa Lee				*
Yo-Yo Ma	*			*
Patsy Takumoto Mink	*			
Ellison Onizuka	*			

Naomi Osaka			*	
Mamie Tape				*
Philip Vera Cruz	*		*	*
Vera Wang				*
Tyrus Wong		*		
Helen Zia		*		

GUIDING QUESTIONS FOR TEXT SELECTION (CHILDREN'S LITERATURE ASSEMBLY, 2019)

- From whose perspective is the story told?
- Whose voices and experiences are present/absent from the text?
- What moral values and socio-political messages are dominant in the text?
- How are cultural practices depicted?
- What is the overall tone of the illustrations? The written narrative?
- How are the lived experiences of historically minoritized populations represented in the text?
- To what degree are complex social situations oversimplified in the text?
- How are complex relationships between characters represented in the text?

GUIDING QUESTIONS FOR STUDENT ENGAGEMENT (CHILDREN'S LITERATURE ASSEMBLY, 2019)

- How are you like ______________ [character]? How are you not like ______________ [character]?
- How does this book make you feel?
- [After selecting a particularly important spread in the book] If you could draw yourself anywhere in this picture, where would you be? What would you be doing? What would you be saying? How would you be feeling?
- Whose voices are present in this book? Whose aren't?
- Whose experiences are represented? Whose aren't?
- How are the issues in this book relevant to you today? To your community? To others?
- What does this book have to say about the world?

FREQUENTLY ASKED QUESTIONS

Here we address common questions that we are asked when working with educators. We expect our readers to hold a range of identities and cultures as well as types of educational expertise. We hope that the frequently asked questions and responses that follow will be useful in clarifying any misconceptions or misunderstandings.

Should I say Asian or Asian American?

We often hear this question when we do professional development workshops with educators. Our answer is: It depends. Is the person/place/thing from the continent of Asia? Then they are Asian. Are they in the United States? Then it could go either way. For example, Noreen's and Esther's parents are Asian immigrants; they still refer to themselves as Asian. Noreen and Esther were born, raised, and educated in the U.S.; they consider themselves Asian American. While Noreen's and Esther's parents have lived in the U.S. for over 40 years, they might refer to themselves as Americans *from* Asia, but they generally do not self-identify as Asian Americans. Some of this distinction is generational, as the term had not reached prominence when many Asian immigrants first arrived in the 1970s. It is important to know that, because the term Asian American emerged during the Civil Rights Movement, for some people the term describes their sociopolitical identity—much like the word "Chicano" may be used by Latine people who hold particular political beliefs.

Most importantly, it is important to ask people how *they* prefer to be identified. Scholars Jennifer Lee and Karthick Ramakrishnan (2020) found that most people in the United States equate Asian American with *East* Asian Americans only. While South Asian Americans considered themselves to be a part of the group, many East Asian Americans did not think the term Asian American included people from Afghanistan, Pakistan, India, Sri Lanka, Bangladesh, the Maldives, Bhutan, and Nepal. This is the case with many concepts that cast a wide net; people tend to associate sweeping terminology with very specific examples. Just as Latines may be conflated with Mexican Americans while meant to recognize people who descend from across Latin America, the umbrella term Asian American is supposed to acknowledge *all* people of Asian descent in the United States. It is important to make sure that students understand who is included in this term and teachers should ensure that South and Southeast Asian Americans are not left out.

To many Asian Americans, ethnic identity may be more important than racial identity, as it more specifically suggests essential characteristics related to history, culture, language, and even religion (Espiritu, 1992). It is crucial for teachers and students to understand that some Asian Americans identify themselves by ethnicities that do not align with a particular nationality. For example, the Hmong people's origins can be traced to the area near the Yellow River of China thousands of years ago. In recent centuries, they migrated to Southeast Asia and settled in countries including Thailand, Vietnam, and Laos. But the place where they lived most recently does not best describe the cultural and linguistic practices of their group, which are distinct from Thai, Vietnamese, and Lao languages and cultures. The largest population of Hmong Americans is in St. Paul, Minnesota, where many refugees arrived after the Vietnam War. Three-time Olympic Gymnastic medalist Sunisa "Suni" Lee is a Hmong American from St. Paul. While Hmong culture is well known in areas with high demographic concentrations like St. Paul, people in other parts of the U.S. may be entirely unfamiliar with who Hmong are and their refugee histories.

People sometimes group Asian Americans with Pacific Islanders. Why aren't you doing that?

Pacific Islanders have their own distinct histories, cultures, and languages that often have little or nothing at all to do with Asia. In the 1970s, Pacific Islanders were lumped together in the same category with Asian Americans by the U.S. Census Bureau. However, due to their vast cultural and experiential differences, the two groups were separated for the 2000 Census. When Pacific Islander data are grouped with Asian Americans, Pacific Islanders are rarely recognized and are often ignored completely. Therefore, putting them together with Asian Americans actually does them a disservice in terms of their distinct needs and experiences. Importantly, for some Pacific Islanders and for Native Hawaiians, their identity is not simply about nationality or ethnicity but also sovereignty. To read more about this distinction, check out Diaz' 2004 article "To P or not to P?: Marking the territory between Pacific Islander and Asian American studies."

I already teach about Asian holidays and food. Why isn't that enough?

In most U.S.schools, Christian holidays and European food are centered and understood as normal. When other cultures and religious traditions are included in the curriculum, they are often presented in ways that are decontextualized and/or exoticized. For instance, Lunar New Year is celebrated in different parts of East and Southeast Asia, but may be taught only as Chinese New Year, and perhaps may be the only time the Chinese are explicitly mentioned to young children. If the distinction is not made between Chinese and Chinese Americans, and if it is not clear that people in the United States celebrate Chinese New Year as part of their culture, students who are not Chinese or Asian American might make assumptions about the holiday and Chinese people.

The same is true when religious holidays like Diwali or Eid are included in school. Even worse, some teachers may spotlight students who belong to those faiths/cultures and expect them to teach the class as an unofficial spokesperson. While some children may be happy to do this, others may feel tokenized or uncomfortable being asked to share things that emphasize how they are different from their peers. Don't put kids on the spot for requests like this—give them time and space to consider whether they want to share about their culture or religion and to consult their families in advance. Additionally, not everyone celebrates holidays in the same way or eats the same foods. We know this to be true for white Christian Americans, yet instruction that stereotypes other ethnoracial and religious groups rather than recognizing diversity within communities is far too common.

Ultimately, Asian Americans have lived in what we now know as the United States since before it was a nation. Their history deserves to be taught in addition to "fun" activities and crafts related to food and holidays; in fact, if taught together, Asian American foods and holidays might be understood not as foreign, but as part of our multicultural and diverse society.

I've heard some people refer to what happened to Japanese Americans during World War II as "internment," while others use the word "incarceration." Why is that and why does it matter?

A euphemism is a word that is chosen in an effort to not offend others; in some cases, euphemisms can downplay the severity or harm of an event in ways that mask issues of power and oppression. That's exactly the case with many of the terms popularly used to describe what happened to Japanese Americans during World War II after the bombing of Pearl Harbor. For example, their forced imprisonment in isolated camps is often described as internment. However, internment is a historical process that only applies to foreign nationals of countries with which the United States is at war. Two-thirds of the Japanese Americans imprisoned by the WRA were U.S. citizens, so "internment" is an inaccurate description of their circumstances. Therefore, scholars of Asian American histories have long preferred the term "incarceration." It more clearly explains that the U.S. government forced Japanese Americans to leave their homes and live in camps surrounded by barbed wire and armed guards for an undetermined amount of time.

Other terms related to Japanese American incarceration are also euphemistic, such as "evacuation" and "removal," which suggest that they were taken from their homes for the purposes of their own safety. This was not the case; in fact, a government-commissioned report released before the bombing of Pearl Harbor found that Japanese Americans were extremely loyal to the United States. If a U.S. government report can recognize the unconstitutionality, wartime hysteria, and racism behind Japanese American incarceration, educators should, too. To use the term "internment" is simply misleading and inaccurate.

Asian Americans aren't in the standards or the curriculum that I'm supposed to teach. Why is this so, and how should I fit them in?

State standards, high-stakes testing, district and school scope and sequencing all contribute to supporting teachers to develop common curricula with a clear focus. They also heighten feelings and realities of constraint as teachers are pressured to "teach to the test" or to stay aligned with district or professional learning community sequencing. In many elementary classrooms, social studies has disappeared as testing, standards, and district curriculum have focused almost exclusively on literacy and math. When present in curriculum, research shows that certain state standards purposefully emphasize dominant narratives of U.S. exceptionalism and progress. Such an emphasis silences the histories of entire communities, including those of more than half our students in addition to many teachers. Educators have long dealt with this challenge by teaching beyond the standards through morning meetings, children's literature, and integrated lessons—to name a few of the ways that are detailed throughout this book.

• References •

An, S. (2016). Asian Americans in American history: An AsianCrit perspective on Asian American representation in U.S. history curriculum standards. *Theory and Research in Social Education, 44*(2), 244–276.

An, S. (2017). AsianCrit perspective on social studies. *Journal of Social Studies Research, 41*(2), 131–139.

An, S. (2021). Selective (un)telling of difficult knowledge of U.S. wars in children's literature: The Korean War as a case study. *The Social Studies, 113*(2), 68–80. https://doi.org/10.1080/00377996.2021.1960256

An, S. (2022a). Re/presentation of Asian Americans in 50 states U.S. history standards. *The Social Studies, 113*(4), 171–184. https://doi.org/10.1080/00377996.2021.2023083

An, S. (2022b). Critical juxtaposing of war and migration: A critical content analysis of Southeast Asian refugee children's literature. *The Social Studies, 113*(5), 249–263. https://doi.org/10.1080/00377996.2022.2046996

An, S., & Rodríguez, N. N. (2021). Anti-Asian violence amid COVID-19 and implications to social studies education. In W. Journell (Ed.), *Post-pandemic social studies: How Covid-19 changed the world and how we teach* (pp. 163–174). Teachers College Press.

Ancheta, A. N. (2006). *Race, rights, and the Asian American experience.* Rutgers University Press.

Anderson, W. H. (1942, February 2). The question of Japanese-Americans. *Los Angeles Times.*

Angel Island Immigration Station Foundation. (n. d.). *Angel Island Immigration Station—San Francisco.* https://www.aiisf.org

Au, W., & Yonamine, M. (2021, March 23). Dear educators, it is time to fight for Asian America. *Rethinking Schools.* https://rethinkingschools.org/2021/03/23/dear-educators-it-is-time-to-fight-for-asian-america

Bajaj, M., Ghaffar-Kucher, A., & Desai, K. (2013). In the face of xenophobia: Lessons to address the bullying of South Asian American youth. *SAALT.* https://www.sikhcoalition.org/wp-content/uploads/2016/11/SAALT-In-The-Face-Of-Xenophobia.pdf

Bajaj, M., Ghaffar-Kucher, A., & Desai, K. (2016). Brown bodies and xenophobic bullying in US schools: Critical analysis and strategies for action. *Harvard Educational Review, 86*(4), 481–505.

Baldoz, R. (2011). *The third Asiatic invasion: Migration and empire in Filipino America, 1898–1946.* New York University Press.

Baldwin, J. (1955). *Notes of a native son.* Beacon Press.

Balgassi, H. (1996). *Peacebound trains* (C. Soentpiet, Illus.). Clarion Books.

Bishop, C. H. (1938). *The five Chinese brothers* (K. Weise, Illus.). Coward-McCann.

Bishop, R. S. (1990, March). Windows and mirrors: Children's books and parallel cultures [Paper presentation]. In *California State University reading conference.* 14th annual conference, San Bernadino (pp. 3–12).

Blue Scholars. (2011). Yuri Kochiyama [Song]. Cinemetropolis [Album]. Independent.

Blumenbach, J. F. (1795). *De generis humani varietate nativa* (3rd ed.). Vandenhoek et Ruprecht.

Borja, M., & Gibson, J. (2020). Anti-Asian racism in 2020. *Virulent Hate + Reports.* https://virulenthate.org/wp-content/uploads/2021/05/Virulent-Hate-Anti-Asian-Racism-In-2020-5.17.21.pdf

Britto, P. (2011). Global battleground or school playground: The bullying of America's Muslim children. *Washington, DC: Institute for Social Policy and Understanding.* http://www.ispu.org/content/Global_Battleground_or_School_Playground_The_Bullying_of_Americas_Muslim_Children#sthash.raLVdu7v.dpuf

Budiman, A., & Ruiz, N. G. (2021, April 29). *Key facts about Asian origin groups in the U.S.* Pew Research Center. https://www.pewresearch

.org/fact-tank/2021/04/29/key-facts-about-asian-origin-groups-in-the-u-s

Busey, C. L., & Walker, I. (2017). A dream and a bus: Black critical patriotism in elementary social studies standards. *Theory & Research in Social Education*, *45*(4), 456–488.

Cahill, C. D. (2020). *Recasting the vote: How women of color transformed the suffrage movement.* The University of North Carolina Press.

California Assembly Bill 268. (1885). The statues of California and amendments to the codes passed at the twenty-sixth of the legislature, 1885. *California State Assembly Archives.* https://clerk.assembly.ca.gov/sites/clerk.assembly.ca.gov/files/archive/Statutes/1885/1885.pdf#page=151

Chang, G. H. (2019). *Ghosts of Gold Mountain: The epic story of the Chinese who built the Transcontinental Railroad.* Houghton Mifflin.

Children's Literature Assembly. (2019, February 12). Position statement on the importance of critical selection and teaching of diverse children's literature. *National Council of Teachers of English.* https://www.childrensliteratureassembly.org/uploads/1/1/8/6/118631535/inclusiondiversityandequitypolicystatement.pdf

Choy, C. C. (2022). *Asian American histories of the United States.* Beacon Press.

Collins, P. H., & Bilge, S. (2016). *Intersectionality.* John Wiley & Sons.

Commission on Wartime Relocation Internment of Civilians. (1983). *Personal justice denied: Report of the Commission on Wartime Relocation and Internment of Civilians.* US Government Printing Office.

Cornbleth, C., & Waugh, D. (2012). *The great speckled bird: Multicultural politics and education policymaking.* Routledge.

Cridland-Hughes, S., & King, L. (2015). Killing me softly: How violence comes from the curriculum we teach. In K. Fasching-Varner & N. Hartlep (Eds.), *The assault on communities of color: Exploring the realities of race-based violence* (pp. 99–102). Rowman & Littlefield.

Cumings, B. (2010). *The Korean War: A history.* Modern Library.

Dahlen, S. P. (2022, March 25). *Spring 2022 Baker Diversity Lecture—Asian Pacific American Library Association* [Video]. University of South Carolina School of Information Science. https://www.youtube.com/watch?v=YPWkDliurqo

Daniels, R. (2005). Words do matter: A note on inappropriate terminology and the incarceration of the Japanese Americans. In L. Fiset & G. Nomura (Eds.), *Nikkei in the Pacific Northwest: Japanese Americans and Japanese Canadians in the twentieth century* (pp. 183–207). University of Washington Press.

David, E. J. R. (2011). *Brown skin, white minds: Filipino-American postcolonial psychology.* Information Age Publishing.

DeSilver, D. (2015, November 9th). U.S. public seldom has welcomed refugees into country. *Pew Research Center.* https://www.pewresearch.org/fact-tank/2015/11/19/u-s-public-seldom-has-welcomed-refugees-into-country

Dingle, M., & Yeh, C. (2021). Mathematics in context: The pedagogy of liberation. *Teaching Tolerance, 66.* https://www.learningforjustice.org/magazine/spring-2021/mathematics-in-context-the-pedagogy-of-liberation

Dr. Seuss Enterprises. (2021, March 2). Statement from Dr. Seuss Enterprises. *Seussville.* https://www.seussville.com/statement-from-dr-seuss-enterprises

DuBois, W. E. B. (1935/1992). *Black reconstruction in America.* The Free Press.

Espiritu, Y. L. (1992). *Asian American panethnicity: Bridging institutions and identities.* Temple University Press.

Espiritu, Y. L. (2014). *Body counts: The Vietnam War and militarized refuge(es).* University of California Press.

Frost, A. (2021). "By accident of birth": The battle over birthright citizenship after *United States v. Wong Kim Ark. Yale Journal of Law & the Humanities, 32*(1), 38–76.

Fujikane, C., & Okamura, J. (2008). *Asian settler colonialism: From local governance to the habits of everyday life in Hawaii.* University of Hawaii Press.

Fujino, D. C. (2005). *Heartbeat of struggle: The revolutionary life of Yuri Kochiyama.* University of Minnesota Press.

Gallardo, G., & Yeh, C. (2022). "Tu lucha es mi lucha": Mathematics for movement building. In T. Bartell, C. Yeh, M. Felton-Koestler, & R. Q. Berry III (Eds.), *Upper elementary mathematics lessons to explore, understand, and respond to social injustice* (pp. 134–143). Corwin Press.

Givens, J. R. (2021). *Fugitive pedagogy: Carter G. Woodson and the art of Black teaching.* Harvard University Press.

Gossett, C., & Lincoln L. C. (Producers), & Gossett, C., & Lincoln L.C. (Directors). (n. d.). *Kiyoshi Kuromiya* [Documentary].

Gotanda, N. (1991). A critique of "Our Constitution is color-blind." *Stanford Law Review, 44*, 1–67.

Gross, M. (2019). Grounding our work theoretically: The peritextual literacy framework. In S. Witte, D. Latham, & M. Gross (Eds.), *Literacy engagement through peritextual analysis* (pp. 3–15). American Library Association.

Hall, J. D. (2005). The long Civil Rights Movement and the political uses of the past. *The Journal of American History,* 1233–1263.

Henkes, K. (1991). *Chrysanthemum.* Green Willow.

Hill, N. E., Castellino, D. R., Lansford, J. E., Nowlin, P., Dodge, K. A., Bates, J. E., & Pettit, G. S. (2004). Parent academic involvement as related to school behavior, achievement, and aspirations: Demographic variations across adolescence. *Child development, 75*(5), 1491–1509.

Hing, B. O. (2005). Deporting Cambodian refugees: Justice denied? *Crime & Delinquency, 51*(2), 265–290. https://doi.org/10.1177/0011128704273468.

Hoot, J. L., Szecsi, T., & Moosa, S. (2003). What teachers of young children should know about Islam. *Early Childhood Education Journal, 31*(2), 85–90.

Hsu, M. Y. (2000). *Dreaming of gold, dreaming of home: Transnationalism and migration between the United States and South China, 1882–1943.* Stanford University Press.

Hsu, M. Y. (2015). *The good immigrants: How the yellow peril became the model minority.* Princeton University Press.

Immerwahr, D. (2020). *How to hide an empire: A short history of the United States.* Vintage.

The James and Grace Lee Boggs School. (2022). *Mission & core ideology.* https://www.boggsschool.org/mission-core-ideology

Johnson, L., & Bryan, N. (2016). Using our voices, losing our bodies: Michael Brown, Trayvon Martin, and the spirit murders of Black male professors in the academy. *Race Ethnicity and Education, 20*(2), 163–177.

Johnson, L. B. (1965, October 3). *Public papers of the Presidents of the United States: Lyndon B. Johnson, 1965.* Volume II, entry 546, pp. 1037–1040. Office of the Federal Register, National Archives and Records Administration.

Joseph, P. (2020). *The sword and the shield: The revolutionary lives of Malcolm X and Martin Luther King, Jr.* Basic Books.

Karuka, M. (2019). *Empire's tracks: Indigenous Nations, Chinese workers, and the Transcontinental Railroad.* University of California Press.

Kaur, V. (2016, September 23). His brother was murdered for wearing a turban after 9/11. 15 years later, he spoke to the killer. *The World.* https://theworld.org/stories/2016-09-23/his-brother-was-murdered-wearing-turban-after-911-last-week-he-spoke-killer

Keevak, M. (2011). *Becoming yellow: A short history of racial thinking.* Princeton University Press.

Khan, R. (2018, October 11). *South Asian immigrant cab drivers in New York City.* Immigration and Ethnic History Society. https://iehs.org/khan-south-asian-cab-drivers

Kieffer, C. (2021, December 2). Afghan refugee resettlement efforts ignites ugly rhetoric despite popular support. *Southern Poverty Law Center.* https://www.splcenter.org/hatewatch/2021/12/02/afghan-refugee-resettlement-efforts-ignites-ugly-rhetoric-despite-popular-support

Kim, E. (2010). *Adopted territory: Transnational Korean adoptees and the politics of belonging.* Duke University Press.

Kim, R. (2021, March 31). Atlanta spa shootings: What Korean-language media told us that the mainstream media didn't. *Rolling Stone.* https://www.rollingstone.com/culture/culture-news/atlanta-shootings-what-korean-language-media-told-us-that-the-mainstream-media-didnt-1149698

King, L. J. (2020). Black history is not American history: Toward a framework of Black historical consciousness. *Social Education, 84*(6), 335–341.

Kochiyama, Y. (2004). *Passing it on: A memoir.* UCLA Asian American Studies Center Press.

Kohli, R., & Solórzano, D. G. (2012). Teachers, please learn our names!: Racial microaggressions and the K–12 classroom. *Race Ethnicity and Education, 15*(4), 441–462.

KQED. (n. d.). *Pacific Link: The KQED Asain Education Initiative.* https://www.kqed.org/w/pacificlink/home.html

Kubota, L. (1969, April). Yellow power! *Gidra.*

Kurlantzick, J. (2017). *A great place to have a war: America in Laos and the birth of a military CIA.* Simon & Schuster.

Lee, E. (2015). *The making of Asian America.* Simon & Schuster.

Lee, E. (2019). *America for Americans: A history of xenophobia in the United States.* Basic Books.

Lee, E. (2003). *At America's gates: Chinese immigration during the exclusion era, 1882-1943.* University of North Carolina Press.

Lee, E., & Yung, J. (2010). *Angel island: Immigrant gateway to America.* Oxford University Press.

Lee, J., & Ramakrishnan, K. (2020). Who counts as Asian. *Ethnic and Racial Studies, 43*(10), 1733–1756.

Lee, J., Wong, J., & Ramakrishnan, K. (2021). Asian Americans' support for affirmative action increased since 2016. *AAPI Data.* http://aapidata.com/blog/affirmative-action-increase

Lee, J. S., & Bowen, N. K. (2006). Parent involvement, cultural capital, and the achievement gap among elementary school children. *American Educational Research Journal, 43*(2), 193- 218.

Library of Congress. (n. d.). *Japanese American internment primary source set.* https://www.loc.gov/classroom-materials/japanese-american-internment

Love, B. (2019). *We want to do more than survive: Abolitionist teaching and the pursuit of educational freedom.* Beacon Press.

Lum v. Rice, 275 U.S. 78. (1927). https://supreme.justia.com/cases/federal/us/275/78

Mabalon, D. B. (2013). *Little Manila is in the heart: The making of the Filipina/o American community in Stockton, California.* Duke University Press.

Maeda, D. J. (2009). *Chains of Babylon: The rise of Asian America.* University of Minnesota Press.

Maeda, D. J. (2012). *Rethinking the Asian American movement.* Routledge.

Marco, M. L., Heeney, D., Binda, S., Cifelli, C. J., Cotter, P. D., Foligné, B., Gänzle, M., Kort, R., Pasin, G., Pihlanto, A., Smid, E. J., & Hutkins, R. (2017). Health benefits of fermented foods: microbiota and beyond. *Current opinion in biotechnology, 44*, 94–102.

Martinez-Cola, M. (2022). *The bricks before Brown: The Chinese American, Native American, and Mexican Americans' struggle for educational equality.* University of Georgia Press.

McCormick, M. M., & West, A. N. (2022). Seen but not seen: Supporting transracial and transnational adoptees in the classroom. *Social Studies and the Young Learner, 34*(4), 26–31.

Mosel, A. (1968). *Tikki Tikki Tembo* (B. Lent, Illus.). Holt, Rinehart and Winston.

Nakamura, R. A. (Director). (2002). *Toyo Miyatake: Infinite shades of gray.* [Film]. Japanese American National Museum, Media Arts Center.

Ngai, M. M. (2014). *Impossible subjects.* Princeton University Press.

Nguyen, L. T. (2012). *Hanoi's war.* University of North Carolina Press.

Niiya, B. (2017). *Asian Americans and World War II.* National Park Service. https://www.nps.gov/articles/aapi-theme-study-essay-10-wwii.htm

Office of the Historian and Office of the Clerk United States House of Representatives. (2017). *Asian and Pacific Islander Americans in Congress 1900–2017.* U.S. Government Publishing Office.

Okihiro, G. Y. (1994). *Margins and mainstreams: Asians in American history and culture.* University of Washington Press.

Osumi, T. (2006). Feast of resistance: Asian American history through food. In E. W-C. Chen & G. Omatsu (Eds.), *Teaching about Asian Pacific Americans* (pp. 19–25). Rowman & Littlefield.

Ozawa v. United States, 260 U.S. 178, 43 S. Ct. 65. (1922). https://casetext.com/case/ozawa-v-united-states

Perna, L. W., & Titus, M. A. (2005). The relationship between parental involvement as social capital and college enrollment: An examination of racial/ethnic group differences. *The Journal of Higher Education, 76*(5), 485–518.

Public Religion Research Institute. (2021, July 8). The American religious landscape in 2020. https://www.prri.org/research/2020-census-of-american-religion

Recorvits, H. (2003). *My name is Yoon* (G. Swiatkowska, Illus.). Frances Foster Books.

Rice v. Lum, 139 Miss. 760, 104 So. 105. (1925). https://cite.case.law/miss/139/760

Rodríguez, N. N. (2017). Not all terrorists: A teacher educator's approach to teaching against Islamophobia and for religious tolerance. In S. B. Shear, C. M. Tschida, E. Bellows, L. B. Buchanan, & E. E. Saylor (Eds.), *(Re)imagining elementary social studies: A controversial issues reader* (pp. 129–152). Information Age.

Rodríguez, N. N. (2022). Social studies comes alive: Using diverse children's literature and primary sources to teach social studies. *Literacy Today,* April/May, 50–51.

Rodríguez, N. N., Falkner, A., & Bohl, L. T. (2022). Reading beyond the book with primary sources. *The Reading Teacher, 75*(6), 749–754.

Rodríguez, N. N., & Kim, E. J. (2018). In search of mirrors: An Asian Critical Race Theory content analysis of Asian American picturebooks from 2007–2017. *Journal of Children's Literature, 44*(2), 16–33.

Rodríguez, N. N., & Kim, E. J. (2021). Beyond the model minority and forever foreigner: Asian American children's nonfiction. In T. Crisp, S. Knezek, & R. P. Gardner (Eds.), *Reading and teaching with diverse nonfiction children's books: Representations and possibilities* (pp. 58–78). National Council of Teachers of English.

Rodríguez, N. N., & Kim, E. (2022). The audacity of equality: Disrupting the invisibility of Asian America. In W. Au, N. H. Merchant, & S. Shear (Eds.), *Insurgent social studies* (pp. 55–74). Meyer.

Rodríguez, N. N., & Swalwell, K. (2022). *Social studies for a better world: An anti-oppressive approach for elementary educators.* W. W. Norton.

Roy, A. (2004). Peace & the new corporate liberation theology: City of Sydney Peace Prize Lecture. *The Centre for Peace and Conflict Studies.* https://sydneypeacefoundation.org.au/wp-content/uploads/2012/02/2004-SPP_-Arundhati-Roy.pdf

Rusling, J. (1903). Interview with President McKinley. *Christian Advocate, 78*, 137–138.

Salinas, C., Blevins, B., & Sullivan, C. C. (2012). Critical historical thinking: When official narratives collide with other narratives. *Multicultural Perspectives, 14*(1), 18–27.

Saranillio, D. (2013). Why Asian settler colonialism matters. *Settler Colonial Studies, 3*(3), 280–294.

Scholastic, Inc. (n. d.) Immigration: Stories of yesterday and today. http://teacher.scholastic.com/activities/immigration/index.htm

Sleeter, C. E., & Grant, C. A. (2017). Race, class, gender, and disability in current textbooks. In M. Apple & L. Christian-Smith (Eds.), *The politics of the textbook* (pp. 78–110). Routledge.

Smithsonian National Museum of American History. (n. d.). *In pursuit of equality—Separate is not equal.* https://americanhistory.si.edu/brown/history/2-battleground/detail/tape-family.html

South Asian Americans Leading Together. (2014). *Under suspicion, under attack: Xenophobic political rhetoric and hate violence against South Asian, Muslim, Sikh, Hindu, Middle Eastern, and Arab communities in the US.* http://saalt.org/wp-content/uploads/2014/09/SAALT_report_full_links.pdf

Stanford University Libraries. (n. d.). Map of the United States showing territorial expansion of a century—1804 to 1904. *Stanford University.* https://exhibits.stanford.edu/nhdmaps/catalog/xr731vr4463

Stanton-Salazar, R. D. (2011). A social capital framework for the study of institutional agents and their role in the empowerment of low-status students and youth. *Youth & Society, 43*(3), 1066–1109.

Takaki, R. T. (1998). *Strangers from a different shore: A history of Asian Americans.* Back Bay Books/Little Brown and Company.

Tang, E. (2015). *Unsettled: Cambodian refugees in the New York City hyperghetto.* Temple University Press.

Tape, M. (1885, April 16). Chinese mother's letter. *Daily Alta California.*

Tape v. Hurley, 66 Cal. 473. (1885). https://casetext.com/case/tape-v-hurley

Tchen, J. K. W., & Yeats, D. (2014). Yellow peril!: An archive of anti-Asian fear. Verso Books.

TeachMideast. (n. d.) *Middle East in focus: History.* TeachMideast.org. https://teachmideast.org/mideast-focus/history

Trieu, M. M., & Vang, C. Y. (2015). A portrait of refugees from Burma/Myanmar and Bhutan in the United States. *Journal of Asian American Studies, 18*(3), 347–369.

Trump, D. (2016, March 9). *Anderson Cooper 360* [Television Broadcast]. CNN.

Tuan, M. (1998). *Forever foreigners or honorary whites?: The Asian ethnic experience today.* Rutgers University Press.

United States v. Thind, 261 U.S. 204. (1923). https://supreme.justia.com/cases/federal/us/261/204

U.S. Census Bureau. (1993). *We, the American Asians.* https://www.census.gov/library/publications/1993/dec/we-03.html

U.S. Census Bureau. (2021). *Asian American and Pacific Islander heritage month: May 2021.* https://www.census.gov/newsroom/facts-for-features/2021/asian-american-pacific-islander.html

U.S. Office of Management and Budget. (1997). Revisions to the standards for the classification of federal data on race and ethnicity. *Executive Office of the President.* https://obamawhitehouse.archives.gov/omb/fedreg_1997standards

Vaughan, R. (1968). The defiant voices of S.D.S. *Life, 65*(16), 80–96.

Venet, A. S. (2021). *Equity-centered trauma-informed education.* W. W. Norton.

Vine, D. (2020). *The United States of war: A global history of America's endless conflicts from Columbus to the Islamic states.* University of California Press.

Wang, F. K-H. (2021, May 31). I am Asian American. No hyphen required. *Mic.* https://www.mic.com/impact/i-am-asian-american-no-hyphen-required-81037228

Wang, H. L. (2014, May 10). *Descendants Of Chinese laborers reclaim railroad's history* [Radio broadcast]. National Public Radio. https://www.npr.org/sections/codeswitch/2014/05/10/311157404/descendants-of-chinese-laborers-reclaim-railroads-history

Wong, T. K. (2015). Reaching undocumented Asian Americans and Pacific Islanders in the United States [White paper]. *Center for Migration Studies.* https://cmsny.org/publications/reaching-undocumented-asian-americans-and-pacific-islanders-in-the-united-states

Wu, E. (2014). *The color of success: Asian Americans and the origin of the model minority.* Princeton University Press.

Wu, E. (2019). It's time to center war in U.S. immigration history. *Modern American History, 2*, 215–235.

Wu, J. T., & Mink, G. (2022). *Fierce and fearless: Patsy Takemoto Mink, first woman of color in Congress.* New York University Press.

Yellow Horse, A. J., Jeung, R., & Matriano, R. (2022). Stop AAPI Hate National Report, 3/19/20–12/31/21. *Stop AAPI Hate.* https://stopaapihate.org/wp-content/uploads/2022/03/22-SAH-NationalReport-3.1.22-v9.pdf

Yi, J. (2021). Memoirs or myths? Storying Asian American adoption in picturebooks. *Journal of Children's Literature, 47*(2), 22–34.

Yoshinaga, I., & Kossa, E. (2000). Local Japanese Women for Justice speak out against Daniel Inouye and the JACL. *Amerasia Journal, 26*(1), 143–157.

Yosso, T. J. (2016). Whose culture has capital?: A critical race theory discussion of community cultural wealth. *Race Ethnicity and Education, 8*(1), 69–91.

Yung, J. (1999). *Unbound voices: A documentary history of Chinese women in San Francisco.* University of California Press.

Zia, H. (2000). *Asian American dreams: The emergence of an American people.* Farrar, Straus and Giroux.

Zinn, H. (2011). *Howard Zinn on war.* Seven Stories Press.

RECOMMENDED CHILDREN'S LITERATURE REFERENCED

Anand, S. (2020). *Laxmi's mooch* (N.H. Ali, Illus.). Kokila.

Cha, D. (1998). *Dia's story cloth* (C. Cha & N. Cha, Illus.). Lee & Low Books.

Cho, T. (2022). *Asian American women in science: An Asian American history book for kids.* Callisto Media.

Conkling, W. (2013). *Sylvia and Aki.* Yearling.

Cronin, D. (2000). *Click clack moo* (B. Lewin, Illus.). Atheneum.

Hirahara, N. (2022). *We are here: 30 inspiring Asian Americans and Pacific Islanders who have shaped the United States* (I. Ferandez, Illus.). Running Press Kids.

Ho, J. (2021). *Eyes that kiss in the corners* (D. Ho, Illus.). Harper CollinsPublishers.

Khaira, R. K. (2021). *Stories of South Asian super girls.* Puffin.

Lai, T. (2013). *Inside out & back again.* HarperCollins.

Landowne, Y. (2010). *Mali under the night sky* (Y. Landowne, Illus.). Cinco Puntos Press.

Lee, U-B. (2019). *When spring comes to the DMZ* (U-B. Lee, Illus.). Plough Publishing House.

Leung, J. (2021). *The fearless flights of Hazel Ying Lee* (J. Kwon, Illus.). Little, Brown Books for Young Readers.

Ludwig, T. (2013). *The invisible boy* (P. Barton, Illus.). Knopf Books for Young Readers.
Mabalon, D. B., & Romasanta, G. (2018). *Journey for justice: The life of Larry Itliong* (A. Sabayan, Illus.). Bridge + Delta.
Maclear, K. (2019). *It began with a page* (J. Morstad, Illus.). HarperCollins.
Markel, M. (2013). *Brave girl: Clara and the shirtwaist makers' strike of 1909* (M. Sweet, Illus.). Balzer+Bray.
Martin, J. B., & Lee, J. J. (2015). *Chef Roy Choi and the street food remix* (M. One, Illus).
Chronicle Books.
Michalak, J., & Florence, D. M. (2021). *Niki Nakayama: A chef's tale in 13 bites* (Y. Jones, Illus.). Farrar, Straus, and Giroux.
Mir, S. (2019). *Muslim girls rise: Inspirational champions of our time* (A. Jaleel, Illus.). Simon & Schuster.
Mobin-Uddin, A. (2005). *My name is Bilal* (B. Kiwak, Illus.). Astra Young Readers.
Moss, M. (2009). *Sky high: The true story of Maggie Gee* (C. Angel, Illus.). Tricycle press.
Moua, D. (2022). *Today is different* (K. Holt, Illus.). Carolrhoda Books.
Myers, W. D. (2015). *Ida B. Wells: Let the truth be told* (B. Christensen, Illus.). Amistad.
Pimm, N. R. (2020). *Fly, girl, fly!: Shaesta Waiz soars around the world* (A. Bye, Illus.). Beaming Books.
Polacco, P. (2015). *Tucky Jo and Little Heart* (P. Polacco, Illus.). Simon & Schuster.
Robeson, T. (2019). *Queen of physics: How Wu Chien Shiung helped unlock the secrets of the atom* (R. Huang, Illus.). Union Square Kids.
Saeed, A. (2019). *Bilal cooks daal* (A. Syed, Illus.). Simon & Schuster.
Smith, I. (2010). *Half spoon of rice* (S. Nhem, Illus.). East West Discovery Press.
Soontornvat, C. (2022). *A life of service: The story of Senator Tammy Duckworth* (D. Phumiruk, Illus.). Candlewick.
Stein, J. D. (2022). *Lunch from home* (J. Li, Illus.). Penguin Random House.
Thompkins-Bigelow, J. (2020). *Your name is a song* (L. Uribe, Illus.). The Innovation Press.

Uchida, Y. (1996). *The bracelet* (J. Yardley, Illus.). Puffin.

Vo, Y. (2022). *Gibberish.* Levine Querido.

Wang, A. (2021). *Watercress* (J. Chin, Illus.). Holiday House.

Woodson, J. (2018). *The day you begin* (R. López, Illus.). Nancy Paulsen Books.

Yang, K. (2018). *Front desk.* Scholastic.

Yang, K. (2021). *Three keys.* Scholastic.

Yang, K. (2021). *Room to dream.* Scholastic.

Yang, K. (2022). *Key player.* Scholastic.

Yang, K. (2022). *Yes we will: Asian Americans who shaped this country* (N. H. Ali et al., Illus.). Penguin Random House.

Yin. (2001). *Coolies* (C. Soentpiet, Illus.). Philomel.

Yoo, P. (2005). *Sixteen years in sixty seconds: The Sammy Lee story* (D. Lee, Illus.). Lee & Low.

Yoo, P. (2009). *Shining star: The Anna May Wong story* (L. Wang, Illus.). Lee & Low.